THE VOLVO PENTA AQUAMATIC BOAT ENGINE

Keith Beardow

Foreword by James R. Wynne

DAVID & CHARLES
Newton Abbot   London   North Pomfret (Vt)

British Library Cataloguing in Publication Data

Beardow, Keith
    The Volvo Penta Aquamatic boat engine.
    1. Inboard-outboard engines
    I. Title
    623.87′23′4   VM771

    ISBN 0-7153-8000-1

Printed in Great Britain
by Biddles Limited, Guildford, Surrey
for David & Charles (Publishers) Limited
Brunel House   Newton Abbot   Devon

Published in the United States of America
by David & Charles Inc
North Pomfret   Vermont 05053   USA

Contents

Acknowledgements

The author gratefully acknowledges the assistance of the following organisations and individuals for providing information and material:

James R. Wynne of Wynne Marine Inc, Miami.

Stig Linde, Lars Eldenius, Ake Edman, Annika Svensson and Börje Nodby of A. B. Volvo Penta, Gothenburg.

Alan Revington, David Peat, Heather Ahern, and David Nichols of Volvo Penta UK Ltd, Watford.

Dick Johnson, of *Motor Boat and Yachting*, London.

Harald Wiklund, Gothenburg.

Roy E. Scherman, London.

Ray Lawrence, London.

Brenda Faulkner, Welwyn Garden City.

Foreword

I was of course more than casually interested when I heard that Keith Beardow was writing a history of the Volvo Penta Aquamatic. I was also concerned that the facts were correct and some of the misconceptions which had developed over the years would be set straight. After reading the first proof, I was impressed with the attention to detail and the amount of effort which Keith expended to make the events of the past twenty-odd years so accurate and interesting.

The story is unique in that the efforts of a few individuals and a major company combined to have far-reaching effects on the marine industry. I seriously doubt that this could happen today; it is somewhat sad that an era when such developments could occur is past. This seems to be the price of progress and increased technical sophistication.

When I look back on the events of 1958 it seems incredible that the collection of parts assembled in my garage would successfully propel a boat and that Harald Wiklund would commit Volvo Penta to manufacturing the unit based on what little I had to show him. This tells how it all happened; I'm proud to have had a part in it.

JAMES R. WYNNE
Miami, Florida, May 1980

Introduction:
The Mouse that Roared

Volvo cars are renowned for their rugged, conservative quality. Apart from their well-known and almost obsessional concern with safety (something Volvo pioneered), the cars can neither be described as innovative nor of mass-market appeal; indeed one memorable advertising slogan during the early 1970s was 'Volvo for the fortunate few'. As a direct result of successfully aiming at a specific market niche, the Volvo car division achieved a small but significant share of a very large total market.

Volvo Penta, of necessity, had to approach the marine engine market from a quite different direction for, compared with the automobile, the number of marine engines used worldwide is tiny. Fortunately, since the first Volvo in 1927 had adopted the four-cylinder marine engine produced by the then separate company of Pentaverken, all subsequent automotive blocks were over-dimensioned and developed to provide for marine application. Nonetheless, to ensure lasting success in marine production and a solid basis for development, Volvo Penta had to capture a large proportion of this relatively small market.

In the late fifties, powerboat manufacture in most western countries was emerging from a highly specialised 'cottage industry' into one of comparative mass-production where rapid assembly by non-specialist labour was an important criterion. The earliest production boats were constructed from resin-bonded plywood or aluminium and were invariably small, high speed powerboats whose hard-chine shape was most adaptable to these materials. The introduction of glass reinforced plastic (GRP, glassfibre, fibreglass) initiated an explosion in powerboat volumes as the wood and aluminium hulls provided ready-made plugs from which a mould could be made. From one mould scores of hulls could now be manufactured in a short time by two or three unskilled laminators.

7

1 Changing styles 1959–62. The coming of GRP and deep-vee hulls during the first three years of the Aquamatic. Compare this early flat-bottomed wooden hull with the illustrations 2 and 4

In North America, Scandinavia and Northern Europe these low-cost boats became available to a much wider section of the community, establishing watersport, which had formerly been the prerogative of the wealthy, as a leading leisure activity.

Volvo Penta knew that to succeed in this fast-expanding market they had to be innovative and geared for high production. They needed to explore methods of reducing engine installation times and simplify means of installing power units. They had to look ahead to apply the same approach to sailing auxiliaries, tugs, cabin cruisers, fishing boats etc, and be equipped to provide service and parts all over the world to the customer.

These combined objectives of innovation and a large share of the market were for Volvo Penta something very different from the Volvo car tradition. Also, unlike the car, complete unto itself, a marine engine is only a component of the greater whole, the boat, which must have priority consideration. Sure of their objectives Volvo Penta have achieved success in both market penetration and ingenuity with all their marine products for many years, but most outstanding of all, and the key to more recent successes, was the adoption of an idea by an American marine engineer that became known as the Aquamatic.

The Aquamatic was the world's first technically and commercially viable inboard/outboard drive. It influenced powerboat design as much as the deep-vee and more than any other form of marine propulsion since the invention of the propeller. The Aquamatic was transformed from an idea into production reality in an unbelievable six months; the Aquamatic was unchallenged by competition for its first three years and, despite intensive competition, it now enters its twenty-first year as market leader with a seventy per cent share in Europe and over fifteen per cent in the heart of 'enemy' territory, North America. Since the first Aquamatic Transmount Drive Model 80 was introduced in 1959 (a cumbersome

2 GRP but still flat

title compared with the later Volvo sterndrive!) developments from the original concept have kept pace with boatbuilders' and owners' requirements. This demands foresight and a keen awareness of trends. Development of new engine models is started long before there are boats suitable to receive them; indeed there have been instances of engines or drive systems being announced before a single boat has existed to use them, namely the Sailboat drive, introduced in 1973, and the twin-into-one Y-drive which was introduced in 1975.

For many years, and throughout the Aquamatic period, the research, design, development and marketing of new engines were the brain-child of Volvo Penta's president, Harald Wiklund, who retired at the end of 1976, and the working team he had assembled. Even the geographical location of Volvo Penta has contributed significantly to technical development of the engines, for Gothenburg is the gateway to Sweden's vast boating paradise, the west coast archipelago. In the country with the highest number of boats *per capita* in the world it is not surprising that the principal leisure pursuit of all Volvo Penta employees is boating.

On most summer evenings, bank holidays, weekends, and for a whole month in July and August, the Volvo Penta marina at Långedrag and the test station at Krossholm are deserted as the Volvo Penta workforce, from sweepers to directors, puts to sea at a spot only a few minutes' drive from their homes. Thus, to the great benefit of the company, every one of the Volvo Penta team is a skilled yachtsman, all use a boat extensively for pleasure, and each has constant first-hand practical experience of the firm's products. This is surely unique. When the Aquamatic version of the B.30 engine, AQ165/270, was under development Wiklund himself carried out all the sea trials and burnt over two tons of fuel in six weeks in the process!

The purpose of this book is to commemorate the Aquamatic coming of age and at the same time to provide past, present and future owners with both an insight into the Aquamatic story and a technical reference for all models produced to date. Much of the information contained herein has not been available previously outside the Volvo Penta organisation and I am indebted to Volvo Penta for it, particularly the chapter covering the future which at the time of my research is still on the secret list.

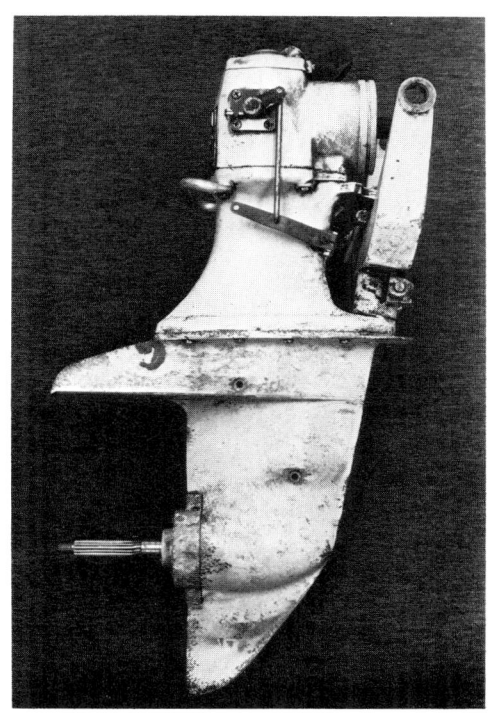

3 Vintage 1959 drive, in constant use before repainting in 1979. Now back
in service

Finally, why *The mouse that roared*? In 1963, the Keikhaefer
Mercury company published a four-page dissertation on what were
in their opinion the demerits of the Aquamatic in comparison to
their Mercruiser 110. At the time the Aquamatic had been in production for almost four years, the Mercruiser but one. The article
began:

Recently brought to our attention was a *Volvo Information Bulletin*
that reminded us of a comedy cartoon scene in which a very puffed-
up mouse tries to roar like a lion. Needless to say, the little rascal
sounds as ridiculous as he looks. Likewise Volvo's comparison of its
pint-sized sports car engine with the Mercruiser 110 and the
Mercruiser 140 would be funny if it weren't so pathetic.

11

4 All GRP and constant deadrise deep-vee

The document concluded:

> *Rookie in the big league.* It takes a lot of natural talent plus savvy
> and years of experience to make the grade in big league competition;
> yet mighty mouse, only a rookie in the marine propulsion game,
> displays his know-it-all attitude by criticising those most experienced
> and successful in the business. Newcomers would benefit by following
> the wise example of the big-league managers who, year after year,
> continue to look to Mercury for the newest and best in marine
> propulsion.

Well, competitive activities are much more sophisticated nowadays,
but *the mouse is still roaring!*

1
Transatlantic Origins

Early in 1958 James R. Wynne, a marine engineer of Miami, Florida, was on the beach. He was a self-employed marine consultant who had found that in between commissions he had copious free time. This had given him the opportunity to explore and develop the accumulated ideas from his years with the Keikhaefer Mercury organisation.

His major accomplishment in 1958 was to design the world's first commercially successful sterndrive, which was to become the Volvo Penta Aquamatic and which he patented in his own name.

This led to consultancy work for Bertram Yachts, Morse and Teleflex controls, and the design of production boats for Crestliner, Coronet, Donzi, Formula, Trojan, Yamaha and many others. Time and time again Jim Wynne proved the worth of his inboard/outboard engine and the new, complementary deep-vee hull designs in gruelling offshore racing. Winner of many classics, Miami–Nassau, Viareggio–Bastia, Cowes–Torquay and other races in America and Europe, he went on to gain eight world powerboat records and become the World Offshore Champion in 1964 and 1966.

Today, as president of Wynne Marine Inc, Jim still specialises in the design of high speed hull and propulsion systems—a far cry from his origins as an aspiring aeronautical engineer whose hobby was boating.

Jim Wynne graduated from Florida University in 1951 with a mechanical engineering degree. Convinced that his future was with aircraft engines he studied for his master's degree at the Massachusetts Institute of Technology and there, via contacts in powerboating, he met Charles Strang, later to become president of OMC but at that time director of research for the Keikhaefer corporation. Strang commissioned Wynne, who had access to MIT facilities, to carry out development work on the power unit of a small pilotless target aircraft. Wynne completed the research and adopted it as his thesis, 'Altitude performance of a small two-stroke engine'.

Wynne's contact with Charlie Strang led to his appointment as chief test engineer with Keikhaefer Mercury. His responsibility covered all boat testing of Mercury outboards and supervision of the test sites in Florida and Wisconsin. By the end of 1957 Wynne was reluctant to surrender the privilege of working with the legendary Carl Keikhaefer, but he was determined to branch out on his own and left the Mercury organisation.

The young test engineer had long pondered on the possible advantages of combining an outboard leg with an inboard engine. He had by now gleaned a great deal of experience of both forms of propulsion and had already carved a considerable reputation for himself in powerboat racing on the East Coast.

In his new-found freedom, Wynne assembled all the data he could find on previous attempts to introduce I/O units. He spent many hours checking and rechecking calculations by other designers, and made many of his own. It was not until he took an in-depth look at the market that he realised there were other than technical reasons for the failure of the early drives. Until the rapid expansion created by the adoption of GRP for boatbuilding, the market had lacked enough boats of the right type to justify series manufacture of I/O units. Previous production efforts had all had one thing in common: manufacture in small numbers at high prices, for the limited number of equally high-priced boats. He knew then that the success of a new I/O would depend, firstly, on wide acceptance by boatbuilders and buyers in both concept and price compared with the alternative inboard or outboard installation; secondly, on a high standard of engineering quality and design strength; and, thirdly, on the ability of the I/O manufacturer to gear up for quantity production in a short time.

The more Wynne thought about the requisite market conditions for the success of his project the more convinced he became that the time was right. Not only did North America have a vast number of powerboats already, but the number was growing astonishingly in the affluent 1950s. During March Wynne sketched out his ideas and decided to construct a working mock-up. His plan was to marry his outdrive to a light four-stroke engine which would be comparable

14

5 James R. Wynne 1959

in power to the larger outboards of the era.

The engine he chose and placed on order was the Penta BB70, then available in the USA as an inboard. He wrote to Volvo Penta asking their co-operation in making a special bell-housing and coupling, suitable for adapting their engine to his experimental drive.

In the fashion of many inventors, Wynne planned to incorporate as many existing components as possible. He utilised a lower drive housing, shaft and propeller from a Mercury outboard and a standard right-angle drive bevel gearbox. Another outboard part, this time the intermediate casting, formed a distance piece between the bevel box and the underwater unit for the external vertical shaft. To mount the whole on the pre-drilled transom Wynne fabricated a mounting collar from angle iron and steel strip. A Rzeppa type of flexible joint was attached to the input shaft to allow the drive to be tilted. This working mock-up was without a reverse gearbox or astern lock. Anti-corrosive alloys and sophisticated inlet and exhaust systems were still for the future.

15

6 Wynne's mock-up with external drive shaft and lock-tab propeller cone

The tests carried out on Wynne's mock-up were as unscientific as the device itself. Prolonged running was out of the question because of the extremely basic lubrication system which consisted only of a lower oil-bath in the underwater unit and an upper reservoir contained within the bevel box. The lower part was adequately cooled by virtue of its immersion but the upper gears were prone to overheat with alarming rapidity. The gear ratio, inherited with the outboard lower casing, was totally unsuitable for the maximum rpm of the B.16 which at 4000rpm gave away 1500rpm to the outboard from which the leg had originated. A consequence of this was the problem Wynne found in selecting a propeller that would transmit sufficient torque at low revs to plane the boat and yet provide the right combination of pitch and diameter for high speed once on the plane. However, Wynne had anticipated this problem and, lacking facilities for original manufacture, he had had to resort to a testing of the principle only. In this respect the trials were a complete success; not only did his idea work in practical application, but the unit steered the boat without excessive

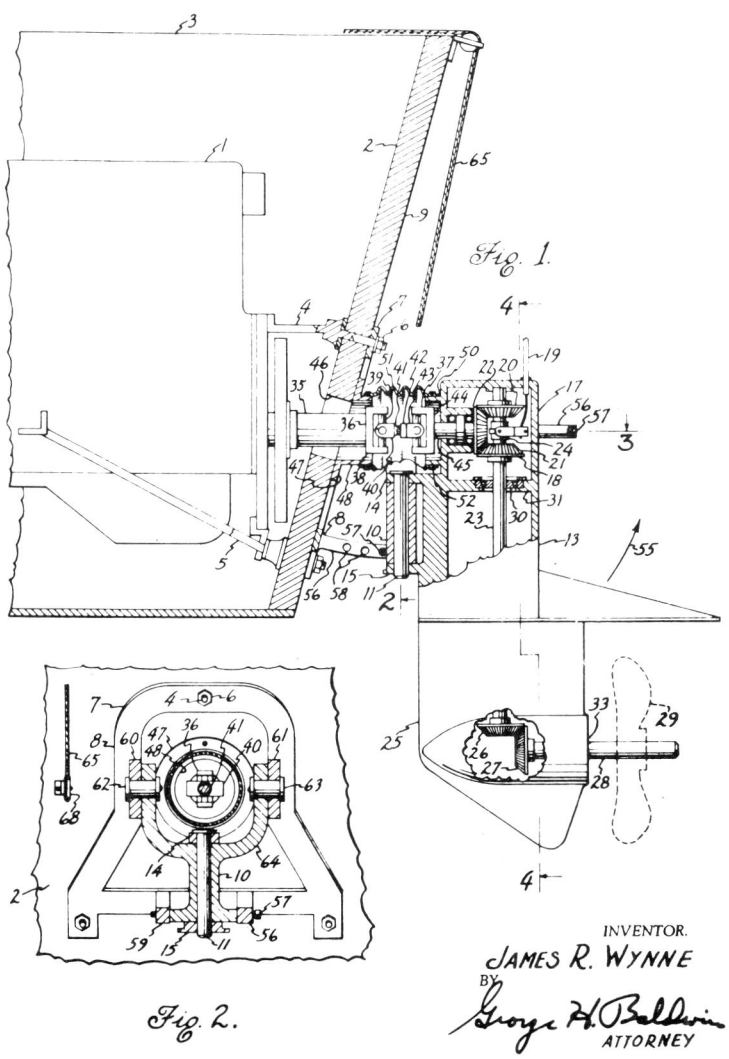

Fig. 1.

Fig. 2.

INVENTOR.

JAMES R. WYNNE

BY

George H. Baldwin

ATTORNEY

7 The drawing finally accepted by the US Patents Office

17

helm loading and, as a result of an unscheduled collision with driftwood, proved that the leg would kick up without damaging the propeller!

Encouraged by his findings, Wynne began making drawings and finalising his calculations. At that time he was sure that he could produce his I/o leg himself and interest engine manufacturers. So convinced was he of the potential of his design that he applied to patent it and forwarded a drawing to the US Patents Office. To this day the drawing is clearly recognisable as an Aquamatic drive: steering yoke, bellows, tilt pin, gearshift and transom shield—all are there. Significantly, the engine is shown suspended on the transom without a conventional engine bed, a feature that was to be unique to the Aquamatic until the advent of six- and eight-cylinder engines and diesels in the late 1960s. With remarkable foresight Wynne also depicted a universal joint, a transmission

8 Early B.16/BB70 engine adapted for Aquamatic drive

design that remained unadopted until the introduction of the Aquamatic 200 series in January 1965.

John Jarnmark, Volvo Penta's US representative, heard of Wynne's i/o model and decided to see it for himself. In May 1958 Wynne showed Jarnmark the unit, now parked in his mother's garage; Jarnmark left shortly afterwards, fired with enthusiasm to report his find to Harald Wiklund, president of Volvo Penta. Wiklund responded immediately by inviting Wynne for discussions in Gothenburg. It is interesting to note that, contrary to legend, Wynne did not offer his invention to OMC and Mercury first, to be subsequently rejected by them. He chose the Volvo B.16 as most suitable for his i/o and thanks to the intuition of Harald Wiklund was invited to discuss his ideas in Sweden.

As the long Florida summer approached, Jim Wynne was obliged to turn some of his attention to his other activity of boat design and development. Wynne had for some time established a dialogue with Ole Botved of Botved Boats A/S of Denmark. The combination of Wynne's ability as a designer and Botved's extraordinary skill in mass-producing boats to a very high standard was to lead to the Botved Coronet range becoming the doyen of European motorboats.

In the spring of 1958, with the Coronet success still ahead of them, Botved invited Wynne to accompany him on an attempt to cross the Atlantic Ocean in a Botved Coronet Explorer powered by two outboard motors. The plan was to embark from Copenhagen and make for the Hudson River in company with the regular Thordén liner. The crossing, in a boat named *Clary Thordén*, equipped with twin Johnson outboards, was completed in 10 days, 16 hours and 18 minutes—not without its share of drama; this was the first and, so far, only Atlantic crossing by outboards.

More important from a historical point of view was the opportunity the Scandinavian trip gave Jim Wynne to visit Volvo Penta to discuss his inboard/outboard. With difficulty, Wynne tracked down Volvo Penta's timber-built offices on the fringe of Gothenburg's vast dock and railhead area; there he was introduced to the then managing director, Harald Wiklund.

Wiklund is a big unpretentious man who invariably looks uncomfortable in business suits, despite his slicked down hair and clean shaven face. At the wheel of a powerboat, his shovel-like hands

9 Harald Wiklund (born 24.4.11) became Volvo spares chief in 1944 and managing director of A. B. Volvo Penta in 1949

and powerful arms dwarf the controls, and the surprising agility of his massive frame contributes to his reputation as an exceptional seaman. When Wynne first met him he had just entered his forty-seventh year and had already begun to demonstrate his uncanny talent for anticipating trends in the boat business, a talent which was later to put Volvo Penta in the forefront of marine engine builders. In 1958 Wiklund well understood that the rapid expansion of GRP boats was favouring the outboard motor suppliers and that Volvo Penta, with only the inboard variety to offer, could not expect to expand apace.

20

The Penta outboard had been dropped when Volvo had bought out Pentaverken in 1929 and was subsequently sold as Electrolux, Penta, Monark, Crescent and Archimedes. The factory was acquired again by Volvo Penta in 1975, and all the brand names were gradually phased out in favour of 'Volvo Penta'. Today the outboards are manufactured by Solo.

When Jim Wynne entered Wiklund's small office the only material evidence of his inboard/outboard that he carried with him was in the form of a copy of his patent sketch and a photograph of the test model. Wiklund was immediately impressed with the designer's analysis of existing and probable market trends and even more convinced by the sound technical reasoning and thorough research that Wynne produced. The two men had discovered a shared enthusiasm; they talked long into the early hours and throughout the next day. Wynne could hardly believe his luck. Not only was Wiklund as go-ahead as himself, but the Volvo Penta factory had both the know-how and the capacity to fully develop his invention. The designer immediately abandoned his plans to build the outdrive himself and a licence was signed for Volvo Penta to develop it.

Harald Wiklund knew that the outboard factories in the USA were already producing to capacity to meet the sudden demand for motors; they were unlikely to divert their efforts in the foreseeable future to a project which, even if it worked, would merely put them in a self-competing position. For an inboard manufacturer, however, the I/O would be the opportunity to compete in the vast marketplace that existed for big outboards, especially with a four-stroke engine to marine specification available in large numbers.

Since the first Volvo car rolled off the line with its Pentaverken marine engine in 1927 all the engines produced by the parent company have been greatly influenced in their design to allow for the marine requirement. The Penta people are now firmly convinced that the marine engine tradition at Volvo has significantly contributed to the reputation of the car for ruggedness. At the same time, the car builders are equally sure that the marine products owe their success to the fame of the car! There is truth in both points of view, but in 1958 the question meant more to Harald Wiklund than friendly rivalry; it meant that he had a guaranteed in-house source of power units because Volvo had geared up their production capacity in anticipation of export orders.

21

Before Wynne left on his transatlantic venture Wiklund had issued instructions to his design and development department to proceed with the preliminary drawings for a prototype. The head of that department was the late Nils Hansson, then in his early fifties, a master of innovation and ingenuity. Nils, who spoke English with a pronounced American accent, was a dapper, shy and very modest engineer. In his youth he had specialised in detailed weaponry design and was reputed to have been 'persuaded' whilst in the USA to carry out work on Capone's 'typewriters'. Hansson and his deputy Abdon Bergstedt were ready with their drawings within six weeks of Wynne's visit; these were then shown to Wiklund along with a technical feasibility study. It was agreed that Hansson should travel to America and discuss the layouts with the inventor and with Volvo Import Inc, who were the Volvo Penta *concessionaires.*

Hansson arrived in New York early in October and showed the drawings to Wynne, who had flown to meet him. Wynne was delighted with Volvo Penta's interpretation of his own sketches and eagerly involved himself in the meeting with Volvo Import. The meeting was not the easiest that Wynne and Hansson had attended. Volvo Import, although enthusiastic about the idea, proposed that a thorough market survey be carried out before they committed themselves to a sales programme. Furthermore, they wanted to discuss the project with their key regional dealers, a point on which Hansson was reluctant to agree. Many of these distributors operated franchises for companies with whom Volvo Penta might well be competing in the near future and Hansson did not intend to forewarn the opposition. Finally, it was agreed that with Volvo Import co-operation Wynne and Hansson would themselves undertake the research and hold limited talks with selected dealers, thus keeping a tight control on the project and avoiding premature rumours.

Volvo Import had also indicated that, in order to 'catch the market' when it opened, the new drive should be launched at the New York Boat Show—a mere two and half months away! Both men saw the logic of this, for the show was America's biggest boating event of the year and the ideal opportunity to give their I/O a good send-off.

When Hansson and Wynne set off on their fact-finding tour in

22

the second week of October, they knew the odds against them achieving the deadline were astronomical. During the next two weeks the two designers travelled from New York to Maine, then inland to the Great Lakes. They talked about their i/o in Annapolis and Chesapeake Bay, then headed south through the Carolinas and Georgia to explain their theories to boatbuilders and dealers in Wynne's native Florida. It was in Florida that they met with Albert Woodson of Plastic Fabrications Inc of Miami. Woodson, who already knew Jim Wynne well and had considerable respect for his abilities, built the famous Thunderbird range of GRP sportsboats and cruisers. By the end of the meeting Woodson, Wynne and Hansson had established that, given the unit in time, the first i/o boat to be exhibited in the New York show would be a Thunderbird Comanche.

Travelworn but very encouraged by the industry's response, Hansson telephoned Harald Wiklund in Sweden and the decision was taken to proceed with detailed construction drawings and a wooden mock-up of the drive assembly to show to Gunnar Engellau, the president of the Volvo corporation. Meanwhile, Hansson returned to the office of Volvo Import in Englewood Cliffs, New Jersey, to arrange the advertising for the forthcoming exhibition. Copy date for the January editions of the leading yachting journals was just one week hence and Volvo Penta had as yet not thought of a name for Wynne's invention! Several names were suggested and tossed around between Hansson and the advertising men but one above all others seemed to stick : Aquamatic. The advertising plans went ahead anyway but it was not until 23 December that the agency was given written authorisation to use the name. These advertisements also needed an illustration of the Volvo Penta Aquamatic; so an artist's impression was utilised, which subsequently was seen to be quite accurate regarding the engine, which existed, but highly inaccurate in its representation of the drive, which did not.

Nils Hansson, on his return to Sweden at the beginning of November, found the Volvo Köping factory on continuous twenty-four-hour shifts, tooling up to the drawings made in his absence by Bergstedt. Within a week of Hansson's arrival Engellau had approved the wooden model of the Aquamatic and given the go-ahead for prototype construction and testing. Three prototypes

From Sweden came the **VOLVO**...

Masterpiece of

INBOARD POWER

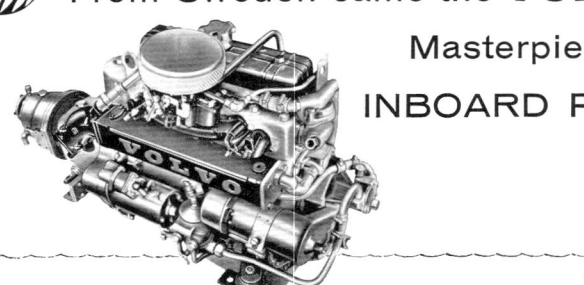

And now the

VOLVO AQUAMATIC

80 HP outboard performance with new inboard TRANS-MOUNT

Sweden's famed 4-cycle marine engine linked to high-efficiency transom drive

There's a new performance now for outboard-type boats . . . more fun coming up for owners. Famed for operating hour after hour at sustained high speeds *with* economy, this Volvo is now engineered into a balanced power package. Here's outboard pep, with inboard safety! Here's 4-cycle smoothness . . . quietness. Here's dependability proven in North Sea storms; here's Swedish craftsmanship in high-efficiency performance on salt or fresh water.

New Volvo AQUAMATIC POWER matches outboard speed at ⅓ the fuel cost

Engine and drive with reverse-reduction gears are mounted in counterbalance on transom. Transom has full height safety; no extra well needed. In actual tests, Aquamatic fuel costs averaged only 67¢ an hour versus $2.15 for conventional outboard power. And no messy oil mixing. Inboard quiet, inboard safety, with tilt protection in water, tilt convenience for beaching and trailer hauling.

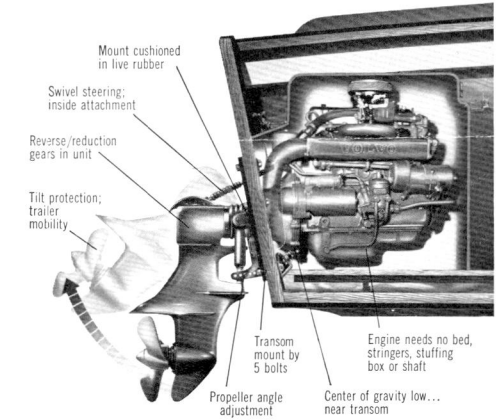

Mount cushioned in live rubber

Swivel steering; inside attachment

Reverse/reduction gears in unit

Tilt protection; trailer mobility

Transom mount by 5 bolts

Engine needs no bed, stringers, stuffing box or shaft

Propeller angle adjustment

Center of gravity low... near transom

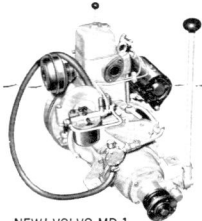

NEW! VOLVO MD-1
5 HP 1-cylinder Auxiliary Diesel

FREE: Write for new folders with Aquamatic details, specifications, diagrams. Complete data for boat builders, owners.

See the fine line of Volvo Engines ...at the NEW YORK BOAT SHOW

Volvo Aquamatic —Volvo Inboards
Volvo Diesels 5-220 HP

VOLVO IMPORT, INC.
Marine Engine Division, 452 Hudson Terrace
Englewood Cliffs, New Jersey

10 Advertisement for the 1959 New York Boat Show with 'artist's impression' of the new Aquamatic drive. The announcement of the famous MD1 was overshadowed

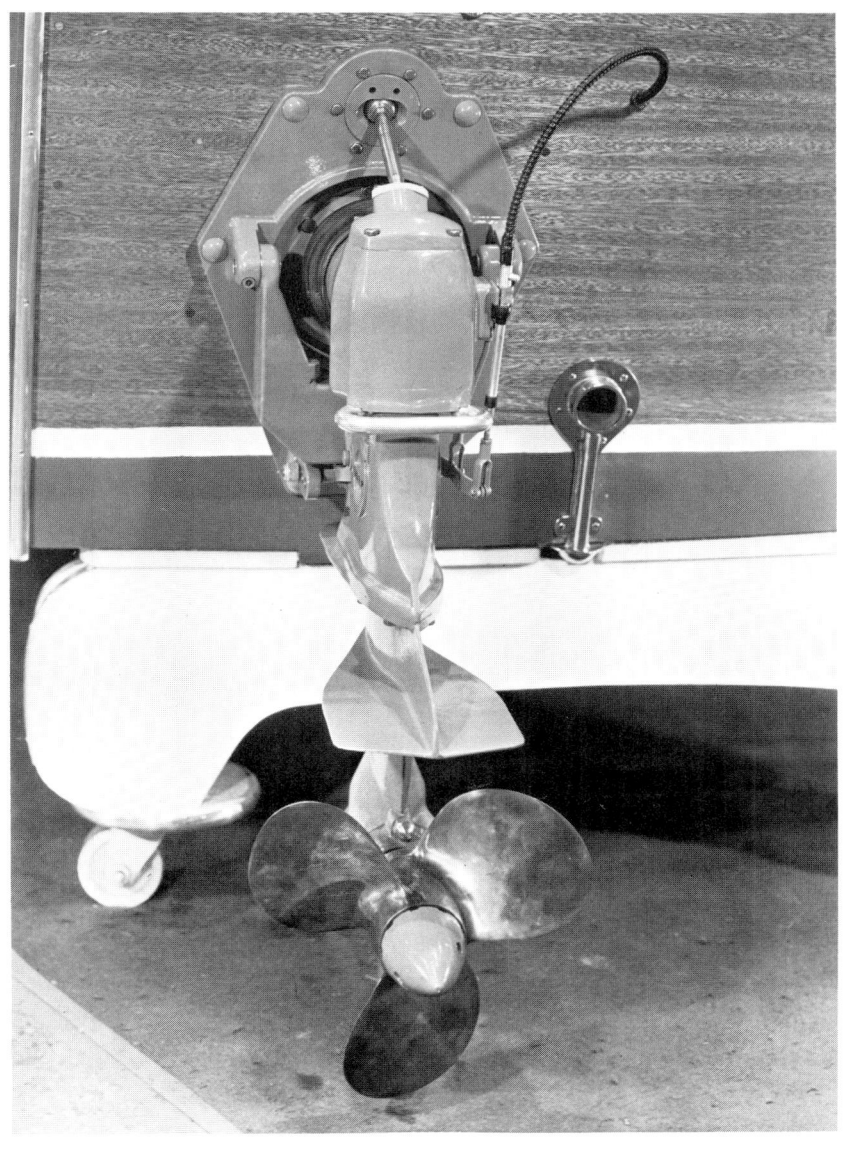

11 The 1959 New York Boat Show. Volvo 'Iron' badge on side of upper housing and first combined inlet and exhaust fitting

were made, the target date for completing the first one being Christmas Day, just six weeks off. After the briefest of running on the bench, No 1 was finished on Christmas Eve and then carefully packed for shipment to the USA with Arne Jones of Volvo Import to supervise it *en route*. No 2, ready at the same time, was assigned to the Volvo Penta test tank. The third pre-production unit was installed in a test boat and run twenty-four hours a day for many consecutive days under the close scrutiny of Hansson's specialists. Miraculously, the Aquamatic had arrived on schedule and without a single technical fault.

The public reaction to the Aquamatic at the 1959 New York show was overwhelming in its enthusiasm, enough for Volvo immediately to set a production target of a thousand units for the current year. Thunderbirds of course had an exclusive option at the time and the first batch of one hundred engines and outdrives was promised to them. Ole Botved decided that his new Coronets would be the first boats in Europe to adopt the Aquamatic as standard, whilst Knut Bogeburg, Norwegian head of the UK's GRP pioneers Tod's of Weymouth, determined to become Britain's first.

Shortly after the New York show had closed its doors, engineers and design staff at the Keikhaefer Mercury offices were making plans for a Mercury I/O, which began testing a year later. Mercury were not the only people who were impressed by Volvo Penta's new winner, for between 1960 and 1962 no less than twenty-two other manufacturers announced new outdrives of which two alone have survived under their original name OMC and Mercruiser. A third, Unicorn's, was adopted by Perkins of Peterborough to become the Perkins Z-Drive, later relinquished by Perkins to Enfield Engineering.

By July 1959, just one year after Jim Wynne's visit to Volvo Penta, the Aquamatic was internationally accepted, technically efficient and well on its way to achieving the 1959 target of a thousand units, with no serious competition for nearly two years to come. Meanwhile the first prototype had been tested for the Miami-Nassau powerboat race. Here is Wynne's report to Volvo Penta a few days after the race:

Saturday 18 April 1959
Report from Jim Wynne on board the Miss Aquamatic
The practicality of the new Volvo Penta Aquamatic inboard/outboard unit for boats was proved today when it finished first in its class in the world's most rugged powerboat race, the famous and fearsome run across the Gulf Stream from Miami to Nassau, a distance of 188 miles.

Every form of sea condition was encountered in this gruelling event with 9 to 10ft seas and winds of up to 20mph, but the 18ft Thunderbird boat with Volvo Penta power was first to finish in the single engine class against boats to 30ft and 215hp. The engine and the drive performed smoothly during the complete $16\frac{1}{2}$ hours of this endurance run. *Miss Aquamatic* was fourth to finish overall, beating some boats twice her 18ft size and with four times her power, proving that a small family cruiser can weather the roughest conditions. Only three large twin engine craft came in ahead of *Miss Aquamatic*, who also beat another craft of the same design, but twin-outboard-powered, by 12 hours.

Of seventeen boats that started only nine could finish the contest. Bucking into the strong easterly winds, the run was made with a total fuel consumption of 64 gallons compared to 162 gallons consumed by the finishing outboard-powered boat.

Jim Wynne, skipper.

2
The I/O Concept

Jim Wynne had foreseen the advantages of combining the best features of the inboard engine and outboard motor without inheriting their disadvantages. Nowadays the I/O system is so commonplace a part of the powerboating scene that it is perhaps worth recalling the pros and cons of the two types which visionary designers worked from, and which Jim Wynne and Volvo Penta converted into practical success.

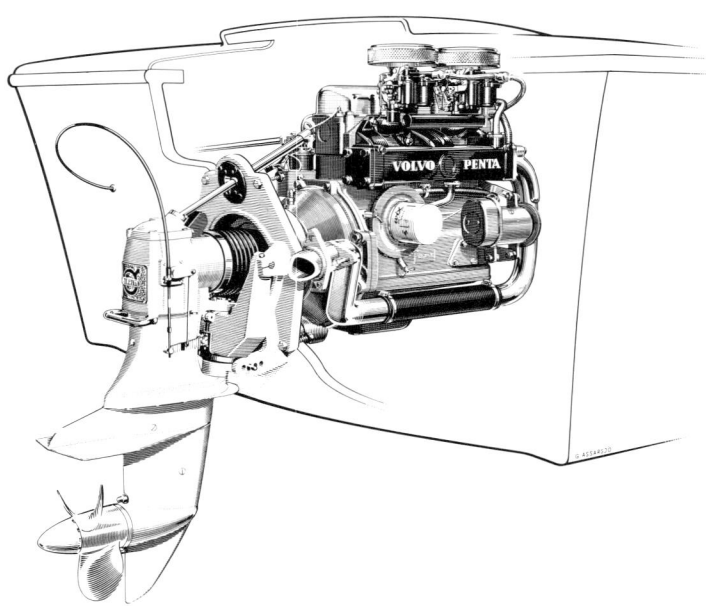

12 1961 Aquamatic 100, showing the continuing concept of simplicity with this first **B**.18 engine

28

The inboard engine

Advantages
robust construction
four-stroke cycle
low fuel consumption
protected from seawater
protected from damp
long service life
simple maintenance
secure from theft
boat has high resale value

Disadvantages
need of stern tube and P bracket
necessity for rudder steering
inefficient propeller thrust angle
underwater gear vulnerable and expensive to repair
engine placed forward restricting space
transmission friction losses high with vee-drive
long and complicated installation

The outboard engine

Advantages
integral propeller and shaft
steering incorporated
propeller thrust parallel with boat angle of attack
ease of repair if damaged underwater
transom-mounted engine allows unrestricted living space
low transmission loss
simple and quick installation*

Disadvantages
light construction
two-stroke cycle
high fuel consumption
exposed to seawater
exposed to damp
short service life
maintenance usually means removal
vulnerable to theft
low resale value

*Not strictly true of high powered outboards which, by nature of their size and weight, cease to be portable.

When the two lists of advantages are combined one can see that they form the basis of the design of the i/o and thus the basis of the Aquamatic. The one comparison that is not included above is that of performance. In a light boat, for example a ski-boat or racing craft, the i/o contribution to total weight is high compared with an outboard motor of equivalent power, and for sheer speed the outboard will be superior. In heavier craft, such as 23 to 35ft cabin cruisers, the engine weight is less critical and the i/o comes into its own. The i/o has a more appropriate propeller interpretation via its reduction gearing and achieves a considerably increased cruising range for a given amount of fuel.

29

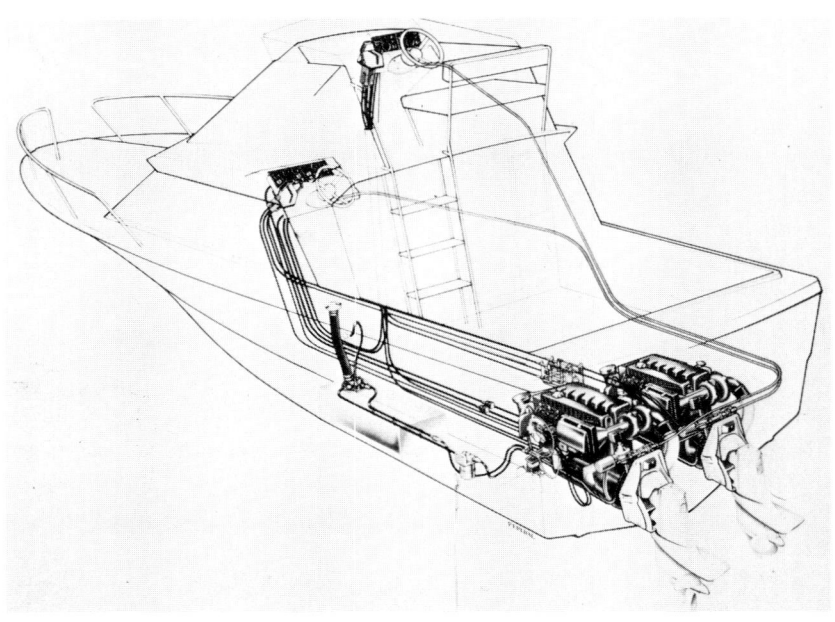

13 Formula boat on test in Sweden

14 The complete package. All the propulsion-linked equipment can be supplied by Volvo Penta, but it is unusual for tank and battery to be included

It is in the field of motor cruisers that the i/o concept had the greatest effect on boat design. Thinking of the most popular cruisers of the 1950s one recalls the variety of transom shapes and angles, unaffected by the engines which were installed amidships. Today, the majority of fast cruisers up to 35ft have an aft cockpit and a flat transom raked at 12° even when they have an inboard engine. The i/o lent itself to improved boat production techniques. Glass-fibre mouldings, prefabricated furniture, mass-produced screens and windows, flow-line assembly etc would all have been relatively ineffective if each engine had required elaborate wiring, meticulous alignment to the propeller shaft, fabricated exhaust and cooling systems, assembly of rudders and steering gear. An added hindrance for the boatbuilder was that he had to rely on several different suppliers for all the components which go to make up the total engine installation. The i/o package enabled the production boat-builder to plan with certainty his installation times and cut them considerably. Further, because the entire engine, transmission, steering and electrics were all contained in the aft compartment, the completion of the forward part of the boat could proceed unhindered.

From the beginning of Aquamatic production Volvo had a unique and inherent advantage which enabled the company to maintain a lead in i/o development for so many years. With two brief exceptions (Perkins in the 1960s and BMW in 1978) Volvo were the only manufacturers of both engine and drive units. This has meant that engine and outdrive design, production capacity, parts avail-ability and price levels of most models have been entirely under Volvo's own control. Although the current AQ120, AQ140, AQ145, AQ170 and AQD40 engines are of pure Volvo origin, the aluminium VPR (Volvo-Peugeot-Renault) petrol engine used in the 264 car is unsuitable for marine adaptation. This fact, allied to the demand for more power, principally from the USA, has prompted the factory to adopt American basic engines for the upper end of the Aquamatic range.

Volvo's early forays into this field were fraught with disaster, particularly in the case of the Buick-based AQ150 V-6 engine. The marinisation of this engine was subcontracted to an American com-pany and in its short lifespan from 1967 to 1970 became the subject of much modification. These early marine engines, first GM-based

15 British progress. Early Project 31 built by Marine Projects of Plymouth on a standard Senior 31ft hull designed for inboard or i/o power. Although pre-production line era, the quality left something to be desired

and later Ford Escort-based, had the drawback of prohibitively expensive spare parts, which were also very difficult to obtain. Having thus burnt their fingers in these early attempts to convert American V-engines, Volvo built their own factory in the US in Norfolk, Virginia, in 1975 and made a firm agreement with GM Chevrolet for commercial blocks and spare parts. To ensure both technical and follow-up efficiency the new range of V-8 engines to emerge from the Norfolk works were sold only on the US home market for the first two years. Today they have proved reliable and eminently suitable worldwide. In contrast to their early problems with American conversions, Volvo have enjoyed a long and highly successful co-operation with Indenor-Peugeot in France. The light and powerful Indenor diesels formed the basis of the AQD19, AQD21, AQD27, AQD29 and AQD32 engines which put Volvo

16 From the same builder in 1979 the excellent Princess 33ft. Maximum advantage has been taken of the low height of the engines, in this case twin AQD40s

Penta ahead of all competition in the field of planing boat diesel engines. Experience with these units provided the basis for Volvo to invest heavily in the creation of their own remarkable 40 series engine and bring high speed Aquamatic diesel development firmly under their own roof. The significance of this very advanced AQD40 justifies a later chapter to itself.

The modern 280 drive is the latest expression of Volvo Penta's twenty-one years of outdrive experience, experience dominated by commonsense technology and the Swedish taste for functional simplicity. The treacherous craggy coastline of Sweden's west coast and the vile weather that prevails there for nine months of the year have dictated that the outdrives must above all be tough. Volvo Penta also appreciate that the Swedish yachtsman, with such a brief summer to spend afloat, does not want to lose leisure time

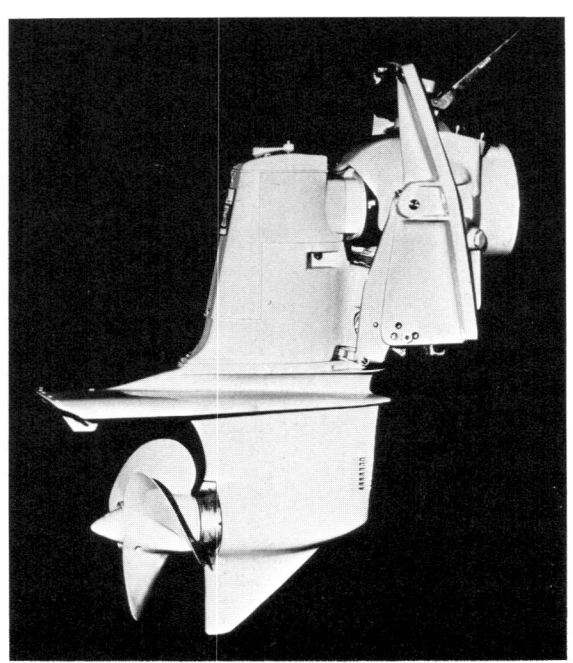

17 The 280 drive

on engine or drive repairs. Even less does he want to feel that he needs a qualification in electro-mechanical engineering before putting to sea! All Aquamatics have been built with such considerations in mind—hence their worldwide reputation for rugged practicality.

Features of the 280 outdrive

The 280 drive is the latest in the line from the 200 drive through 200B, 250 and 270. When the 200 unit was introduced in 1964 it was designed for engine torques up to 250Nm (Newton metres). In 1968 the 250 drive raised the figure to 300Nm, whilst the 270 drive in 1970 raised it yet again to 400Nm. Mechanically similar to the 270, the 280 drive has a larger cavitation plate and an improved hydrodynamic design of the lower unit. This alone gives the 280 up to three knots more speed than its predecessor with a similar

18 This idyllic setting in Gothenburg's archipelago underlines why Swedish
yachtsmen want to make the most of their leisure time

engine. A new steering system reduces steering effort by thirty-four
per cent. All Aquamatic units consist of three main components:
the engine, which has the forward mounting feet attached and is
carried on the transom shield by a bell housing; the drive unit,
which contains the gearbox and reduction gears and passages for
cooling water and exhaust gas and water discharge; finally, the
transom shield, which performs the function of bringing engine
and drive together.

The drive line
Engine power is transmitted to the drive via a UJ joint on a splined
shaft which engages with corresponding splines in the flywheel
damper assembly. From the UJ, power is carried to the upper bevel
gears, which contain the cone clutch mechanism, and to the vertical

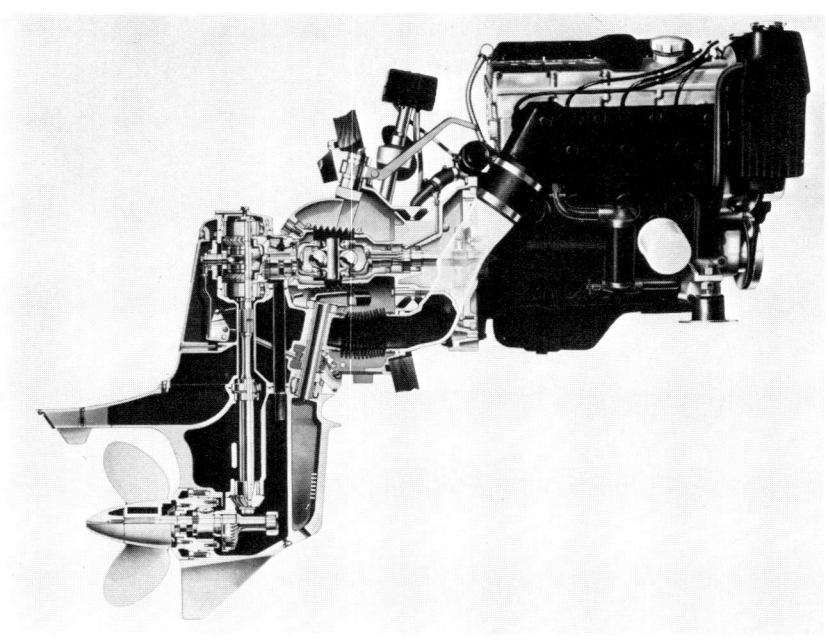

19 AQ140/280 showing the interlink of the mounting collar between engine and drive

drive shaft which in turn engages with the lower bevel gears carrying the propeller shaft. The lower gears provide the various reduction ratios.

The transom shield
The shield consists of an aluminium, gravity die cast plate in alloy to Swedish Society of Engineers (SIS) 4244 standard. The shield is hardened after casting due to the extremely high loading requirement. The forces to be transmitted to the boat hull under normal conditions can be up to 6000Nm. Extreme operational stresses such as the boat leaving and re-entering the water with engine racing in a heavy sea can induce loads of up to 15,000Nm. Under such circumstances inertia forces of up to 15g on the hull have been measured. On the instant of re-entry a transverse shock load is applied to the propeller that is more than twice the normal load

36

level. The effect of this can be reduced greatly by the helmsman throttling back whilst airborne.

Inevitably, both transom and shield have to be strongly constructed, and securely bolted together. This is achieved by six heavy peripheral bolts through both, leaving only one large central hole for connecting engine to drive. A large rubber sealing ring is compressed between the plate and transom surface. Where the bell housing enters the central orifice in the shield, two large rubber O-rings are clamped between cones: one on the housing, the other in the shield itself. This provides the double facility of vibration damping and preventing ingress of water. Originally, this method of mounting, with the assistance of a small rubber stop under the bell housing, was sufficient to carry the entire engine. However, higher engine powers and heavier engines prompted the introduction of an additional mounting at the forward end of the engine.

As the shield also carries the mechanism for steering and kick-up, the drive is necessarily mounted via dowels to a pivoting yoke which carries the steering tube. The yoke is cast from a very high

20 Shock loads on drive and shield

37

strength and costly aluminium alloy Alcan C.135. Tilting of the drive is effected by an electro-mechanical lift unit which lifts the drive to its full 60° in approximately six to eight seconds. A small friction clutch is built into the lift unit to allow low speed trolling ahead when entering shallow water with the drive tilted. Above idling rpm the propeller thrust overcomes the friction and pushes the drive down to its normal running position. Ideally, the line of propeller thrust underway is parallel to the angle of attack of the boat but sometimes it is necessary to compensate boat trim by moving the tilt pin fore and aft $+$ or $-4°$ in the holes provided. Kick-up when hitting an obstacle in the water is provided by the retaining pawl mechanism. When running ahead the thrust from the propeller keeps the drive tucked in against the tilt pin and the pawl is disengaged. Should the drive begin to 'trail' as in deccelerating, the spring loaded pawl locks onto the pin. Should the drive hit an obstacle the acceleration of the drive away from the transom is so great that it kicks up before the pawl operates. A rubber stop is provided at the top of the transom shield to act as a shock buffer and to absorb the kinetic energy when the drive kicks up. The outdrive is locked down mechanically when astern gear is selected.

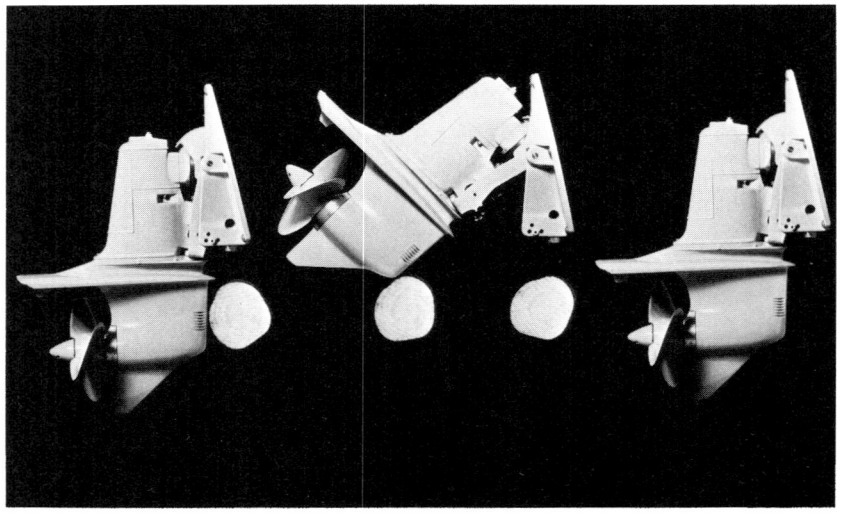

21 Photographic simulation of tests carried out over tethered log

22 Reserve water intake just below the point of the torpedo

Steering the unit is usually carried out by means of a push-pull cable system from the steering wheel to the tiller, sometimes via a reduction gear linkage to reduce load. Later versions of the 280 drive have a .8 or .5 reduction link incorporated in the shield. The maximum angle to which the drive may be turned lock to lock is 30° port or starboard. Although this is less than with other stern drive systems Volvo have limited it for safety reasons. The lower unit of the drive has the shape of an aerofoil section which creates 'lift' towards the outside of the turn as the drive angle changes. This lift factor enables very tight turns to be made with relatively small helm movements. The greater the speed of the boat the more effective does this design feature become.

Cooling water for the engine is drawn (pressurised when underway) from an intake in the leading edge of the drive. Should this become blocked a reserve intake under the nose of the torpedo ensures a continuous supply but with a perceptible increase showing on the temperature gauge to warn the helmsman. The water is then transferred from the intake through the steering tube via a hose connection to a transfer tube in the shield and carried via a raised pipe (above the waterline) before connecting with the weed trap and/or the water circulating pump on the front of the engine.

Exhaust manifolds on the engines are generally water-jacketed and cooled by raw water. The cooling water mixes with the exhaust gases in a special water-injection elbow before being discharged together. At the injection point the exhaust gas is at a much higher temperature than the water, thus causing a high evaporation rate. The refrigeration effect on the exhaust gas results in a slowing of gas flow by almost half, thus lowering back-pressure. At high speeds, where the water volume is much higher, back-pressure is reduced by the exhaust bypass pipe in the shield, which allows excessive gas and water to discharge directly overboard. The bulk of the emission passes through the exhaust bellows and via channels in the outdrive to the outlet at the trailing edge of the cavitation plate. The plate is designed to create a cavity under the water surface to receive the gases, an improvement of over three decibels' sound deadening compared with the 270 drive.

At low speeds and when manoeuvring, the flow of cooling water is low, allowing the bypass pipe to act as an extra exhaust pipe. This in turn reduces the exhaust pressure and volume at the main outlet, thus eliminating the adverse effect of exhaust gas around the propeller when going astern. All connections, controls and electrics are intentionally contained inside the shield for both protection and accessibility.

The drive unit
Like all the earlier Aquamatic drives, the 280 drive consists of three basic units: the upper housing, containing the gearbox and gear shift mechanism, the UJ coupling and input shaft; the intermediate housing, which contains the steering yoke and tilt fork, the retaining pawl and part of the exhaust channelling; finally the third unit, the lower housing with its reduction gears, propeller shaft, water intake and exhaust discharge.

Significantly, Volvo Penta has adhered to a simple mechanical cone clutch gearbox and placed it in the upper housing. Not only is this, the most expensive part of the drive, above the waterline

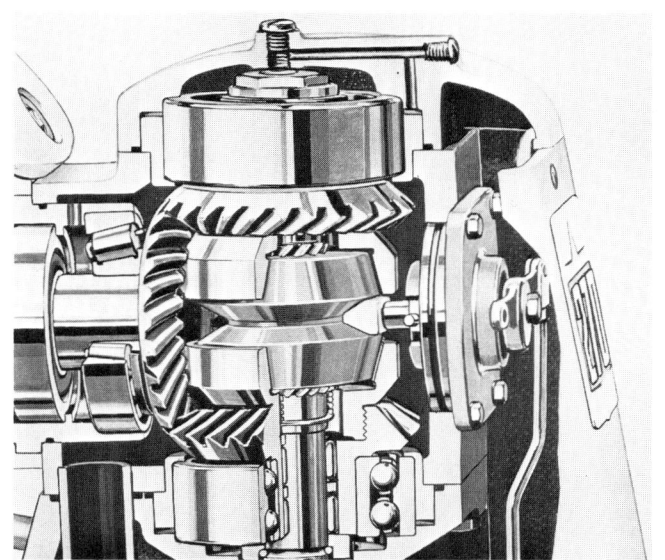

23 Patented cone clutch ahead-neutral-astern gearbox on 270 drive

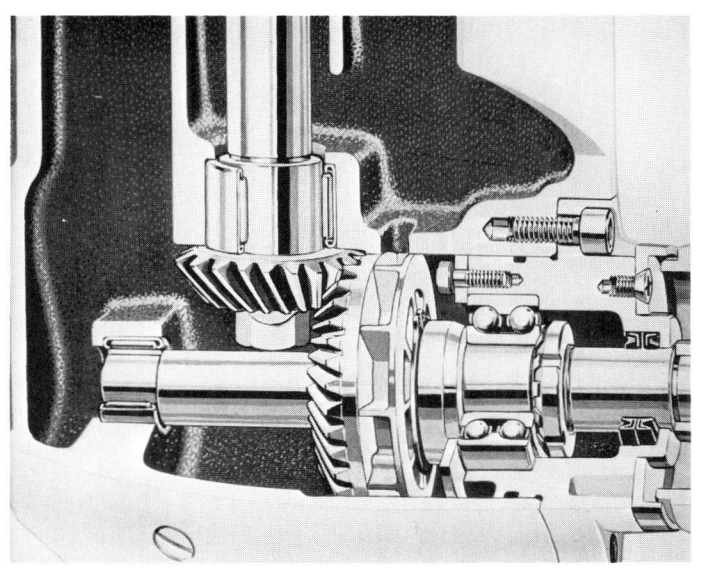

24 The relatively simple lower unit

41

and out of harm's way (the lower unit on any sterndrive can, of course, be destroyed by reversing into something), but it allows the gearbox and clutch to be as big and tough as required without affecting hydrodynamic shape. The relatively less costly lower unit can bow to hydrodynamic constraints as it merely contains the bevel reduction gears.

The blanks from which both upper and lower gears are made are forged in such a way that impurities are concentrated into the centre of the blanks. During machining the centre is cut away leaving only the purest material in the teeth. Helical gears are used to reduce noise level—the greater the helical angle the lower the noise. Upper gears have an angle of 35° but the lower gears, which are required to run in both directions of rotation, have an angle of 20°. The lower unit is immersed when running, which tends to deaden gear noise. After forging, cutting and case hardening the gears are lapped in and thereafter kept in their matched sets. Although there is no effective reduction ratio in the upper gears the primary gear (input) has 26 teeth and the secondary gears have 27 teeth to allow even wear. The reduction ratio is obtained from the lower gears wherein the secondary gear (propeller shaft) has 31 teeth and alternatives of 15, 17 or 20 teeth on the primary gear give ratios of 2·146 : 1, 1·893 : 1 and 1·61 : 1 respectively.

The lower unit is a hydrodynamically designed aerofoil section containing the streamlined pod around the bevel gears. At speed the blade of the lower unit has a marked rudder action which, combined with the aerofoil shape, improves turning stability. At low speeds the rudder effect is negligible and steering sensitivity very poor without the aid of propeller thrust. To offset the influence of steering torque with single (LH) engine installations an adjustable trim tab is provided under the cavitation plate, aft of the propeller. The amount of engine torque consumed by the steering, depending on gear ratio and propeller size, falls between ten and fifteen per cent.

To adjust the trim tab it is necessary to turn it, a small amount at a time, in the direction that the boat is tending to go, ie if the boat is running off to the right the trim tab should be offset to starboard. Because the tab can only be fixed in one position its effect cannot be constant throughout the speed range. Ideally, the tab should be adjusted to give neutral torque at about eighty per

cent of the boat speed. This would mean acceptable steering loads at higher speed but inevitably torque reaction would still be experienced at lower speeds, particularly when the boat is just approaching planing speed. When running straight ahead at eighty per cent of the maximum knots the drive will actually be offset by .5° to 1°.

The aluminium castings used in the drive have to be extremely tough and corrosion-resistant. To meet this requirement Volvo Penta use virgin gravity die casting aluminium to standard SIS 4244 thus obtaining a high corrosion-resistance with minimum risk of porosity. The castings are hardened in the process of surface treatments which consist of a series of epoxy-based baking varnishes in the following sequence:

1 Application of primer
2 Filler applied and baked to 180°C
3 Grinding and rubbing down
4 Further primer hardened to 180°C
5 Two layers of finishing varnish baked to 160°C.

For protection against weed growth Volvo Penta offers a non-metallic anti-fouling paint as an accessory.

Many of the exposed components on the drive are made from stainless steel, for example, propeller shaft, all bolts and thread inserts, retaining pawl mechanism. These components have a galvanic tension difference with the aluminium alloy of just over half a volt. To prevent the possible electrolytic effect of these and possible alien items (iron piles in a marina, a nearby steel hull etc) on the aluminium, the drive is fitted with zinc sacrificial anodes. The anodes, one in the shape of a ring forward of the propeller and the other an ingot under the transom shield, have a higher galvanic potential than the other materials; thus it is the higher tension zinc which discharges towards the lower tension steel and aluminium and intentionally is allowed to corrode away.

To facilitate oil level checking when afloat (with care) a dipstick is located in the drive top cover. The rear-face cover is also removable whilst afloat to enable the gear selection to be adjusted or the rotation of the drive to be changed.

The engines
The Volvo Aquamatic engines are characteristically simple and accessible. The seawater circulating pump is always positioned at

26 Stainless steel bolt and helicoil

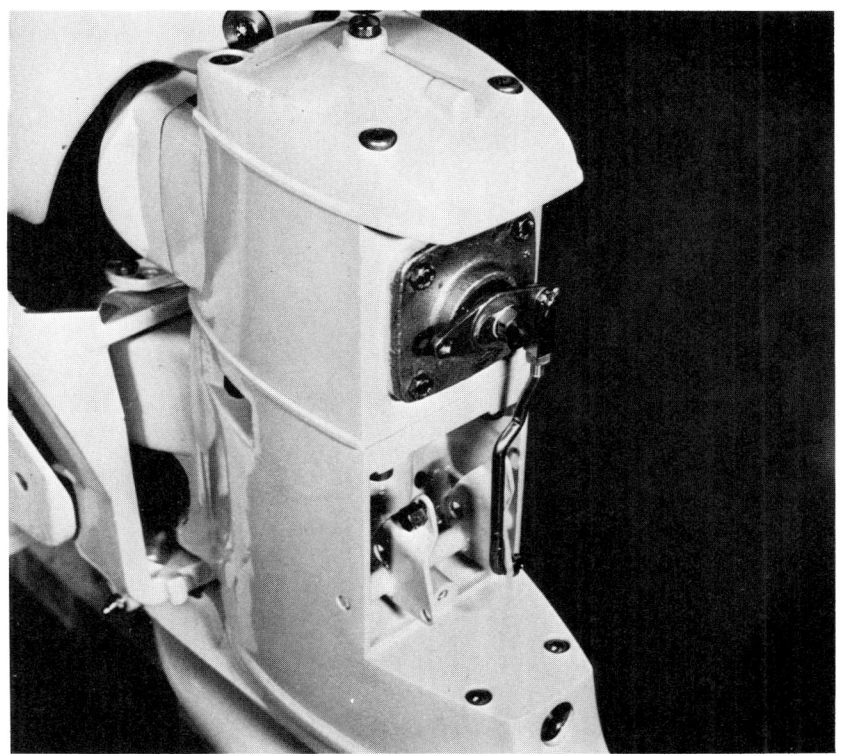

27 To change rotation relocate the vertical link-rod on the right

the front of the engine; items that frequently require checking, such as dipsticks, weed traps, oil and fuel filters, are all brought within easy reach.

Since 1963 all engines have been equipped with plug-in water-proof wiring harnesses between engine and instrument panel. Later engines, including those paired with the 280 drive, have the additional feature of a quick-change fuse block or, in some cases, a reset button, eliminating conventional fuses.

In the Volvo laboratories in Skoevde and Gothenburg and at the marine test station on Krossholm Island the quest for improvement is continuous and exhaustive. Aquamatic drives are run non-stop under full load for weeks at a time. They are tested in sub-zero

45

temperatures, thrashed through ice-covered seas, and recklessly driven over obstacles time after time. The test boats are specially constructed in steel to withstand the constant punishment. One of the boats is fitted with a ten-litre turbo-charged diesel which through a series of step-up and reduction gears can simulate conditions of load, rpm, torque and horsepower far in excess of anything an Aquamatic would encounter in service. The Aquamatic has come a long way since the idea was mooted in 1958, but it still recognisably conforms to Jim Wynne's original and patented concept.

3
Trials and Tests

Jim Wynne's prototype I/O unit was run for about five minutes on its initial test. The AQD40 in various prototype forms was developed over five years and travelled the equivalent of eight times around the world. Wynne was testing an idea. With the D.40 Volvo Penta was testing a sophisticated piece of engineering technology which had to be commercially viable, reliable and safe. Most modern testing is carried out in Volvo's engine test laboratory with simulated conditions of load and stress. At the Krossholm marine test centre the testing is clinically precise and laboriously meticulous, but occasionally some tests are spectacular enough to use for publicity purposes. This was particularly so in the early days of the Aquamatic when its builders wanted to prove a point. One of the principal claims by Volvo Penta has always been that of fuel economy. By 1961 many counter-claims were being made, and outboard manufacturers accused Volvo of exaggerating the meanness of their four-cycle engine.

NASCAR, the National Association for Stock Car Auto Racing Inc, was established in the United States in 1949 to give organisation and direction to the rapidly growing sport of stock car racing. NASCAR had become the world's largest auto racing organisation, with a membership of some 8000 in 1961. This organisation with its extensive experience in running economy and performance tests for major auto and auto-equipment manufacturers had become interested in the marine industry. Volvo Penta was the first marine firm to take advantage of the facilities of this independent authority.

Utilising Lake Lloyd in the centre of the Daytona Speedway, NASCAR's new marine research division tested the boats of eleven major builders, all of them equipped with the Volvo Penta Aquamatic 80.

Making up the fleet from manufacturers that represented some sixty per cent of the United States' annual boat production were craft from Thompson Brothers (Wisconsin), Hydrodyne, Glasspar, Larson, Thompson Brothers (NY), Skee-Craft, Cruisers, Grady-White, Sabre Craft, Grumman and Coronet.

The tests were set up to justify the fuel-economy claims for the 80hp four-cycle, four-cylinder Volvo Penta engine. They did just that according to William C. France, director of the marine research division, who commented on the performance of the new outdrive: 'The eleven craft ranged from a 17ft runabout to a 22ft cabin cruiser and averaged 1880 pounds each, yet they attained an average of $5\frac{1}{4}$ gallons of fuel per hour'.

According to published trials by outboard manufacturers, the average two-cycle outboard of comparable horsepower consumes $8\frac{1}{2}$ to $9\frac{1}{2}$ gallons an hour, and oil has to be mixed with the gasoline.

'Even more impressive was the performance of the craft at reasonable cruising speed,' France continued. 'We found that at 3500 revolutions per minute the boats averaged almost 23 miles per hour, used only 2·8 gallons of fuel an hour and averaged better than eight miles per gallon of fuel.' France also mentioned that the

28 The first NASCAR tests. *Left to right* Hydrodyne, Skee-Craft, Grumman, Thompson

29 The first NASCAR tests. Jim Wynne drives for test crew and their
equipment aboard Grumman Sportster

eleven boats had been set up for the average user with no attempt
to feature either exceptional speed or fuel economy. Thus these
figures represent the performance that the normal user could expect
to receive from his own Volvo Penta powered rig.

France stressed that the fuel economy and speed figures in the
Volvo Penta Aquamatic tests were taken simultaneously, thus
eliminating the possibility of different adjustments for speed and
economy: 'This was an extremely well-balanced test that is indica-
tive of the future of American boating. The varying size and style
cf the eleven craft let us get figures on just about every type of
craft in the rapidly growing segment of inboard/outboards . . .
No attempt should be made to compare performance of the

TABLE 1   THE FIRST NASCAR TESTS

| | | | 3000 RPM | | | | 3500 RPM |
	Weight Lbs	Length Feet	Avg.fuel cons. GPH	Avg. speed MPH	Knots	MPG	Avg.fuel cons. GPH
Thompson "P" "Off Shore"	1890	19'	2.20	18.604	16,156	8.46	2.91
Hydrodyne "runabout"	1385	17'	2.12	23.189	20,137	10.94	2.73
Glasspar "Seafair Sedan"	1588	17'	2.09	19.241	16,709	9.21	2.88
Larson "Cabin Cruiser"	1835	19'	2.36	15.178	13,181	6.43	2.89
Thompson "C" "Cruisette"	2123	19'	2.09	17.257	14,986	8.26	2.80
Skee-Craft "Sebring"	1868	19'	2.05	18.418	15,994	8.98	2.69
Cruiser "Commander"	1850	17'	2.24	17.881	15,528	7.98	2.85
G & W "Atlantic"	2188	20'	2.09	15.084	13,099	7.60	2.77
Coronet "Explorer"	2555	22'	2.16	14.365	12,475	6.67	2.92
Sabre Craft "Debutante"	2020	19'	2.09	19.436	16,878	9.30	2.67
Grumman "Sportster"	1380	19'	2.01	20.042	17,404	10.02	2.72
Average	1880		2.14	18.972	15,686	8.53	2.80

TABLE 2   THE SECOND NASCAR TEST

Boat	Weight (Lbs)	Length (Ft)	3000 RPM GPH	MPH	MPG	3500 RPM GPH	MPH	MPG	4000 RPM GPH	MPH	MPG
AFI Special	1935	19'6"	2.385	19.311	8.096	2.930	23.860	8.143	3.800	28.186	7.417
Coronet Explorer	2687	22'	2.770	15.289	5.519	3.370	20.855	6.188	4.165	25.234	5.818
Dorsett Daytona	1335	16'	2.095	19.423	9.271	2.670	25.199	9.437	3.42	29.796	8.712
Glasspar Sunliner	1525	17'	2.530	18.959	7.493	3.130	23.743	7.585	3.935	28.827	7.325
Glastron Futura	1300	16'	2.250	21.844	9.710	2.920	27.958	9.570	3.560	32.661	9.170
Grady-White Capri	2150	19'	2365	13.101	5.539	3.015	18.313	6.073	3.550	22.238	6.264
Hydrodyne 1700	1440	17'	2.135	20.371	9.541	2.815	26.098	9.271	3.560	30.737	8.633
Thompson Utility	1960	18'	2.205	17.967	8.148	2.780	23.334	8.393	3.345	28.081	8.394
Vega 21	2360	21'	2.605	16.163	6.204	3.205	20.785	6.485	4.205	25.434	6.048
Average	1854	18'5"	2.371	18.047	7.724	2.981	23.349	7.905	3.726	27.910	7.531
Formula 233 (Twin Engines)	3835	23'	4.930	18.641	3.840	5.975	24.644	4.124	7.135	29.668	4.202

| 3500 RPM | | | 4000 RPM | | | | W.O.T.(4500 RPM) | | | |
| Avg. speed | | | Avg. fuel cons. | Avg. speed | | | Avg.fuel cons. | Avg. speed | | |
PH	Knots	MPG	GPH	MPH	Knots	MPG	GPH	MPH	Knots	MPG
3.379	20,302	8.06	3.65	27,649	24,010	7.60	5.16	31.880	27,685	6.18
7.464	23,850	10.06	3.57	32.263	28,017	9.05	5.37	35.426	30,764	6.60
4.301	21,103	8.45	3.52	28.544	24,788	8.16	5.27	33.277	28,898	6.31
0.252	17,587	7.03	3.55	24.807	21,542	6.99	5.54	30.020	26,069	5.42
2.118	19,207	7.50	3.50	26.288	22,828	7.49	5.04	30.045	26,091	5.96
3.507	20,413	8.74	3.34	27.165	23,590	8.16	5.11	32,097	27,873	6.28
2.723	19,733	7.99	3.58	26.556	23,061	7.43	5.18	30.100	26,139	5.82
9.858	17,245	7.17	3.37	24.762	21,503	7.35	5.49	30.115	26,152	5.49
0.288	17,618	6.95	3.50	24.633	21,391	7.04	5.45	27.911	24,238	5.13
3.990	20,833	8.99	3.40	28.657	24,886	8.43	5.25	33.173	28,807	6.33
4.803	21,539	9.14	3.46	29.816	25,892	8.62	4.85	33.185	28,818	6.84
2.971	19,948	8.19	3.49	27.376	23,773	7.85	5.24	31.566	27,412	6.03

| 450C RPM | | | W.O.T.(4927) RPM | | |
PH	MPH	MPG	GPH	MPH	MPG
.710	31.768	5.635	6.230	32.549	5.224
.565	27.459	4.934	7.230	28.892	3.996
.515	33.847	7.496	6.765	36.734	5.430
.505	32.979	5.990	6.895	34.522	5.006
.390	36.585	4.360	7.010	39.656	5.660
695	25.977	5.532	7.035	28.544	4.057
530	33.955	7.495	7.475	37.267	4.985
715	33.198	5.808	6.570	33.885	5.157
905	29.776	5.042	6.440	30.753	4.775
170	31.727	5.810	6.850	33.644	4.921
140	34.602	3.785	14.195	37.375	2.632

30 The second NASCAR tests. Chief timekeeper Joe Epton talks to the crew of the Thompson Utility

31 The second NASCAR tests. *Left to right* Grady-White Capri. Glasspar Sunliner, Coronet Explorer

32 Sarasota, Florida. Jim Wynne lowers the drive on the Hydrodyne test boat

33 Into the reeds at Sarasota. Wynne drives the Hydrodyne into the reeds at 35mph

Aquamatic on the larger boats present.' France found that the 22ft cruiser attained a speed of 28mph yet used less than $5\frac{1}{2}$ gallons of fuel at full throttle. At 3500rpm the craft went over 20mph yet used less than three gallons an hour.

A quarter-mile course was measured on the lake's surface and electronic eyes installed to measure times to $\frac{1}{100}$ of a second and speeds to $\frac{1}{1000}$ of a mile per hour. Mechanics installed a super-accurate tachometer and gasoline temperature gauges, and tapped a fuel flow meter into the fuel line. Each boat then took north and south runs through the course at 3000, 3500 and 4000 engine revolutions per minute, plus full throttle. These showed the speed and fuel mileage one would get at barely planing speed, easy cruise, fast cruise and all out. After each boat completed its run, officials ran the timing figures through a calculating machine, recorded air and water temperature and barometric pressure. The relevant details may be found in Table 1.

Nearly two years later the tests were repeated with ten selected boats, this time with the new 110hp B.18 unit AQ110/100 (Table 2).

34 The Sarasota trials complete, Jim examines the drive for damage

35 Surely it shoud be the skier . . . ?

Soon after the first NASCAR tests Jim Wynne set about an even more spectacular test programme to prove the toughness of the I/O unit. At Sarasota, Florida, the Aquamatic was installed in a 17ft Hydrodyne fibreglass sports boat, and put through two days of tortuous trials. The craft was run across an island eight times, across a sandbar and beach twenty-two times, over a solid oyster bed four times, through four-foot high marine growth a dozen times and, finally, through underbrush and over the lawn at Sunshine Springs, ending up some sixty feet from shore! After any one of these tests the conventional inboard would be a boatyard patient for several days, requiring shaft, propeller and rudder replacement and engine realignment. When the testing programme was completed the only damage to the Aquamatic was paint scraped off the skeg of the outdrive. Both boat and engine-outdrive combination were strictly standard and no effort was made to 'beef up' either for these tough tests.

Drivers Jim Wynne and Herb Crosby of Midwestern Industries, manufacturers of the Hydrodyne boat, alternated at the controls

36 The Volvo Penta marine test centre at Krossholmen

37 The quay at Krossholmen. Steel-hulled test boats painted blue and numbered

38 Steel boat with ten-litre turbocharged diesel and step-up gears to simulate punishing torque and rpm loads on the 270 drive

while the craft seemed to spend almost as much time moving over solid ground as it did through water. The exciting and spectacular publicity from such testing, interspersed with Wynne's racing successes, secured the reputation of the Volvo I/O.

By the end of the 1960s Volvo Penta had set up its marine test centre at Krossholmen on the Rivö Fjord in the Gothenburg archipelago. The test centre consists of three main units in an available area of 143,000sq ft (13,300sq m). The main units are an assembly hall and workshop, a storage hall, and an office with a central radio installation (for maintaining contact with test boats). The latter is rather quaintly constructed from an old ship's bridge and overlooks a small natural harbour with views beyond to the buoyed test

39 & 40 Test boat beached at full speed followed by visual inspection of drive

41 Production-line testing of instrument panel circuitry

circuits. A bigger harbour and quay is located adjacent to the assembly hall with a five-ton crane to lift test boats in and out of the water.

Five special test boats are kept at Krossholmen, all steel-hulled to withstand the harsh treatment of the year-round test programmes. Up to twenty-five other boats of various types and sizes are based at the centre including a selection of racing craft for testing engines at speeds in excess of fifty knots. The test drivers are all skilled technicians and use electronic instruments and sensors to register information about mechanical stresses, vibrations and temperatures

42 Quality, style and performance. Don Shead (an early racing associate of Jim Wynne) designed this superb Sunseeker 28 for Poole Powerboats of England. Experiences at Gothenburg while testing a diesel Sunseeker 23 enabled Poole Powerboats to achieve over thirty knots in this new boat with twin AQD40 engines. A classic example of Volvo Penta test facilities helping a production boatbuilder

at various critical points throughout the engines and drives. Besides their technical expertise and ability to handle a variety of craft the test drivers have to be pretty tough. They work outside all the year round, in winter snowstorms, sub-zero temperatures and ice-covered seas. During tests over thick logs or running up a beach at full speed, forces of up to 8g have been recorded. To supplement the Krossholmen programme, research is carried out in the tropics, the Middle East, the Mediterranean and in Florida.

Krossholmen could never replace the hours of component checking, tank testing and laboratory work that are spent before and during the production cycle of an Aquamatic unit; but it performs the vital function of in-use testing under simulated conditions far more severe than the engines are ever likely to meet in service.

4
The Fast and the Famous

Minutes after the start of the 1959 Miami–Nassau powerboat race a 30ft cruiser with two 300hp inboard engines had caved in her hull and was running for the beach. Seconds later an outboard-powered boat turned back. Altogether that day, eight of the seventeen starters that set out from Government Cut into the 20mph easterly wind and 10–15ft seas of the Gulf Stream were destined to retire. With fifty-four miles to go before the first refuelling stop Jim Wynne and co-driver Bill McKeown (editor of the US magazine *Popular Boating*) determined not to join them. They were driving a cathedral-hulled 18ft Thunderbird Miami cruiser powered by the New York show Aquamatic. Above all other considerations Jim desperately wanted to prove his invention; this gruelling race, described as the most rugged in the world, gave him an early opportunity. From the beginning, neither Wynne nor McKeown believed they had a chance for the big prizes in this 188 mile marathon. Entries were by invitation only to the twenty most experienced boat/crew combinations out of the total of thirty-six applications. Besides being, at 80hp, the lowest-powered boat in the race, their little Thunderbird was full of equipment for an extended out-island cruise planned from Nassau, should they finish.

However, halfway across the Gulf Stream on the first leg to Cat Cay they found they were gaining on more powerful craft. By the time they checked in at 11.44am, 4hr and 19min after the start, they were leading their class. Delaying only 3min to clear customs, *Miss Aquamatic* pointed her nose towards the next checkpoint, Frazer's Hog Cay, 96 miles away across shallow banks and through a brutally confused and steep sea. Shortly after leaving Cat they rendered radio assistance to an injured crewman on another boat before resuming their course for the first navigational check, the Northwest Light, 75 miles out. This lonely beacon was always

43 *Miss Aquamatic*, boat no 15, the cathedral-hulled 18ft Thunderbird Miami designed by Richard Cole, powered by an AQ80. Boat no 11 in the background is the Cox/Joyce outboard Miami

difficult to see and inability to obtain a sighting was to be a problem for some of the other competitors. Finally, just after dusk, the Thunderbird tied up at Frazer's Hog. To their amazement, Wynne and McKeown learnt that they were only the fifth competitor and the first single-engined boat to reach this stage. Realising they were in with a chance after all, they ignored advice to stay overnight and decided to press on for the last and roughest 38 mile haul to Nassau. To this day Wynne claims that he was thankful that he was unable to see the massive waves in the pitch-black night, but by this time both men had a great deal of confidence in their boat and its single Aquamatic I/O.

When they arrived in Coral Harbour, Nassau, only one person remained to greet them on the quay, as no more finishers had been expected before dawn. *Miss Aquamatic* had won her class and finished fourth overall with three of the fastest and most powerful twin-engined boats in front of her. Their closest rival, another Thunderbird, with two outboards, crewed by Bob Cox and Ed Joyce, arrived twelve hours later. Wynne had proved his point spectacularly; his Aquamatic had stood up to the cruellest of tests with faultless reliability.

After the race, Bill and Jim embarked on a 400 mile cruise through the Bahamas, spreading Aquamatic lore. Whilst in Georgetown, Great Exuma, during the local regatta week Wynne delightedly entertained HRH Prince Philip, Duke of Edinburgh aboard *Miss Aquamatic.*

1960

For the 1960 Miami–Nassau race Wynne had decided to use a bigger boat and install twin Aquamatic engines. This would mean competing in an unlimited class and against boats with engines up to 700hp. He was still puzzling how to overcome this apparently insurmountable disadvantage when Arthur Hartwell of New England Marine in Providence, RI, introduced him to the Hunter. Hartwell claimed that the Aquamatic-powered 16ft GRP Hunter could achieve 35 knots through 3ft seas. Wynne frankly doubted it as to that time no planing hull could stay in one piece under such conditions. Nonetheless, a meeting with George O'Day whose Marscot division of George D. O'Day Associates Inc was producing the boat, resulted in Wynne accepting to test a Hunter 16 in Miami. Even more interesting to Wynne was the news that a mould for a 23ft Hunter was being constructed. As Jim and Bill McKeown again planned to visit the Out Island Regatta after the race, they had set down their accommodation and equipment needs for this cruise and concluded that they required a 22–24ft cabin boat.

Wynne spent an afternoon trying the Hunter 16 and became enthralled with its speed and stability. The absence of pounding in a short steep chop was a startling new experience that meant to Jim that both boat and crew could withstand higher speeds in rougher water than had hitherto been possible. In a later test report for *Popular Boating* he described the Hunter boats as 'fantastic': the deep-vee concept had arrived. This was to change the basics of high speed powerboat design and lend fame and opportunity to such as Dick Bertram, Don Aronow, Renato (Sonny) Levi, Don Shead and of course, one of its greatest converts, Jim Wynne.

The man behind the new hull shape was C. Raymond (Ray) Hunt of Boston, Mass., who had become well known as designer of the sailing yacht *Easterner*, the 1958 America's Cup contender. Ray Hunt had experimented for several years with high speed hulls and, in conjunction with George O'Day and colleagues Palmer and

Duncan Scott, had produced the Marscot Hunter. The deep-vee with constant dead-rise all the way aft allowed the boat to pitch into the sea without presenting a large, flat, horizontal area to slam. Longitudinal strakes, sometimes called planing strips or spray rails, provided lifting 'steps' for the hull and helped maintain both lateral and fore-and-aft stability at speed. The new vee-section did not in itself create higher speed than a conventional hull—more power was required to plane it—but it did allow more power to be used at higher speeds in adverse conditions. Deep-vee hulls truly revolutionised powerboat design and were to be demonstrated most convincingly by, first, Dick Bertram and, secondly, Jim Wynne in the 1960 Miami–Nassau contest.

Christened *Aqua Hunter* the new boat, with its twin Aquamatic engines, spent its shakedown period at Fort Lauderdale preparing for the big race. Bill McKeown and Jim spent the evening before the race planning their strategy. By a process of elimination they concluded that two of the larger high-powered boats offered the most serious opposition. Forrest Johnson's *Prowler* was a very real threat with its twin 325hp engines and was likely to put up a hard fight with the other serious contender, Dick Bertram's *Moppie* skippered by veteran and twice winner of the race Sam Griffith. Navigator for *Moppie* was the skilful Carleton Mitchell of ocean sailing race fame; the third crew member was Bertram himself.

Moppie (said to be named after Dick Bertram's wife's hairstyle) was another hull designed by Ray Hunt, built by Bertram especially for this contest. McKeown and Wynne knew that, if the going became rough, nothing would catch the 30ft Bertram. Before retiring to bed, *Aqua Hunter*'s strategy was forged—cling to *Prowler* and see what happened.

Soon after the start on Wednesday 13 April, twenty-two boats plunged into heavy seas at the mouth of Government Cut, forcing all but two to slow down and several to turn back. Even Forrest Johnson eased back, allowing *Aqua Hunter* to pass and follow *Moppie*, which was already edging away rapidly in front.

Despite a compass problem, *Aqua Hunter* arrived at Cat Cay in 2hr 55min, 8 minutes behind the leader. After only a three-minute customs stop an uneventful but rough trip across to Frazers Hog preceded an extremely rough final leg across the Tongue of the Ocean to the Coral Harbour Channel. During this final phase

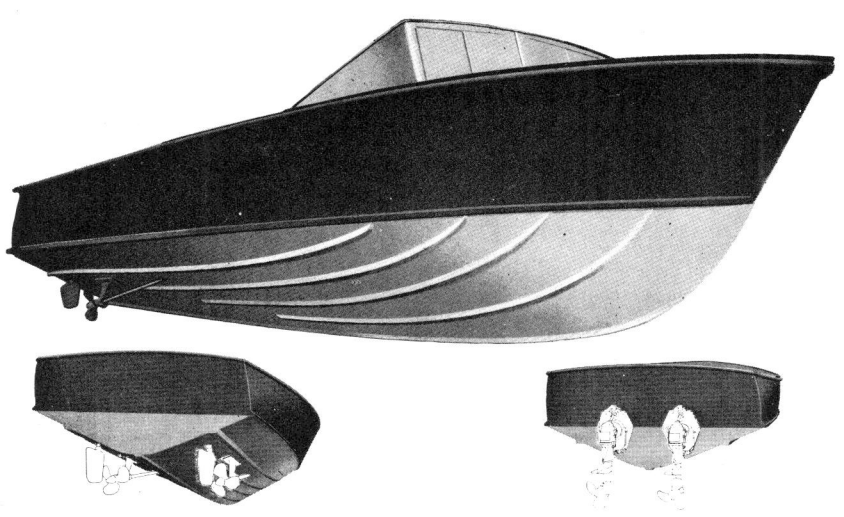

44 The winning shape. First place: (*left and above*) *Moppie;* second place: (*right*) *Aqua Hunter*

Wynne found it necessary to ease the engines back from their full-song 4500rpm to 4000 and then 3700rpm. For some reason not immediately obvious, the electric bilge pump failed and Bill McKeown spent an uncomfortable and deluged thirty minutes half in, half out of the engine compartment, hand-pumping the spray accumulation overboard.

To a tumultuous welcome *Aqua Hunter* docked at 5.25pm after completing the race in 10 hours and 25 minutes. Dick Bertram and Sam Griffith had finished in an incredible 8 hours. Each boat had won its class. The third boat to finish, Bob Cox and Ed Joyce's 22ft Thunderbird Scout, docked 12 hours later. They were the first outboard boat ever to be placed in an overall rating position as well as achieving their class win.

Once again Jim Wynne had proved his Aquamatic against sterling opposition. Inadvertently, both Dick Bertram and Wynne had conclusively proved the superiority of the deep-vee hull, a form they were to adhere to in all their future powerboat exploits.

The deep-vee bug had soundly bitten both Miami–Nassau

45 Jim Wynne driving the Marscot Hunter 16 to victory in the 1960 Miami Orange Bowl Regatta

winners. Shortly after the race Dick Bertram put the 30ft Moppie into production and asked Jim Wynne to assist Ray Hunt in developing a 25ft hull with twin i/os. The result of this joint effort culminated in the famous Bertram 25 in which type Wynne was to secure first in class in the first London *Daily Express* International Offshore Powerboat Race from Cowes to Torquay in the following year.

In December 1960 Wynne entered the Orange Bowl Regatta in Miami, Florida. Driving a 16ft Hunter with his beloved Aquamatic, Jim achieved four new world records for 1, 3, 6 and 9 hours in the nine-hour marathon. Only seventeen boats finished out of the fifty-five starters, the mirror-like conditions calling for sustained full throttle, which caused many engines to fail rapidly. The Hunter, averaging 38.8mph, won Class One against more powerful boats and was the only boat to finish without a refuelling stop. This was only the second time since the event was initiated in 1954 that this had been achieved.

The powerboat racing highlight of 1961 was the newly established *Daily Express* International Offshore Powerboat Race from Cowes in the Isle of Wight to Torquay in South Devon. Sir Max Aitken, son of Lord Beaverbrook, ex-World War II fighter ace and proprietor of the *Daily Express*, was to become a regular contestant and frequent prizewinner in this classic.

On the morning of 19 August the wind was blowing WNW force 5 and gusting to force 6 causing some discussion among the organisers about postponing the event; but doubts were dispelled and the forty-odd starters crossed the famous Royal Yacht Squadron line all-out for Torquay. Conditions proved to be very rough indeed, the short steep seas of the Solent and the English Channel subjecting crews, hulls and machinery to severe punishment. Much of the time the boats were airborne, their screws clear of the water, only to plunge back with bone-jarring and shuddering regularity into the troughs. Not surprisingly, the powerful deep-vee boats pulled ahead, led by Tommy Sopwith's *Thunderbolt*. *Thunderbolt*, designed by Ray Hunt and built in the UK by Bruce Campbell of *Christina* fame, was a 25ft LWL GRP hull powered by twin Crusaders totalling 650hp. Close on Sopwith's heels *A'Speranziella,* Sonny Levi's mount from Italy, was a strong challenger until fuel pump trouble prompted her retirement. Two other front runners, both Hunt designs, retired with engine trouble: Peter Twiss, the ex-Fairey Aviation test pilot, in *Huntsman No. 8* (owned by Billy Butlin) was forced to withdraw, and Wynne's old rival Sam Griffiths in Bertram's *Glass Moppie* suffered a burnt-out clutch. Wynne, in *Yo-Yo* the new Bertram 25 with its two diminutive AQ100 I/os, did not have cause to retire and reached Torquay in second place, only twenty-six minutes behind the overall winner, *Thunderbolt*. He collected two silver medals and cash prizes for second overall and first petrol-engined boat under 5.25 litres.

Fresh from this notable success, Wynne decided to draw on the experience he had gained working with Hunt on the Bertram 25 project and set about designing his own boat for the 1961 Miami nine-hour marathon which he had won so convincingly the previous year in the Hunter 16. So began the first of the highly successful Wyn-Mill series. The Wyn-Mill was developed around the Aquamatic, becoming the first purpose-built I/o runabout designed

46 *Yo-Yo*, the Bertram 25 developed by Ray Hunt and Jim Wynne

for racing speed and endurance. To this day, the 17ft Wyn-Mill with its Wynne adaptation of the deep-vee principle, looks as finely honed and purposeful as it did almost twenty years ago. *Wyn-Mill* and later *Wyn-Mill II* were to continue to dominate the Orange Bowl nine-hour event in Class One, Jim Wynne achieving four consecutive victories in four years with Aquamatic-powered entries.

During the autumn of 1961 a small group of British enthusiasts had competed in the Paris six-hour endurance race on the River Seine. The race was a débâcle of smashed boats, overheated engines and damaged outboards. The tortuous circuit under the Seine bridges and the hazards of driftwood and flotsam took a severe toll of the small racing boats. The prize for the best British boat went to Donald Shead and David Barton driving a 14ft Yarecraft with a Perkins 35hp outboard. Narrowly beaten for this award was

47 The first 17ft Wyn-Mill

a Fletcher Arrow in the hands of Ken Fisher and Norman Fletcher himself, who was in subsequent years to become Britain's foremost sportsboat builder and an internationally acclaimed ski-boat designer. It was, however, Don Shead who realised the potential advantages that the I/O could bring to the Paris six-hour event. Don had met Jim Wynne during the 1961 Cowes–Torquay race and had suggested that the Wyn-Mill design would be suitable for Paris. The association between Don Shead and the American was to lead to Shead's first foray into boat design and put him on the road to becoming Britain's premier international powerboat designer. At about this time the Italian Sonny Levi became involved in the Wyn-Mill project; he too was to achieve worldwide fame for advanced hull designs including the beautiful Levi 25 and later the Triana hulls and some of the exotic and expensive Rivas.

1962

Early in the year Wynne visited England in response to Don Shead's suggestion for the Paris race. With him he brought the plans for the 17ft Wyn-Mill and arranged for a three-boat team to be constructed in the UK.

Souters of Cowes would build two boats, one for Wynne and one for Shead; the third would be built by Camper and Nicholson for Tommy Sopwith. While this went ahead Wynne's attention turned once more to the Cowes-Torquay race set for 8 September.

Altogether six Volvo-powered boats were entered for the 1962 event, among which were the Bertram 25 *Yo-Yo II* driven by Wynne and owned by F. Gillam, Don Shead's *Trident* and regular Cowes–Torquay enthusiast Fred Carvill's tiny *Bella II*. Fred never actually won any substantial prizes but, like many others, competed year after year, epitomising the amateur spirit of the early Cowes–Torquay races.

The winner of the 1962 event was *Tramontana* owned by R. S. Wilkins and driven by J. K. Quill. Powered by twin CRM engines of 1154hp each, she finished in 5hr 20min. Second place went to Peter Blond, owner and driver of the 30ft *Blue Moppie*, timed in at 16¼min behind the leader, and third overall was *Yo-Yo II*, finishing after 6hr and 55min. Wynne's third position was one of his most amazing achievements taking into account the engine capacity of the first two boats across the line. *Tramontana*'s engines displaced

48 The second Wyn-Mill in the 1962 Miami nine-hour race

a massive 114.5 litres and *Moppie* a total of 13.3 litres. The two Volvos in *Yo-Yo* added up a mere 3.6 litres!

The following month, October, saw the three Wyn-Mills start in the hazardous Paris six-hour event. Sopwith was in overall lead until struck by engine trouble. Don Shead also led for a while before retiring from the same cause. By the fifth hour Jim Wynne was leading the field but losing speed due to a clogged fuel feed. Wynne finished second overall taking the first inboard prize and the Index of Performance.

In December Wyn-Mill once again achieved a Class One win in the Miami nine-hour race.

1963

The first event of 1963 was the Miami–Nassau race, which was won by Odel Lewis in a Mercruiser-powered Bertram 25. John Bakos in his second-placed boat had also used 450hp Mercruisers to good effect, thus helping Keikhaefer to establish the reputation of the big Mercs. Mercruisers later, right up to the late 1970s, came to dominate the higher power ranges for offshore racing boats, reaching a peak of achievement in the era of Don Shead's Enfield Marine boats and Don Aronow's superb *Cigarettes*. Indeed it was Aronow who took third place in that 1963 Miami–Nassau race in a 27ft boat with twin Interceptors. He had seen the Wyn-Mill and, impressed with the design, had commissioned Jim Wynne and his partner Walt Walters to design what was to become the Formula range and the famous Donzi line.

The Cowes–Torquay event for 1963 continued to be dominated by the big inboard engines, this time the two 400hp Dearborn Interceptors of Sonny Levi and Attilio Petroni's *A'Speranziella*. Second spot was taken by *Blue Moppie* once again, with an 800hp Ford engine, brilliantly handled by Billy Shand-Kydd and that very British sporting gentleman Keith Schellenberg. *Yo-Yo II* followed in third position propelled by two of the new AQ110s.

Outboards took first three places in the Paris race on 6 October. Len Melly and John Merryfield scored the first British win, followed by O. Rocca and D. Francois of France who held another British twosome, J. James and A. Venables, to third place. Jim Wynne in *Wyn-Mill* won the Index of Performance with Don Shead and David Barton runners-up in another similar boat.

71

1964

In his fifth year of racing exclusively Aquamatic-powered boats Wynne was finding that more and more of his time was devoted to boat design. He felt that, although the Aquamatic had opened up opportunities to himself and other leading designers, the time was approaching for him to concentrate on promoting his hulls. No one could deny that he had well and truly proved the Aquamatic, often giving himself extraordinarily hard rides pushing boat and engine to the limit in order to keep up with bigger and more powerful opposition. Nineteen sixty-four was to be the last year in which Jim raced with Volvo engines, a year of superb performances.

In July Sonny Levi invited Wynne to take part in the Italian classic, the Viareggio–Bastia–Viareggio race across the Bay of Genoa from the Italian mainland to Corsica and back. First man home was future world champion Vincenzo Balestrieri in the Interceptor-powered *A'Speranziella*; second was Sergio Sonnino in the Italcraft-Chrysler *XL*; third, with less than a third of the power from the twin Volvos, came Jim Wynne in the Levi-designed *Settime Velo IV*.

Within a month Wynne was is England preparing for the *Daily Express* race to Torquay. Wynne designs were now beginning to feature second only to Ray Hunt in the pre-race listing. Among the 1964 entrants were four Wynne-Walters designs; *Migrant* a Daytona-powered Formula for the Earl of Lucan; Billy Shand-Kydd's *Lucinda*, another but this time single-Daytona-powered Formula; and Don Aronow's *Claudia II* Formula, shared with D. P. Miller. Wynne, with former transatlantic partner Ole Botved, was driving a new 24ft Coronet which was aptly called *Coronet Wyn-Mill*.

The weather was windless, allowing a flat calm sea that would most favour the big powerhouses. The millpond conditions also promoted one of the most exciting finishes ever to be seen in off-shore racing. *Lucky Moppie*, with Dick Bertram at the helm, headed the fleet into Torbay only to lose his way in the last seconds to the finishing line. The mistake cost him the race as the Gardner brothers in their Bertram 31, *Surfrider*, slipped through to take first place. *Lucky Moppie* came second with *Claudia II*, D. P. Miller's Formula, third. Only three minutes separated first and third boats home. After the race was over the press hailed Jim Wynne

49 *Coronet Wyn-Mill.* Wynne and Ole Botved showing off their trophies after the 1964 Cowes-Torquay event. This was the first public showing of the new Coronet 24

and Ole Botved as the day's heroes. When they passed Southsea, eight miles from the start, they were in 25th position; by Ventnor, IOW, 19th; at Bournemouth, 17th; abeam of Portland, 11th; they finished in Torquay in 8th position. The average horsepower of boats ahead was 650hp compared with their two AQ110s. *Coronet Wyn-Mill* won first prizes for fuel economy and Index of Performance and second prize in the Concours d'Elegance for the best designed, maintained and equipped boat. The three awards combined culminated in a major trophy for the 'best all-rounder'.

The 1964 Paris six-hour race had its share of excitement and success for Volvo but was marred by the death of Kirié who, driving the Aquamatic-powered *Kirié*, hit a bridge pier. After the recovery team had extricated him from his sunken boat it was too late; he died shortly afterwards in hospital. John Merryfield and Len Melly won the event for the second time in a Levi-designed 16ft outboard. After an unplanned beaching had his boat, *Thunderball*, temporarily out of control, Jim Wynne succeeded in re-launching to finish second overall and winner of the restricted inboard (R1) class. Second in this class were Frenchmen Bouillant and Delettrez with their Wyn-Mill and third were Fox and May of Britain in a Shakespeare-Mercruiser. Appropriately in 1964 Jim Wynne became the first World Offshore Champion.

1965

By now the international offshore races had become the domain of the high speed missiles, expensive to build and prohibitive to maintain and run for all but the very wealthy. Within very few years company sponsorship would become a necessity; racing machines would no longer contribute to the development of everyday fast cruisers and sportsboats. By this time too Jim Wynne had turned his attention to more powerful boats; he took first place in Viareggio–Bastia–Viareggio with a 32ft boat of his own design, *Maritime*, powered by twin Daytonas and owned by Merrick Lewis. *Maritime* was the world's first all-aluminium offshore racing boat. His previous year's boat, *Settimo Velo V*, now re-engined with big Mercruisers, was driven to second place by Rene Jacoby and her daughter; the veteran *A'Speranziella* took third prize. In the rough conditions over half of the fleet, including Aronow in *Donzi 007*, Bertram's *Brave Moppie* and Lady Violet Aitken in the re-engined *Yo-Yo II*, suffered breakdowns.

By the end of the summer the Cowes–Torquay race had a prolific line-up of Wynne-Walters designs. *Lucinda* had passed into the hands of Mrs N. Gardner, whilst Shand-Kydd sported a new Donzi, *Lucy Too*. Other Formula boats included Lord Lucan's *Migrant* and the well-known *Broad Jumper*. J. Robinson had entered a Wynne Coronet but the engines were by Aston Martin. Jim himself drove the aluminium *Maritime*, which had served so well in Italy. T. J. Threlfall in the Levi-designed, R. W. Clarke-built *Poseidon* secured the best all-rounder and fuel economy prizes for Volvo.

Although the Aquamatic was now losing out to the big Daytonas, Interceptors and Mercruisers offshore, new successes awaited in France. For the first time in its history, the Paris six-hour race was won outright by an R1 inboard-class boat. Raymond Guyard and Serge Monier of France in their Volvo-powered Luizzi broke a long-standing record to establish 287.8 miles at an average speed of 47.9mph. Second boat overall was a Mercury outboard-powered

74

Levi, driven by the up-and-coming James Beard. Third prize and second in Class R1 was attained by Don Shead and John Quick in another Levi, but this time Volvo Penta powered.

The Guyard Luizzi, this time in the hands of Raymond's sons Alain and Daniel, gained a convincing first overall and first in Class R1 at the first international Rouen twenty-four-hour marathon. Although the Rouen course was better than Paris, and certainly less cluttered with debris, the twenty-four-hour race was and is a gruelling trial for man and machine.

1966

It was in Rouen again that the Volvos achieved their prime victory of 1966. The Guyard family entered two new Rocca boats with Aquamatic engines, one to be driven by Raymond and Raymond Jr, the other by Alain and Daniel. Despite the temporary hospitalisation of Raymond *père* as the result of injury in a shunt, the Rocca-Volvo of R. and R. Guyard took first place, first in R1 and the Index of Performance, having covered 1066 miles at an average of 44.4mph. Brothers Alain and Daniel were a close second, having set a new lap record of 53.16mph.

In Paris, the R1 class was won by Blanchet and Jourdan of France in an Oioli-Volvo, but with an overall position of tenth. Don Shead and James Beard finished second overall in their Levi-Volvo but were unplaced as a result of an homologation problem. Significantly, the outright winner was Molinari in a Mercury-powered catamaran of his own creation. The high performance catamaran was to set new standards in circuit and offshore races, with Molinari and James Beard in the van of twin hull development.

By the end of 1966 Jim Wynne had won another world championship but not on the strength of the Aquamatic. Indeed, racing boats and racing speeds had moved away from the concept of boating for which Aquamatic had been intended. Volvo-Penta rarely made international racing headlines again.

Nonetheless, the Aquamatic made local headlines with ever increasing frequency. As offshore racing evolved away from most pockets, racing enthusiasts continued to organise local events inshore and on inland lakes. 'Round the cans' racing grew and grew until it became impossible to keep track of all the events in the US and Europe where Aquamatic successes were attained.

50 Fast! Ex-world heavyweight champion Ingmar Johansson and son with their Aqua-matic

51 Faster! The late Donald Campbell who was to hold the world waterspeed record in 1964 seen here talking to Per Nyström of Volvo, Gothenburg 1960

52 Fastest! Yuri Gagarin, the first spaceman, orbited the world at 18,000mph on 12 April 1961. Shortly afterwards he became the first Russian to own an Aquamatic in his Coronet

To assist with the promotion of club racing the Volvo Car Competition department, formed in the 1950s and since 1962 under the leadership of the Swedish rally driver Gunnar Andersson, extended its activities in 1970 to include the tuning of Aquamatic units. The original i/o design team of Nils Hansson and Abdon Bergstedt developed a new, very slender twin-shaft lower unit for the 250 drive which later progressed through the 270E to the 280E. Gunnar Andersson and his colleagues applied to the engines the fruits of their experience in rally-tuning cars to provide powerboat enthusiasts with a range of high powered sports engines based on the B.20 and B.30 blocks.

The B.16 engines used by Jim Wynne in the early races were very much factory standard AQ80s. Not until 1961 did Volvo Penta tune this model to produce 88hp, naming it the Aquamatic 80 Sport. Early B.18s were also tunable with factory supplied parts. The AQ100 could be souped up by fitting twin SU HS6 carburettors, a 'C' camshaft, new pistons, harder valve springs, and by shaving the cylinder head to give an 11:1 compression ratio. By the time the AQ110 was introduced in 1963 most of the above modifications were included in the production engine, leaving only carburettors, compression ratio and ignition tuning needing attention. The gain in output was around 15bhp. Very little work was done in the early 1960s to modify the drive units especially for racing. The changes that were incorporated on production legs during this period were admirably suitable for the sports enthusiast. With the advent of the 100 drive with cylindrical shaft and pin, it was discovered that few racing propellers were available for this fitting and, more important, the underwater shape of the old 80 unit offered slightly less resistance at higher speeds. In consequence many AQ110S engines were fitted with 'slimline' lower units which were in fact bottom ends of AQ80 drives complete with splined shaft.

As the mid-sixties approached several proprietary firms were finding ways of wringing more and more power from the B.18 engines, in some cases boring out to two litres and cutting dangerously close to the water jacket. Higher power and increases of up to 6000rpm caused a disturbing phenomena with the outdrives, whereby the vertical drive shafts would drill themselves very neatly through the top covers, to the frequent embarrassment of both racers and Volvo

AQUAMATIC 80 SPORT

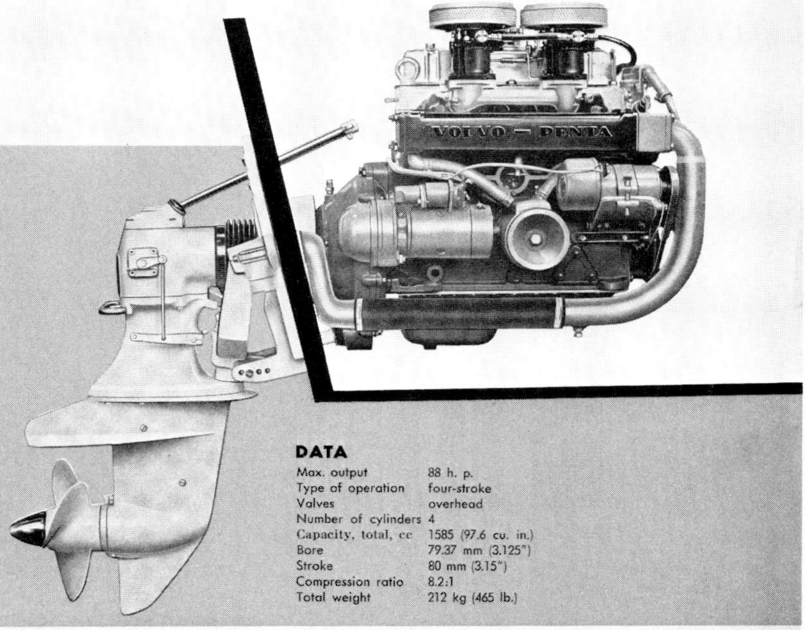

DATA

Max. output	88 h. p.
Type of operation	four-stroke
Valves	overhead
Number of cylinders	4
Capacity, total, cc	1585 (97.6 cu. in.)
Bore	79.37 mm (3.125")
Stroke	80 mm (3.15")
Compression ratio	8.2:1
Total weight	212 kg (465 lb.)

- Cuts fuel cost over 50 %
- More speed — more power for your money
- Easy trailing and beaching
- Rugged 88 h. p., 4 cycle engine
- Needs no expensive oil mixture
- Inboard economy — outboard mobility
- More elbowroom in your boat
- Easy to install.

The renowned Volvo Penta Aquamatic is now available in a new version — the Aquamatic 80 Sport.

The Aquamatic Sport has an output of 88 h. p. and is fitted with two Zenith type 34 VN down-draught carburetters.

This engine has been produced specially for boat-owners who need the extra power necessary to attain planing speed more quickly or to attain top speed more quickly when towing water-skiers.

The Aquamatic 80 Sport is the engine for those who want something extra — something that is more than just an ordinary power unit — and is ideal for those desiring high speed but, at the same time, outstanding fuel economy.

There is now no doubt whatsoever that the Aquamatic has become a "star". Boating people all over the world have learned to appreciate the unique properties represented by this system. In one gruelling international endurance test after another, the Aquamatic has won world records and in official economy tests, it has astonished the experts. The Aquamatic 80 Sport is manufactured by a company which has more than 50 years experience of marine engines.

Volvo Penta leads the way.

53 The original 1961 Volvo sales leaflet introducing the AQ80 Sport

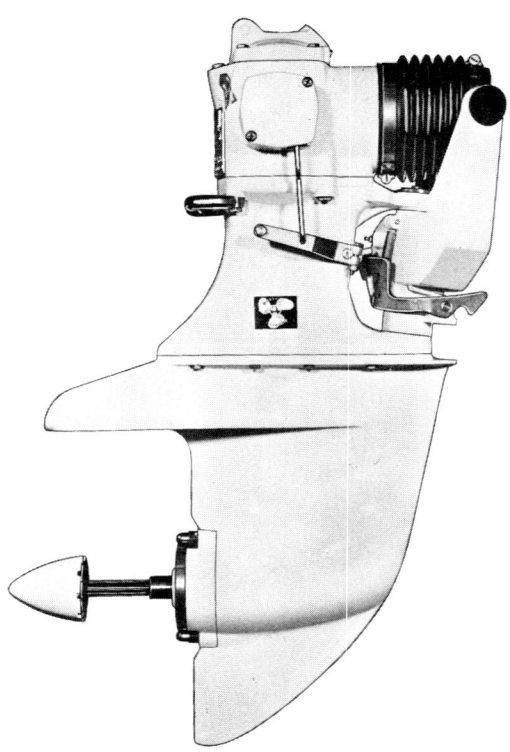

Penta. A modification to prevent this was introduced in 1964 and incorporated in the first production competition outdrive—the 100CTH. At the same time, to discourage the somewhat random attempts by outsiders to tune their engines, Volvo Penta announced the AQ135/100CTH which in stage two condition developed 138bhp DIN at 5800rpm.

It became the responsibility of the Volvo Competition Service department to continue the development of the B.20 and B.30 engines where Volvo Penta had left off in 1968. During their operational span from 1970 to 1978 Gunnar Andersson's team concentrated on basically two models, each being tunable to stages one and two and both suitable for E-series drives. As an alternative, the four-cylinder engine could be coupled to the 170R drive or a modified 100CTH. For technical data on the B.20 and B.30 sports engines see pages 211–15.

5
Model for Model

In all, sixty production engines have been combined with a range of twenty-three different drive-units over a twenty-one-year period. The drives have evolved from the original dog-clutch 100 unit, through the almost disastrous 200 drive which became the subject of a worldwide modification scheme. The 250 and 270 units, the gear cones of which were too well made at first and had to be roughed up, led to the faultless 280 and 750 series. The developments from these have been many and varied to adapt the drives

55 Cutaway 100 drive (dog-clutch)

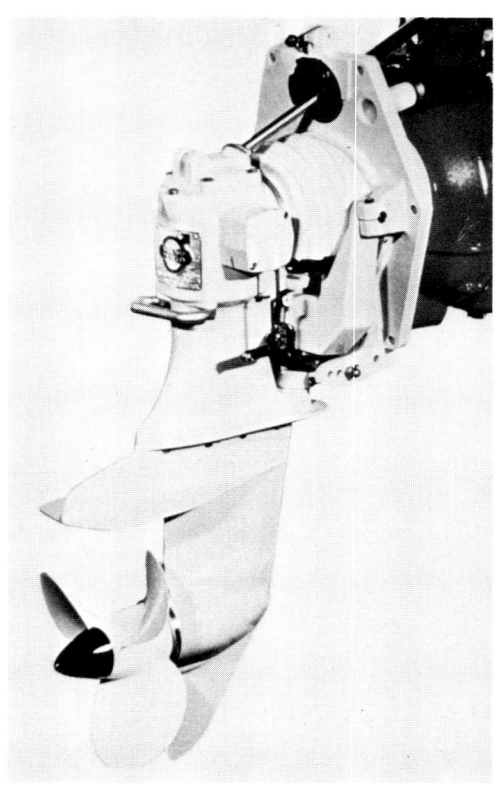

56 Last of the 100 series, the 100B. Phased out of production in 1977 the 100 drive received little modification during its eighteen years

for racing, special extended rigs for catamarans and even hydrofoils. The following tables list every engine and drive type produced by Volvo Penta and offered as original equipment. The tables do not include 'specials' such as Arden or Rudd conversions, neither do they provide for semi-approved 'one-offs' that have emerged from time to time such as the AQ170/270E, AQD3/100B, the Pratt & Whitney gas turbine/270 and more recently the MD40/280B. Drives combined with other manufacturers' engines have also been omitted, eg Eaton, Chrysler, Waukesha, Weissman-BMW, Holman and Moody. Most of the Glastron US engines (which were distinguished by their blue-grey paint finish) can be found under their respective Volvo Penta designations. For more detailed information see pages 162–73.

Summary of engine types and designations

1 Petrol engines

AQ designation	basic engine	comp. ratio	carburettor or injection pump	hp	drive type	product period	
AQ60F	B.18	6:1	1 Zenith 30VNN	60	100	1962–8	for kerosene fuel
AQ80	B.16.B	8.2:1	1 Zenith 34VN	80	100	1958–63	first production model
AQ80S	B.16.B	8.2:1	2 Zenith 34VN	88	100	1961–3	competition version of AQ80
AQ90	B.18.A	7.6:1	2 Zenith 36VNP	90	100	1962–4	low-compression AQ110
AQ95	B.18.B	10:1	1 Stromberg 150CD	95	100	1964–6	
AQ95A	B.18.B	9.7:1	1 Stromberg 150CD	95	100	1966–8	
AQ100	B.18.B	9.5:1	2 Zenith 36VN	100	100	1961–3	first B.18 engine
AQ105A	B.20.B	9.5:1	1 Stromberg 150CD	105	100	1968–9	
AQ110	B.18.B	10:1	2 Zenith 36VN	110	100	1963–6	
AQ110S	B.18.B	11:1	2 Stromberg 175CD 2 SU H56	125	200B, C 100S	1962–4	competition with 'slimline' drive
AQ115A	B.20.B	9.5:1	1 Solex 44PA2	115	100 100B	1969–75	
AQ115B	B.20.B	9.5:1	1 Solex 44PA2	115	100B	1976–8	
AQ120	B.18.B	9.7:1	2 Stromberg 175CD	120	100 200C	1966–8	
AQ120B	B.21	9.3:1	1 Solex 44PHN	120	270D	1978–	'economy' version of AQ140
AQ130A	B.20.B	9.5:1	2 Stromberg 175CD	130	100 250D	1968–70	first B.20 engine
AQ130B	B.20.B	8.4:1	2 Stromberg 175CD	115	100 250D	1968–70	low-compression AQ130

AQ designation	basic engine	comp. ratio	carburettor or injection pump	hp	drive type	product period	
AQ130C	B.20.B	9.5:1	2 Solex 44PA2	130	250D 270D	1969–76	
AQ130D	B.20.B	9:1	2 Solex 44PA2	130	280D	1976–7	competition version
AQ135	B.18.B	10.8:1	2 Solex twin-barrel	135	100CTH	1964–8	first B.21 engine
AQ140A	B.21	9.3:1	2 Solex 44PHN3	125	280D	1976–	first B.23 engine
AQ145A	B.23	9.3:1	2 Solex PA1	138	280D	1979–	
AQ150A, B	Buick V-6 225cu in 3.7 litres	9:1	1 Rochester 2 barrel	150	200B 250B	1965–9	
AQ155	B.20.B	11.2:1	2 Solex 45DDH twin-barrel	155	100CTH 170R	1969–77	competition version
AQ165A	B.30.A	9.2:1	3 Stromberg 175CD	165	250C	1968–9	first in-line six
AQ170A	B.30.A	9.2:1	3 Solex 44PA1	170	250C 270C	1969–73	
AQ170B	B.30.A	9.2:1	3 Solex 44PA1	170	270C	1973–5	
AQ170C	B.30.A	9:1	3 Solex 44PA2	170	280C	1976–8	
AQ180	B.36.B	9.5:1	2 Carter WGD	180	200B	1963–4	Volvo's own V-8
AQ190	Ford US 302cu in 5 litres	8:1	1 Holley 2V	190	280B	1976–7	
AQ195							
AQ200	B.30.A	11.2:1	3 Solex 45DDH twin-barrel	200	250E 270E 280E 280TE	1969–77	competition version
AQ200A, B	Chevrolet 307cu in 5.1 litres	8:1	1 Carter twin-barrel	200	280B	1976–7	
AQ200D	Chevrolet 305cu in 5 litres	8.5:1	Rochester 2GE	200	280B	1977–	
AQ210A	Chris-Craft 307cu in 5.1 litres	8:1	1 Carter twin-barrel	210	270B	1970–5	first US V-8

Model	Engine	Compression	Carburettor	Power (bhp)	Type	Years	Notes
AQ225A	Chevrolet 307cu in 5.1 litres	8.2:1	1 Carter four-barrel	225	280B	1975–7	
AQ225B	Chevrolet 307cu in 5.1 litres	8.2:1	1 Rochester	225	280B	1975–6	
AQ225C	Chevrolet 307cu in 5.1 litres	8.2:1	1 Rochester			1976–7	
AQ225D	Chevrolet 305cu in 5 litres	8.5:1	1 Rochester Quadrajet	220	280B	1977–	
AQ230	Chevrolet 307cu in 5 litres	8:1	1 Rochester Quadrajet	220	280B		limited US production
AQ240	Ford US 351cu in 5.8 litres	8:1	1 Holley 4V	240	280B	1976–7	
AQ255A	Chevrolet 350cu in 5.74 litres	8:1	1 Holley 4V	250	280B	1976–7	
AQ255B	Chevrolet 350cu in 5.74 litres	8.5:1	1 Rochester Quadrajet	250	280B	1977–8	
AQ260	Chevrolet 350cu in 5.74 litres	8.5:1	1 Rochester Quadrajet	260	280B	1978–	
AQ280	Chevrolet 350cu in 5.74 litres	9:1	1 Rochester Quadrajet	280	280B	1977–8	
AQ290	Chevrolet 350cu in 5.74 litres	9:1	1 Rochester Quadrajet	280	280B	1978–	

57 AQ180/200 – the Volvo V-8

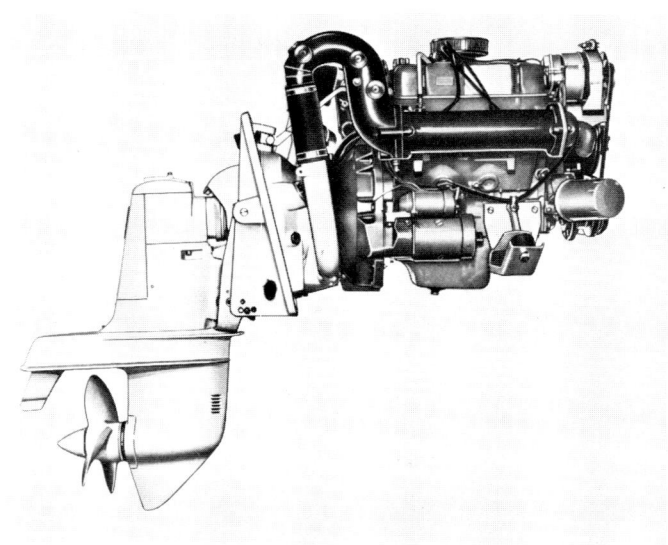

58 AQ150B/250 – the third and final version of the Buick-based V-6

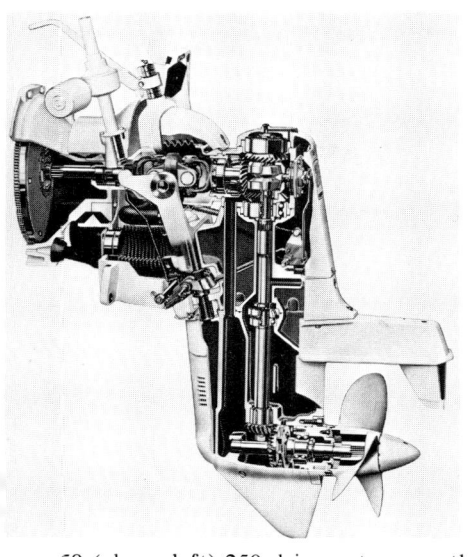
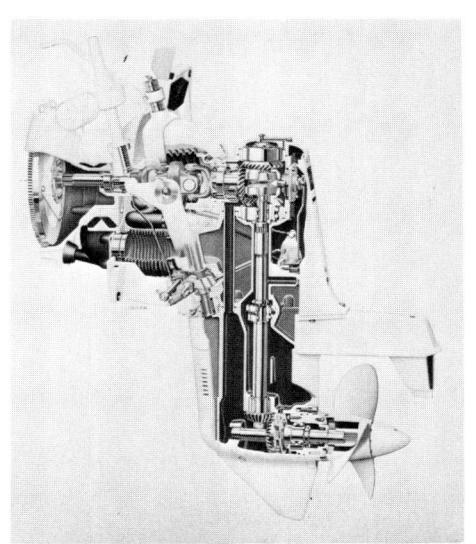

59 (above left) 250 drive cutaway – the first model to have a blue-grey paint finish; 60 (above right) Cutaway 270 drive; 61 (below left) Section through tiller-steered 280 drive; 62 (below right) The big one – cutaway of the 750 drive

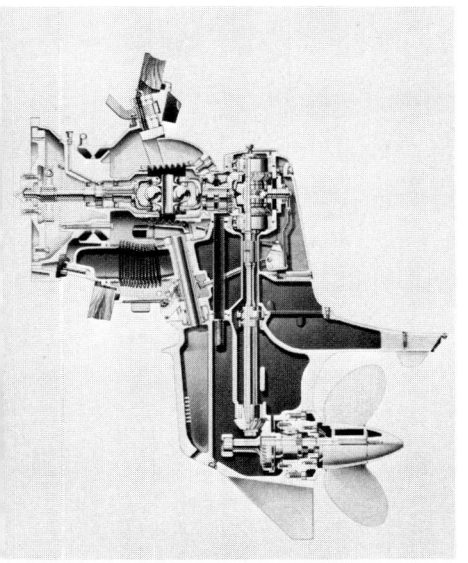
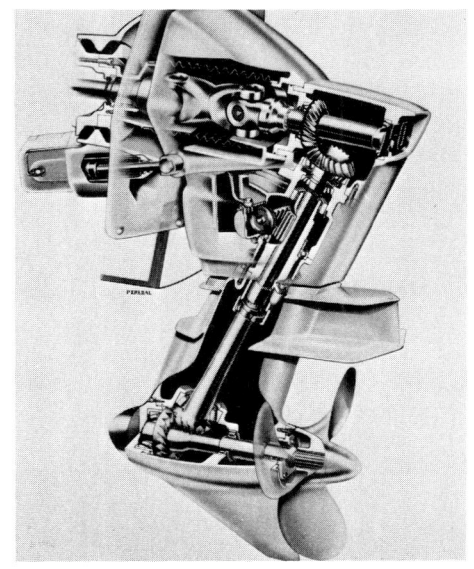

2 Diesel engines

AQ designation	basic engine	comp. ratio	carburettor or injection pump	hp	drive type	product period	
AQD19	Indenor XDP4/88	21:1	CAV Rotodiesel Silto PM	68	100	1963–8	
AQD21	Indenor XDP4/90	22:1	CAV Rotodiesel	75	250D 270D 280D	1968–	
AQD27	Indenor XDP6/85	21:1	Silto PM	83	100 200BC	1963–6	
AQD29	Indenor XDP6/88	21:1	CAV Rotodiesel	92	200C 250D 270D	1966–9	
AQD32	Indenor XDP6/90	22:1	CAV Rotodiesel	106	250D 270D 280D	1969–	
AQD40	TMD 40 3.9 litres	21:1	Bosch EPVE	130	280B	1977–	
AQD2B	MD2B	16:1	Bosch PFR	25	100B	1971–6	
AQD2B	MD2B	17.5:1	Bosch PFR	23	100B	1976–9	
AQD70B	TAMD70B	14.5:1	Bosch PE6P	250	750	1972–5	
AQD70C	TAMD70C	14.5:1	Bosch PE6P	280	750	1975–	
AQD70BL	THAMD70B	14.5:1	Bosch PE6P	250	750	1972–5	horizontal
AQD70CL	THAMD70C	14.5:1	Bosch PE6P	270	750	1975–	horizontal

3 *Outdrive units*

type	red. ratio	max. torque	product period	
100	1.66:1	200Nm	1959–71	In 1962 several significant changes were made: a) introduction of handed drive (RH) b) combined oil reservoir for upper and lower housings c) tilt-up angle increased from 45° to 60°. In 1963 the patented silent-shift cone clutch was incorporated.
100B	1.66:1	200Nm	1971–8	
100CTH	1.67:1	—	1964–	
170R	1.26:1	145lb/ft	1969–	competition slimline unit
	1.41:1	145lb/ft	1969–	competition slimline unit
200B	1.59:1	250Nm	1964–8	competition slimline unit
200C	1.85:1	150Nm	1964–8	
200D	1.35:1	250Nm	1964–8	
250A	1.35:1	330Nm	1968–70	
250B	1.61:1	330Nm	1968–70	
250C	1.89:1	250Nm	1968–70	
250D	2.15:1	180Nm	1968–70	
250E	1.18:1	290lb/ft	1968–	competition
	1.45:1	290lb/ft	1968–	competition
270B	1.61:1	430Nm	1970–4	
270C	1.89:1	330Nm	1970–4	
270D	2.15:1	260Nm	1970–4	re-introduced in 1978 with AQ120B
270E	1.18:1	290lb/ft	1970–	competition
	1.45:1	290lb/ft	1970–	competition
280B	1.61:1	430Nm	1973–	
280C	1.89:1	330Nm	1973–	
280D	2.15:1	260Nm	1973–	
750	1.89:1	720Nm	1971–	

NB 1 Power trim available on 270 and 270E, 280 and 280E.
2 Competition 'E' versions of 280 drive produced in limited numbers.

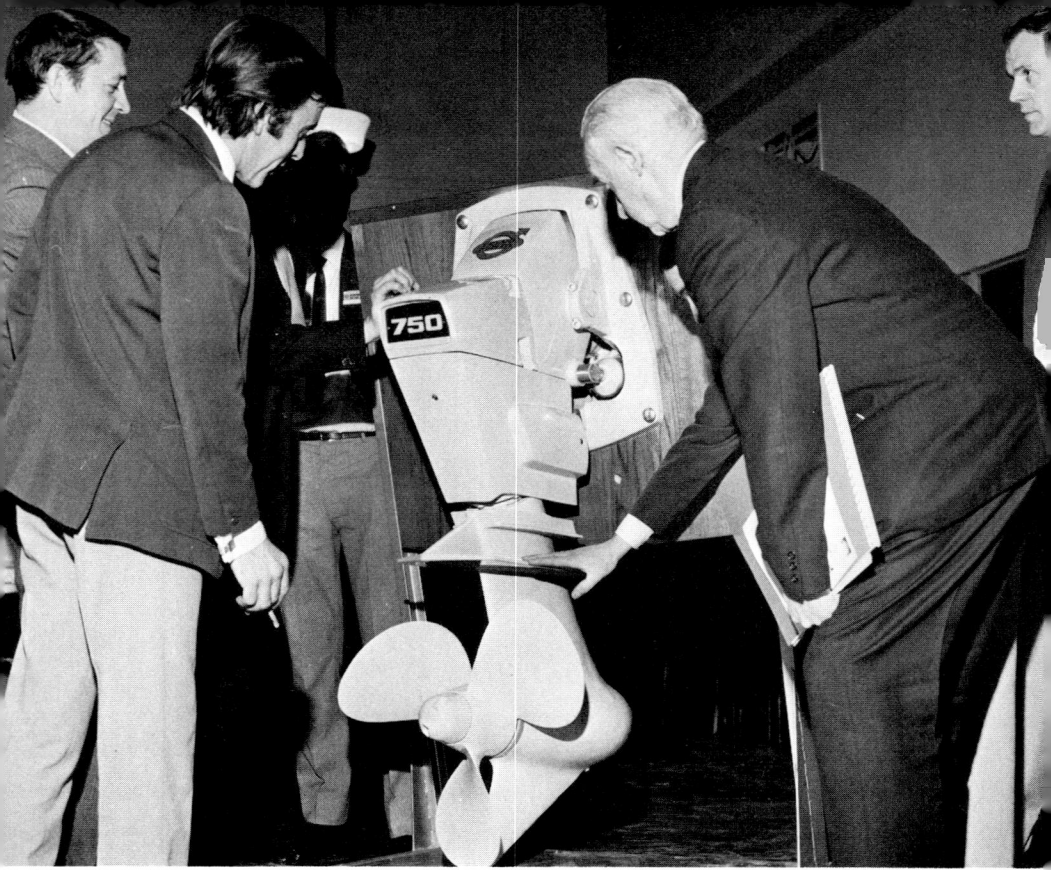

63 British journalists examining the 750 drive at its launching at the London Boat Show, January 1970

Outboard drive extensions

In some circumstances it is desirable to mount the engine higher on the boat transom while maintaining the same position of the propeller relative to the boat-bottom. This particularly applies to boats with a very deep vee and to catamarans where the engine is mounted between the hulls. If the engine is mounted low down in relation to the waterline, water may be drawn into the cylinders thus causing considerable damage.

As a general guide the water level should never be above the lower part of the black rubber pad at the top of the mounting collar when the boat is at rest and fully laden.

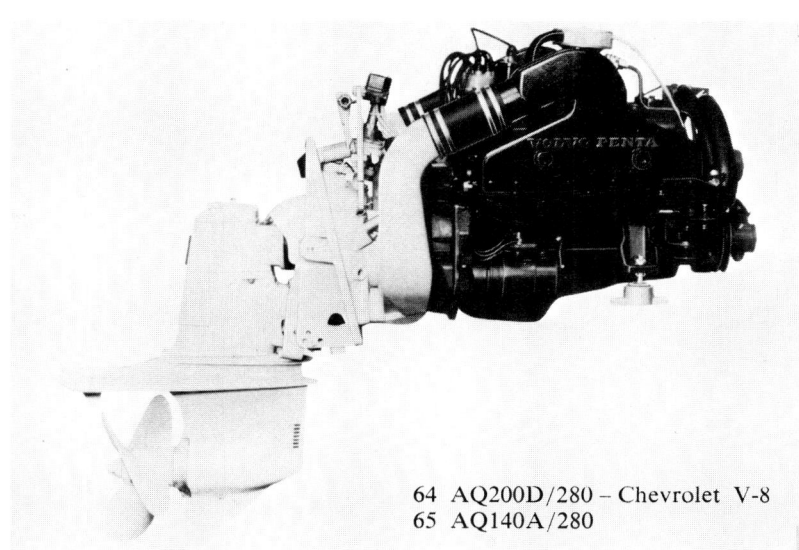

64 AQ200D/280 – Chevrolet V-8
65 AQ140A/280

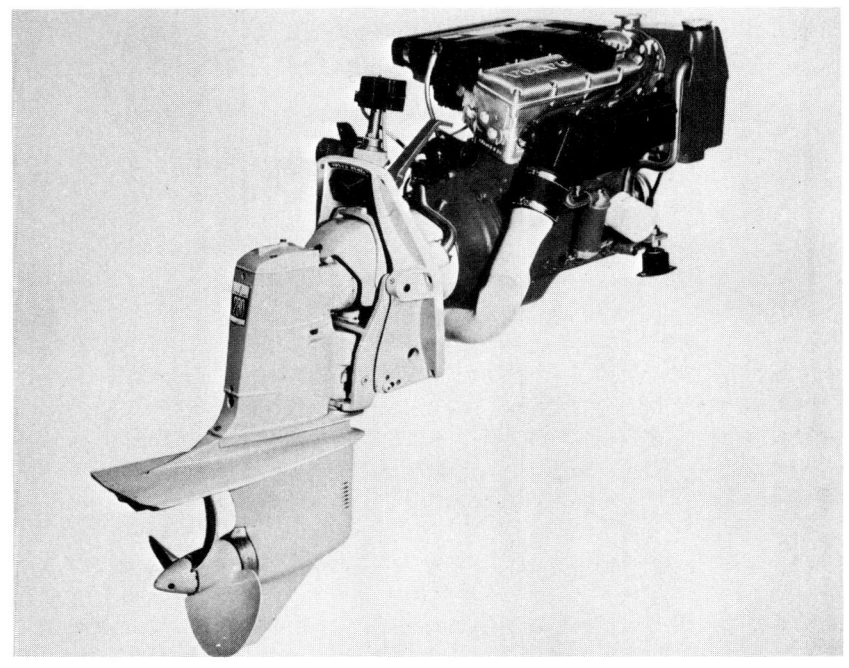

91

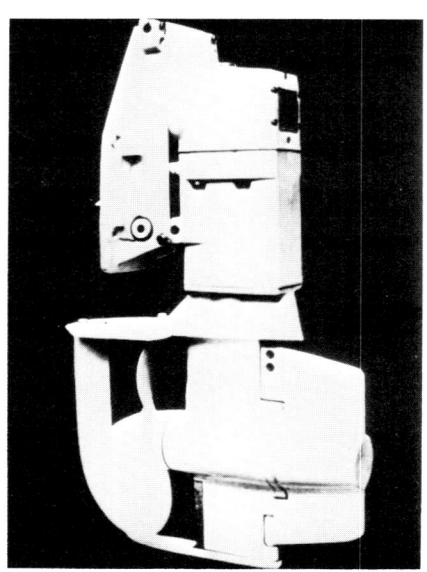

66 Top of the shop. AQ290/ 280 featuring the 1979 power trim and new steering mechanism

67 Yes – it was Volvo Penta! An experimental 'puller prop' drive, the 700. Never adopted for production, it led to the 750

Extension kits
Model 100 drive:
  (25mm) 1in, part no. 814044
  (150mm) 6in, part no. 809965
  (300mm) 12in, part no. 897233
  (350mm) 14in, part no. 814053

Model 200, 250 drives:
  (25mm) 1in, part no. 814133
  (100mm) 4in, part no. 814318
  (200mm) 8in, part no. 897830*

*Not to be used with AQ150/200. Can only be used on 250 series after consultation with AB Volvo Penta.

Model 270 and 280 drives:
  (25mm) 1in, part no. 839548
  (100mm) 4in, part no. 814318
  (200mm) 8in, part no. 897830

When 280 drives are combined with V-8 engines:
280B, standard, a maximum of 4in can be used
280B, trim, a maximum of 1in can be used

For 280 drives on other engines:
280B, standard, max. 4in extension
280D, standard, max. 8in extension
280D, trim, max. 2in extension

6
Propellers

(For propeller selection tables and curves see pages 104–24)

There are many different permutations of propeller designs to meet myriad combinations of horsepowers, speed and thrust requirements. At one end of the scale are the large 3, 4 and 5 bladed propellers used to propel workboats, tugs and fishing vessels. A large diameter slow-revving screw with a large blade area maximises the thrust available from the engine within the design speed limit of the vessel's hull form. The shape of the hull predetermines the speed at which the boat may pass through the water and thus precludes the utilisation of a propeller designed for more speed than the hull can produce. At the other end of the spectrum is the propeller developed for racing powerboats. These propellers are of relatively small diameter but carry a fierce pitch and are allowed to revolve at high rpm. Such propellers are usually of the 'super-cavitating' or 'surface' type and enable powerboats to 'propride' with the hull virtually clear of the water. As a general rule of thumb propeller diameter means 'thrust' and pitch means 'speed'.

Between the above extremes and within the criteria of the rule are an infinite selection of styles, shapes, dimensions and materials to comply with the constraints of blade area ratios, optimum tip velocity, whether equipoise or turbine, reduction ratios and available apertures. Despite an abundance of data and knowledge of the science of propeller design, naval architects will readily concede that the subject retains a certain mystique. Too often a specially made propeller needs corrective work after a boat's initial sea trial. Fortunately for the Aquamatic owner, all the groundwork has been done in advance by Volvo Penta, who have not only developed a wide range of propellers but have provided detailed selection guidelines, which are included at the end of this chapter.

94

68 Propeller selection. *Left to right* standard propeller for 100 drive, standard for 200-280 drives, high speed type for 280, and 23in diameter propeller for 750 drive

When a prototype boat is initially tested by the builder to assess its performance and optimum propeller size the results obtained can be inaccurate and misleading. In the first place the boat is light, both because owner's effects are not aboard and because the hull has not 'soaked'. Soaking can have a pronounced effect on a timber hull; less obvious is the fact that over a season a GRP hull will also absorb water, to a more limited extent. Prototype testing is often a hurried affair and is invariably carried out with fuel and water tanks part full and with rarely more than two people aboard —a weight condition which almost certainly will be exceeded when the boat passes into family ownership!

Finally, the test boat would have a brand new engine and drive-unit installed neither of which would have been run-in or finely adjusted. An experienced builder will take weight factors and engine stiffness into account when making a propeller recommendation to his customers. He cannot, however, guess the usage, crew size or equipment that the owner will apply. The wise owner should take the trouble to discuss these points with the builder or retailer before the boat is delivered and the propeller(s) fitted. An owner would also be well advised to ascertain whether his boat was tested in salt or fresh water as this can have a significant effect on the propeller size due to the differing density and consequently different flotation levels. High temperature and humidity will cause a marked loss of engine power, particularly to diesel engines, which will necessitate a reduction of prop. size. If a boat is to be used in tropical or equatorial regions Volvo Penta can advise on the compensatory propeller.

Once the boat is delivered to the owner, it is in his interest to ensure that the propeller allows the engine to reach its recommended maximum rpm range whatever the boat speed—see following tables. The phrase 'rpm range' has been used deliberately, as the 'continuous cruising speed' recommendation varies between engine models. Generally Volvo Penta describe their continuous cruising speeds by referring to a specific number of rpm below the maximum *obtainable* for a given boat and and not necessarily the maximum engine speed indicated in the data. This can be best illustrated by an example: take a typical medium-vee boat with a single AQ170/280 installed. Initial trials show that the best performance is obtained with a propeller that enables the engine to peak at 4810rpm (whereas the maximum permissible rpm is 5000). The continuous cruising speed for this engine would then be 4810 minus 300 = 4510. It is not 5000 minus 300 = 4700!

In light craft where speeds in excess of thirty knots are envisaged, the four-cylinder B.18, B.20, B.21 and B.23 engines may be allowed

69 Speed testing a new boat over the measured mile at the Volvo Penta test centre

to reach 5500rpm, in which event the continuous cruising rpm would be 5500 minus 300 = 5200.

Volvo-built petrol engines are designed in such a way that the valves begin to rotate in their helical springs at certain rpm levels. This prevents 'hot spots' forming on the valve seats at high loading, making for longer valve life and preventing compression loss. Clearly, if the engine is overloaded below this rotation rpm, damage can result and such damage would not be covered by the engine warranty. The valve rotation point varies from engine to engine but generally it commences just below the recommended rpm ranges given in the table.

Petrol engines (Swedish origin)

Engine	max. rpm range	cruising rpm
B.16 1600cc	exactly 4500	4500
B.18 1780cc	4500–5100 (5500 in light craft)	deduct 300
B.20 1986cc	4500–5100 (5500 in light craft)	deduct 300–500
B.21 2130cc	4500–5100 (5500 in light craft)	deduct 300–500
B.23 2310cc	4500–5100 (5500 in light craft)	deduct 300–500
B.30 2980cc	4200–5000	deduct 300–500
B.36 3600cc	5000	deduct 300

Diesel engines (French origin)

Engine	max. rpm, pleasure	heavy duty rpm	cruising rpm
AQD19	4500 (1 hour)	3000	deduct 300
AQD21	4500	3000	deduct 200
AQD27	4000 (1 hour)	3000	deduct 200
AQD29	4000	3000	deduct 200
AQD32	4000	3000	deduct 200

Diesel engines (Swedish origin)

Engine	max. rpm range	cruising rpm
AQD2	2500	2500
AQD40	3500–3600	deduct 200

Vee petrol engines (American origin)

Engine	max. rpm range	cruising rpm
V-6 Buick	4200	deduct 200
V-8 Ford	3700–4000 (important to be as near 4000 as possible)	3600
V-8 Chevrolet	4000–4400	deduct 300–500

Propeller materials and types

All Volvo Penta Aquamatic propellers are manufactured from a tough aluminium alloy which has a high corrosion-resistant property. Since 1973 the factory has produced propellers exclusively for the Aquamatic rather than rely on outside supply. This has led to an extremely high standard of quality control and the development of the High Speed range which provides a more efficient propulsion for any given boat/engine combination. Volvo Penta insist on the use of their own propellers at all times to the extent of invalidating the engine warranty if other types are used. It is interesting to note that a single-engine installation from the Volvo stable requires a left-handed (or anti-clockwise looking forward) propeller as a result of their inboard tradition. Inboard/outboard units from principally outboard manufacturers invariably are right-handed. Volvo Penta were alone for many years in their provision for handed (counter-rotating) screws. In a twin installation the port propeller should rotate left-handed and the starboard should rotate right-handed.

Volvo Penta propeller with $13/_{16}$in splined hub. This aluminium propeller was introduced for the original 1959 version of the 100 series drive in three-bladed form. It was later adopted with modified blade configurations for the racing drives, 100CTH and 250/270E, with two or three blades. The blade area ratio (ie the area of the propeller diameter circle occupied by the blades) is .50 (or 50 per cent blade and 50 per cent void).

Volvo Penta propeller with cylindrical shaft and shear pin. Aluminium two- or three-bladed propeller designed for later model 100 and 100B outdrives. Blade area ratio .50.

Volvo Penta propeller with $1\frac{1}{8}$in splined hub. The standard propeller for the 200, 250, 270 and 280 drives. Made from aluminium and incorporating a bronze hub mounted in rubber bushing to cushion gearchange and load stresses on the drive and engine. Available with two or three blades. Its highest efficiency is in moderately loaded planing, semi-planing and workboats. Blade area ratio .50.

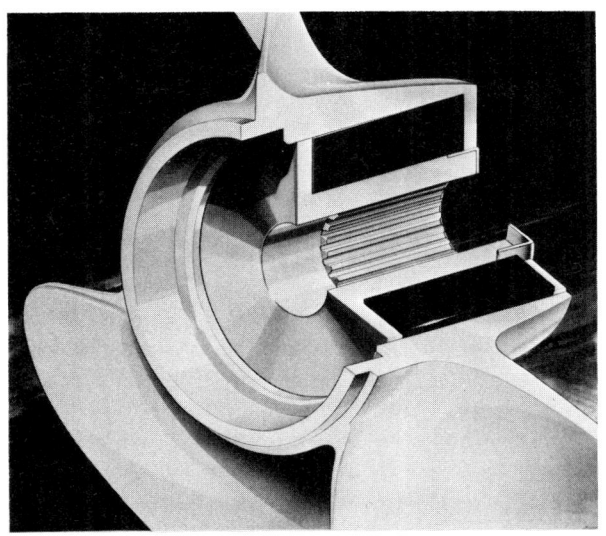

70 Cutaway drawing of the $1\frac{1}{8}$in splined bronze hub with bonded rubber bushing

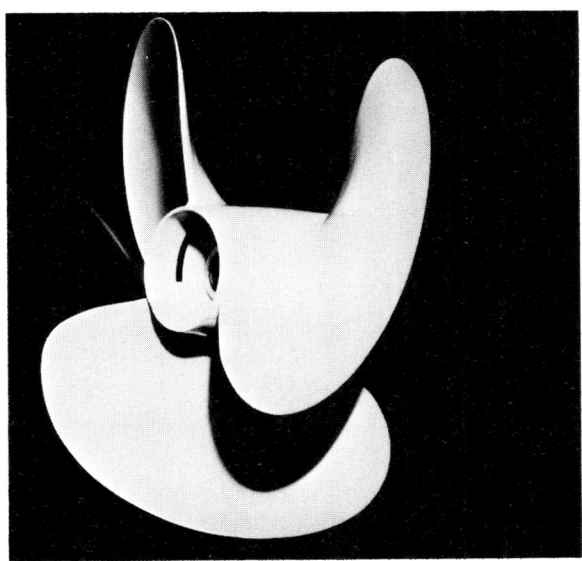

71 Long-hub, high speed propeller

Volvo Penta high speed propeller. Similar to the foregoing mechanically but with a specially designed blade profile and higher blade area ratio. This propeller can achieve a speed increase of up to three knots on fast boats, a higher cruising speed and faster planing times, even for heavier craft. Blade area ratio .63 to .80 depending on speed range. Suitable for 200, 250, 270, 280 and, in limited sizes, 100 drives. Long-hub versions are for 280 drive only, with cone part no. 850785.

Volvo Penta cupped propeller. In certain circumstances involving high speed boats with high powered engines a point is reached where the optimum propeller diameter and blade area to absorb the total available power need to be so great that the propeller cavitates or 'slips' excessively, thus becoming less efficient. One simple method of overcoming this effect is to curve or 'cup' the tip and trailing edge on each blade. This ensures that, whilst the size and area of the propeller is sufficient to plane the boat, a considerable increase in thrust is developed when it is planing. Cupped propellers were introduced to meet this requirement parallel with the new V-8 programme. Available for left-hand rotation only, 200–280 drive.

Volvo Penta stainless steel propeller. Introduced early in 1979 for use in single and twin installations where a high pitch is desirable. Not only is stainless steel tougher than the standard aluminium but it eliminates flexing of the blades due to the high loads induced by coarse pitching. These propellers are restricted to the 280 drive only and because of their long hub require a special cone, Volvo part no. 850785.

dia. x *pitch*	*part no.* LH	*part no.* RH
14 x 23in	850951	851007
14 x 25in	850952	851008
15 x 21in	850953	not available

Radice aluminium propeller (Italy). A high quality propeller that has been recommended and supplied as a standard by Volvo Penta in the past. With some sizes the diameter and pitch stamped on the hub does not give the same rpm and performance as the equivalent Volvo Penta prop. Volvo Penta/Radice propellers were stamped with code letter C after the L or R for rotation.

Michigan aluminium propeller (USA). Another high quality propeller adopted by Volvo Penta before their own production started. As with Radice, size in relation to performance differed from the Volvo Penta equivalent. Volvo Penta / Michigan propellers were stamped with code letter D after L or R.

Austral aluminium propeller (Australia). Once used by Volvo Penta when other suppliers unable to meet demand. Volvo Penta / Austral propellers were stamped with code letter B after L or R.

Bronze propellers. The traditional propeller material which has an unfortunate and devastating effect if used with an Aquamatic in salt water. The zinc sacrificial anodes fitted to the drive will disintegrate rapidly leaving the drive to corrode under electrolytic action. The exception to this occurs where Aquamatic engines are used in competition and highly specialised bronze propellers are essential. Normally the boat would be in the water for a short time or the propeller would be removed at the end of the event.

Nylon propellers. These propellers are still under development and have shown that they can be subject to distortion at high loading.

NB: the code letters DC which appeared on some Aquamatic propellers in the early 1970s referred to Michigan propellers which had been 'pitched up' to match those of Radice origin. This occurred during the changeover from Michigan to Radice supply.

Some do's and don'ts

Do keep spare propellers on board, they are easy to change and can save a lot of misery and anguish. Remember that the spinner, lockwasher or bolt are easily dropped when changing propellers and spares are relatively cheap to have just in case.

Do by all means have your damaged propellers repaired but make sure they are done by a qualified specialist. 'Dressing' the blade edges can cause imbalance and damage the drive. If a propeller is considered too large for the boat beware of the temptation to have the diameter reduced. As this is done the pitch is effectively increased, giving no advantage. Such a prop. should be re-pitched.

Don't blame the engine or propeller for a falling-off of performance towards the end of the season until the bottom of the boat has been inspected. Even the first layer of slime preceding fouling can cause the loss of three or four knots. On a 'marginal' boat it can mean the difference between planing and not planing. Before carrying out speed and propeller trials make sure the hull and drive are clean and the engines in tune.

Don't forget to adopt the correct procedure when fitting propellers to early 100 and 200–280 series drives. The lockwasher is provided with a number of locking tabs which do not coincide with the number of splines on the shaft. This is done intentionally to allow a 'vernier' adjustment of the lockwasher. To fit the propeller correctly the spinner should be fully tightened with the lockwasher in place and a mark made on the prop. boss adjacent to one of the tab recesses in the spinner. The spinner should then be slackened off far enough to allow the lockwasher to slide off the splines and turn. Try the lockwasher in several positions moving it round one spline at a time until one of the tabs aligns with the mark on the propeller boss. Leaving the washer in this position, re-tighten the spinner. It is then only necessary to bend down two or three of the lock tabs to keep it in place.

Although Volvo are tetchy about the use of non-Volvo propellers, they can hardly be accused of despotism. They have clearly spent a great deal of time and capital on making sure that their customers have the best selection of the most advanced propellers available.

Propeller selection tables and curves

In the middle 1960s Volvo Penta began to assemble trials data on a wide range of European boats to enable them to draw up simplified standards for propeller recommendations. The first list with its rather unspecific 'general propeller recommendations' was published for internal use in April 1968 with a further supplement added in December 1969. These lists are reproduced here, along with the excellent and accurate curves of later years; to assist owners to select the correct propellers for both obsolete and current boats.

Each of the curves comprises three main elements: a length/ speed graph, a propeller bar, and an average displacement graph. The first principle when using the curves is to check the displace-

102

ment of the boat against the second diagram, eg a 25ft planing boat (all the diagrams are suitable only for craft with planing hulls) with twin AQ120 engines should displace between 2.8 and 3.1 tons if the speed curve and propeller selection bar are to give an accurate read-out. Assuming the boat in question is within the above displacement guidelines, it is only necessary to read from the lower scale of the length/speed graph the speed range that can be expected by projecting vertically downwards from the two points where the diagonal 'twin installation' band intersects the 25 knot line. In this example a range of 26.9 to 28.2 knots is indicated. By projecting the same two vertical lines upwards to the propeller bar it can be seen that either a 14in dia. × 17in pitch or a 15in × 17in propeller would be suitable. The final choice between the two alternatives rests with the actual displacement figure. If the boat is light (2.8–2.9 tons) it would probably attain the higher speed, 28+ knots; thus the smaller propeller and consequently higher engine rpm would provide a better performance. Conversely, a heavier boat would make better use of the larger blade area of the 15in propeller with a reduced maximum engine rpm.

If it should prove that the same 25ft boat is either heavier or lighter than the displacement guideline the curves can still be used to find speed and propeller recommendations. In order to do so one has to assume that the boat has either a greater or lesser length in relation to the displacement curve; so if the boat weighs 4 tons this is equivalent to the displacement guideline for a 29–30ft craft. Vertical readings from the length/speed graph will project 21–22 knots with a (preferably) 15×15in propeller. Similarly, if the boat weighs only 2.25 tons, the projection gives 29.2–30.6 knots with a (preferably) 14×19in propeller at the position on the graph for a 23ft boat.

The three examples above are drawn in for guidance on the diagram, AQ120B/270D, where (A)=boat with average displacement; (B)=boat with heavy displacement; (C)=boat with light displacement.

PROPELLER SELECTION TABLES AND CURVES

STANDARD PROPELLERS IN RELATION TO BOAT MODELS

Boat builder	Boat model	Engine type	Installation S= Single T= Twin	Propeller	Alt. propeller
Kristiansands Mek. Verkstad A/S Kristiansand S. Norge	Alfa 24'	AQ 110/100	S	13x11x3	13x12x3
		AQ150/200	S	14x16x3	
Arendals Lettmetall-industri A/S Arendal, Norge	AliCraft 21'	AQD 19/100	S	13x11x3	13x12x3
	AliCraft 26´ Norlight	AQD 29/200	S	14x13x3	14x12x3
	AliCraft 28' Norstar	AQD 29/200	T	15x13x3	14x14x3
Ancas A/S Arendal, Norge	Ancas Queen 24' Daycruiser incl	AQ 120/200	S	13x12x3	14x12x3
		AQ150/200	S	14x16x3	
	Ancas Queen 30'	AQD 29/200	T	15x14x3	14x14x3
		AQ150/200	T	14x15x3	
Österskärs Båtvarv AB Österskär Sverige	Biscaya I (27´) 8,30 x 3,05	AQ 110/100	T	13x12x3	13x11x3
	Biscaya II (29´) 8,80 x 3,05	AQ 120/100	T	13x12x3	13x11x3
		AQ 110/200	T	13x13x3	
		AQ 120/200	T	13x13x3	
		AQ 150/200	T	14x16x3	
		AQD 27/100	T	14x11x3	
		AQD 29/200	T	14x12x3	
Vinga Marin AB V:a Frölunda Sverige	Blue Nile 24' 7, 20 x 2, 60	AQ 95/100	S	13x10x3	
Båt-Industri Köping, Sverige	Cascade 19'	AQ 95/100	S	13x12x3	
	Cascade 23'	AQ 95/100	S	13x11x3	
		AQ 120/100	S	13x12x3	
		AQ 120/200	S	13x13x3	
		AQ 150/200	S	14x16x3	
Marieholms Bruk Marieholmsbruk Sverige	Catalina 22'	AQ 120/100	S	13x12x3	
		AQ 120/200	S	13x13x3	
Capirbåtar AB Ankarsvik Sverige	Capir (19') 5,70 x 2,2	AQ 95/100	S	13x12x3	
		AQ 120/100	S	13x13x3	
Åbo Båtvarv Åbo, Finland	Caprice 23' 7, 10 x 2,65	AQD 29/200	T	14x16x3	
Marieholms Bruk Marieholmsbruk Sverige	Concord 16'	AQ 120/100	S	13x14x3	

Boat builder	Boat model	Engine type	Installation S=Single T= Twin	Propeller	Alt. propeller
Botved Boats A/S Slagelse Danmark	Coronet 21' Daycruiser	AQ 120/200	S	13x12x3	14x12x3
		AQ 120/200	T	13x15x3	14x15x3
		AQ 150/200	S	15x15x3	
	Coronet 21' Explorer II	AQ 120/200	S	13x11x3	14x11x3
		AQ 120/200	T	13x14x3	14x14x3
		AQ 150/200	S	15x14x3	
	Coronet 24' Weekender	AQ 120/200	T	13x15x3	14x14x3
		AQ 150/200	S	14x15x3	14x14x3
	Coronet 24' Cabin De Luxe	AQ 120/200	T	13x14x3	
		AQ 150/200	S	14x15x3	14x14x3
	Coronet 30' Oceanfarer	AQ 150/200	T	15x14x3	
Draco Fiberplast Flekkefjord Norge	Draco 21' Sportling	AQ95/100 AQ120/100 AQD19/100	S S S	13x11x3 13x12x3 13x11x3	13x12x3 13x13x3 13x12x3
AB Exoverken Kalmar Sverige	Exotic 28'	AQD 27/200	T	14x14x3	14x13x3
		AQD 29/200	T	14x15x3	
		AQ 150/200	T	14x16x3	
Åbo Båtvarv Åbo, Finland	Fair Lady 19' 5,7x2,2	AQ 120/100	S	13x13x3	13x12x3
Finmar/Pemar Åbo, Finland	Finmar Sea Cabin 5,7x2,2 (19')	AQ 120/100	S	13x13x3	
		AQ 95/100	S	13x12x3	
	Finmar Day Cruiser 5,7x2,2 (19')	AQ 95/100	S	13x12x3	
		AQ 120/100	S	13x13x3	
AB Fisksätra Varv Saltsjöbaden Sverige	Firally Cabin 20' 6,00x2,20	AQ 95/100	S	13x11x3	13x12x3
		AQ150/200	S	14x17x3	
A/S Fjord Plast Arendal Norge	Fjordling 17'	AQ 95/100	S	13x12x3	
		AQ 110/100	S	13x13x3	
		AQ 120/100	S	13x13x3	
	Fjord Day- cruiser 21' Fjord Olympic 21'	AQ 120/200	S	13x13x3	14x13x3

Boat builder	Boat model	Engine type	Installation S= Single T= Twin	Propeller	Alt. propeller
A/S Fjord Plast Arendal Norge	Fjord Consul 26'	AQD 29/200	T	14x16x3	
		AQ 120/200	T	13x13x3	
		AQ 150/200	T	14x17x3	
	Fjord Diplomat 30'	AQ 150/200	T	14x16x3	
		AQD 29/200	T	14x14x3	
Gullringsbåtar Gullringen Sverige	Gullringen 19' (Plast)	AQ 95/100	S	13x12x3	
		AQ 120/100	S	13x13x3	
Herwa Plast Grimstad Norge	Herwa Grimsö 18'	AQ60F/100	S	13x8x3	
	Herwa Grimsholm 22'	AQ95/100	S	13x12x3	
		AQ120/200	S	13x13x3	
Harry Hallberg AB Ellös, Sverige	Malö (21') 6,35 x 2,50	AQ 95/100	S	13x12x3	
Monark Varberg Sverige	Monark 54 (17') 5,12 x 2,02	AQ 120/100	S	13x14x3	
	Monark 66 (22') 6,5 x 2,5	AQ 120/100	S	13x12x3	13x13x3
AB Bergslagsbåtar Kopparberg, Sverige	Nora 17'	AQ 120/100	S	13x13x3	13x12x3
Nordsjöplast A/S Sarpsborg Norge	Nordkapp 17' 5,15 x 2,45 (Daycruiser el. Hardtop)	AQ 95/100	S	13x12x3	13x13x3
Ockelbo Lundgren AB Ockelbo Sverige	Ockelbo 16'	AQ 95/100	S	13x13x3	
	Ockelbo 19'	AQ 95/100	S	13x12x3	
	Ockelbo 21'	AQ 120/100	S	13x12x3	13x13x3
		AQ 120/200	S	13x13x3	13x14x3
Orrskär Båtar AB Norrfjärden Sverige	Orrskär 24' (Minor)	AQ 60 F/100	S	13x8x3	
	Orrskär 26' (Standard)	AQ 60 F/100	S	13x8x3	
		AQ 95/100	S	13x10x3	
		AQ 120/100	S	13x11x3	
	Orrskär 27' Plast (Major)	AQ 60 F/100	S	13x8x3	
		AQ 95/100	S	13x10x3	
		AQ 120/100	S	13x11x3	

Boat builder	Boat model	Engine type	Installation S= Single T= Twin	Propeller	Alt. propeller
AB Fisksätra Varv Saltsjöbaden Sverige	Primör 18'	AQ 95/100	S	13x12x3	
		AQ 120/100	S	13x13x3	
		AQ150/200	S	14x19x3	
	Primör 23'	AQ 120/100	S	13x11x3	
		AQ 120/200	S	13x12x3	
		AQ 150/200	S	14x17x3	
Selco A/S Lilleakerveien 6 Lysaker/Oslo Norge	Selco Daycruiser 18'	AQ 110/100	S	13x13x3	
	Selcab 18'	AQ 110/100	S	13x12x3	
Storebro Bruks AB Storebro Sverige	Solö Lyx II (25') 7,5x2,6	AQ 120/100	S	13x11x3	
	Solö Aqua Cabin (24') 7,30 x 2,50	AQ 60 F/100	S	13x8x3	
		AQ110/100	S	13x11x3	
Söderkvists Varv Oxelösund Sverige	Söder I (30') 9,0 x 2,8	AQ 60 F/100	S	13x8x3	
		AQ 95/100	S	13x10x3	
		AQ 120/100	S	13x10x3	
		AQD 19/100	S	13x8x3	
		AQD 29/200	S	14x12x3	
		AQ 120/200	S	13x12x3	
Thorskogs Bruk Lilla Edet, Sverige	Thorskog 23'	AQ 120/100	S	13x12x3	
Vinga Marin AB V:a Frölunda Sverige	Vinga Cabin 20' 6,10 x 2,35	AQ 95/100	S	13x11x3	13x12x3
Arendals Plast- industri A/S Arendal Norge	Windy 22'	AQ 120/100	S	13x12x3	13x13x3
	Windy 24'	AQ 120/200	T	13x14x3	
		AQ 150/200	S	15x15x3	14x16x3
AB Bröd. Börjesson Bjästa, Sverige	Örnvik (19') 5,70 x 2,20	AQ 95/100	S	13x12x3	
		AQ120/100	S	13x13x3	

SINGLE INSTALLATION

Engine	Boat Length – Pleasure Boats						Work boats House boats
	16' – 18'	19' – 20'	21' – 23'	24' – 26'	27' – 28'	29' – 30'	
AQ 60 F/100	13x10x3	13x8x3	13x8x3				13x8x3
AQ 95/100	13x13x3	13x12x3	13x11x3	13x10x3			13x10x3
AQ 120/100	13x14x3	13x13x3	13x12x3	13x11x3			13x10x3
AQ 120/200 C	13x15x3	13x14x3	13x13x3	14x11x3			i4x10x3
AQ 150/200 B		14x19x3	14x18x3	14x16x3	14x15x3		14x12x3
AQD 19/100	13x11x3	13x10x3	13x8x3				13x8x3
AQD 29/200 C			14x14x3	14x13x3	14x12x3	14x11x3	14x11x3

TWIN INSTALLATION

Engine	20' – 22'	23' – 24'	25' – 26'	27' – 28'	29' – 30'	30' – 33'	Work boats House boats
AQ 60 F/100	13x10x3	13x8x3	13x8x3	13x8x3			13x8x3
AQ 95/100	13x14x3	13x13x3	13x12x3	13x11x3			13x10x3
AQ 120/100	13x15x3	13x14x3	13x13x3	13x12x3	13x11x3	13x10x3	13x10x3
AQ 120/200 C	13x16x3	13x15x3	13x14x3	13x13x3	14x11x3	14x10x3	14x10x3
AQ 150/200 B	14x21x3	14x20x3	14x18x3	14x17x3	14x16x3	14x15x3	14x12x3
AQD 19/100		13x11x3	13x10x3	13x8x3			13x8x3
AQD 29/200 C		14x17x3	14x16x3	14x15x3	14x14x3	14x13x3	14x11x3

The recommendations are to be regarded as a guide for selecting a propeller in relation to a boat of given length. When many factors such as the boat design will have a great influence on the propeller dimension the right dimension should be determined only through testing.

Boat builder	Boat model	Engine type	Installation S-Single T-Twin	Propeller
Alholmens Varv Norrköping Sverige	Ali 26 Alholmen	AQ130/250 AQ170/250	T S	14 x 18 15 x 15
Appleyard Lincoln & Co Cambridgeshire England	Alysian 27 Super sportsman	AQ130/250	T	14 x 16
Arendal Lettmettallindustri Arendal Norge	Norsport 18 Norsun 21 Norstar 28	AQ130/250 AQ170/250 AQD21/250 AQ130/250 AQD32/250	S S S S T	14 x 17 14 x 21 15 x 13 14 x 17 15 x 19
Arendals Plastindustri Arendal Norge	Windy 22 DC Windy 24 Day Windy 24 Cab	AQ130/250 AQ130/250 AQ170/250 AQ130/250 AQ170/250 AQ170/250 AQ130/250 AQ170/250	S T S T T T T S	14 x 17 14 x 19 15 x 17 14 x 18 14 x 16 14 x 21 14 x 18 15 x 15
AB Bergslagsbåtar Kopparberg Sverige	Nora 17 Daycruiser Nora 20 Daycruiser	AQ115/100 AQD21/250	S S	13 x 13 15 x 14
Botved Boats A/S Slagelse Danmark	Coronet 21 Plymate Coronet 21 Daycruiser Coronet 24 Flybridge Coronet 24 Kabin Coronet 24 Family Coronet 27 Seafarer Coronet 32 Oceanfarer	AQ130/250 AQ130/250 AQ130/250 AQ130/250 AQ130/250 AQ170/250 AQD32/250 AQ170/250	S T T T T T T	15 x 15 14 x 18 14 x 17 14 x 17 14 x 18 15 x 16 15 x 17 15 x 16
AB Bröderna Börjesson Bjästa Sverige	Örnvik 570 Cabin Örnvik 570 Daycruiser	AQ115/100 AQ130/250	S S	13 x 13 14 x 18

Boat builder	Boat model	Engine type	Installation S—Single T—Twin	Propeller
Båt-Industri AB	Cascade 19	AQ115/100	S	13 x 13
Köping	Cascade 23 Sport	AQ130/250	S	14 x 14
Sverige		AQ170/250	S	15 x 16
	Cascade 23 Kabin	AQ130/250	S	14 x 14
		AQ170/250	S	15 x 16
S. M. A. P.	Neptune Daycruiser	AQ170/250		14 x 18
Domazan				
Frankrike				
Draco Fiberplast	2000 Day Cab 20	AQ115/100	S	13 x 15
Flekkefjord	Hardtop	AQ130/250	S	14 x 17
Norge	Sportling	AQ170/250	S	14 x 20
		AQD21/250	S	15 x 14
Essex Yacht Builders Ltd	Express	AQ115/100	S	13 x 12
Essex	Fisherman	AQ115/100	T	14 x 15
England		AQD21/250	S	15 x 11
	Blue Nile 23	AQ130/250	S	15 x 13
	Cleopatra 26	AQ130/250	T	14 x 17
	Caribbean	AQD21/250	T	14 x 15
	Cleopatra 26	AQ130/250	T	14 x 17
	Sportsrider	AQD21/250	T	14 x 15
	Cleopatra 30	AQ130/250	T	14 x 14
	Mediterranean	AQ170/250	T	14 x 18
		AQD32/250	T	15 x 17
Fletcher Ltd	15/105	AQ115/100	S	13 x 14
Walsall	V172	AQ130/250	S	14 x 18
England		AQ170/250	S	14 x 20
Fairway Fabrications Ltd	Fairway Gillie	AQD32/250	S	14 x 13
Sheffield				
England				
Finmar-Pemar	Finmar 17 Sportsman	AQ115/100	S	13 x 15
Åbo	Finmar-Sea cabin 19	AQ115/100	S	13 x 15
Finland		AQ130/250	S	14 x 18
		AQ170/250	S	14 x 19
	Finmar Daycruiser 19	AQ115/100	S	13 x 15
		AQ130/250	S	14 x 18
		AQ170/250	S	14 x 19

Boat builder	Boat model	Engine type	Installation S- Single T- Twin	Propeller
Finmar-Pemar Åbo Finland	Finmar Family Cruiser 26	AQ115/100 AQ130/250 AQD21/250	S S S	14 x 12 14 x 12 14 x 12
AB Fisksätra Saltsjöbaden Sverige	Primör 18 Firally Cabin 20 Primör 23	AQ115/100 AQ115/100 AQ130/250 AQ130/250	S S S S	13 x 13 13 x 12 14 x 17 14 x 17
A/S Fjord Plast Arendal Norge	Fjordling 17 Fjord Wing HT 19 Fjord Wing HT cabin 19 Fjord Wing SP 19 Fjord Holiday 21 Fjord Holiday DC 21 Fjord Attaché 24 Fjord Weekender 24 Fjord Consul 26 Fjord Diplomat 30	AQ115/100 AQ130/250 AQ115/100 AQ130/250 AQ115/100 AQ130/250 AQ115/100 AQ130/250 AQ130/250 AQ130/250 AQ170/250 AQD32/250 AQ115/100 AQ115/100 AQ130/250 AQ130/250 AQ130/250 AQ170/250 AQD32/250 AQ130/250 AQ170/250 AQ170/250 AQ130/250 AQD32/250 AQ170/250 AQD32/250	S S S S S S S S T S S S T S T T S T T S T T T T T	13 x 14 14 x 19 13 x 15 14 x 19 13 x 15 14 x 19 13 x 15 14 x 19 14 x 16 14 x 20 14 x 18 15 x 17 13 x 13 13 x 15 14 x 16 14 x 21 15 x 16 15 x 14 15 x 18 15 x 16 14 x 17 14 x 21 14 x 16 15 x 17 15 x 17 15 x 17
Gullringsbåtar Gullringen Sverige	Gullringen 19 Gullringen Cab 19	AQ115/100 AQ130/250	S S	13 x 13 14 x 17
Herwa Plast A/S Grimstad Norge	Grimsö 18	AQ115/100	S	14 x 12

Boat builder	Boat model	Engine type	Installation S→Single T– Twin	Propeller
Sigurd Isacson AB Lidingö Sverige	Delta Daycruiser	AQ115/100	S	13 x 15
Italcantieri Trieste Italien	Bora GT 260-S Bora GT 330-S Bora Diesel S	AQ130/250 AQ170/250 AQD32/250	T T T	15 x 16 15 x 17 16 x 14
Jeanneau 21 Frankrike	Europa Junior	AQ170/250	S	14 x 18
AB Sv. Järnvägsverkstäderna Linköping Sverige	Maritim 26	AQ170/250	S	15 x 16
Thure Lindströms Båtbyggeri Bergå Finland	Pacific 22 Pacific 25	AQ115/100 AQ130/250	S S	14 x 11 14 x 13
Marieholms Bruk Marieholmsbruk Sverige	Concorde 15 Catalina 22	AQ115/100 AQ130/250	S S	13 x 15 14 x 17
Marine Project Plymouth England	Marine Project 31 Pilgrim 30	AQD21/250 AQD32/250 AQ130/250 AQ170/250	T T T T	14 x 13 14 x 17 13 x 14 14 x 17
Marino AB Helsingfors Finland	Marino Super V-18 Marino Daycruiser V-21	AQ130/250 AQ130/250 AQ170/250	S S S	14 x 17 14 x 16 14 x 17
Monark-Crescent Varberg Sverige	Crescent 54 Crescent 53 Cabin Crescent 66 Lyx	AQ115/100 AQ130/250 AQ115/100 AQ170/250	S S S S	13 x 15 14 x 18 13 x 15 15 x 17

Boat builder	Boat model	Engine type	Installation S−Single T−Twin	Propeller
Nordsjöplast A/S Sarpsborg Norge	Nordkapp 17 Prince DC Nordkapp 17 Prince HT Nordkapp 22 King DC	AQ115/100 AQ115/100 AQ130/250 AQ170/250	S S S S	13 x 14 13 x 14 14 x 15 14 x 19
Norrbottens Plastindustri Luleå Sverige	Laxen 17 Hajen 21	AQ115/100 AQ130/250	S S	13 x 15 14 x 19
Ockelbo-Lundgren AB Ockelbo Sverige	Ockelbo T 17´I Ockelbo S 19 I/HT 19Í Ockelbo DC 21/C 21 Ockelbo DC 21/C 21	AQ115/100 AQ115/100 AQ130/250 AQ170/250	S S S S	13 x 15 13 x 15 14 x 17 14 x 18
Orrskär Båtar AB Norrfjärden Sverige	Orrskär 27´ Orrskär 27´	AQ170/250 AQD21/250 AQD32/250 AQ130/250 AQ170/250	S T S S S	15 x 15 15 x 13 15 x 15 15 x 13 15 x 15
Oundle Marina Ltd Nr. Peterborough England	Fairline Fury 25	AQ115/100 AQ115/100 AQ130/250	S T S	13 x 15 13 x 15 14 x 14
Polar Plast A/S Arendal Norge	Polar-17NT	AQ115/100	S	13 x 11
Poole Powerboats Ltd Dorset England	Sovereign 18 Sportsman Sovereign 18 Dayboat	AQ115/100 AQ115/100 AQ130/250	S S S	13 x 15 14 x 12 14 x 17
Reedcraft Norfolk England	Gulf Streamer	AQ115/100 AQ130/250 AQ130/250	T S T	13 x 14 14 x 15 14 x 16
Y.F. Ritz Frankrike	Y.F. Ritz	AQ130/250		14 x 19

Boat builder	Boat model	Engine type	Installation S-Single T-Twin	Propeller
Selco A/S	Selco 18 Daycruiser	AQ130/250	S	14 x 18
Lysaker/Oslo		AQ115/100	S	13 x 14
Norge	Selco 18 Hardtop	AQ130/250	S	14 x 18
	Selcab Stnd	AQ115/100	S	13 x 14
		AQ130/250		14 x 18
	Selcab d. l.	AQ115/100	S	13 x 14
		AQ130/250	S	14 x 18
	Queen 24	AQ130/250	S	15 x 16
		AQ130/250	T	14 x 18
		AQ170/250		15 x 16
	Daycruiser 24	AQ130/250	S	15 x 16
		AQ130/250	T	14 x 18
		AQ170/250	S	15 x 16
	Queen 30	AQ170/250	T	15 x 16
Skagerack A/S	Skagerack 21	AQ130/250	S	14 x 17
Stokke				
Norge				
Skibsplast A/S	Seamaster Daycruiser 17	AQ115/100	S	13 x 15
Kristiansand				
Norge				
Slemmestad Fiberglas A/S	Day 21	AQ130/250	S	14 x 16
Asker/Oslo				
Norge				
Storebro Bruks AB	Solö Lyx II	AQD32/250		15 x 16
Storebro				
Sverige				
Söderkvist Varv	Oxelö 26	AQ130/250	S	14 x 14
Oxelösund		AQ170/250	S	14 x 17
Sverige		AQD21/250	S	14 x 11
Strömmens Verkstad A/S	Trifoil 120 18´	AQ130/250	S	14 x 13
Oslo		AQD21/250	S	15 x 13
Norge				

Boat builder	Boat model	Engine type	Installation S-Single T-Twin	Propeller
Trident Marine Dorset England	Levi/Triana 25	AQ130/250 AQ170/250	T T	14 x 16 14 x 19
Vinga Marin AB Göteborg Sverige	Vinga Cabin 21´	AQ130/250	S	15 x 13
AR Zeis S A Cannes Frankrike	Lambro de Luxe 27´ Lambro Sport	AQ130/250 AQ170/250 AQD32/250	T T T	14 x 17 15 x 18 15 x 17
AB Åbo Båtvarf Åbo Finland	Carita 17 Fair Lady 19 Caprice 24 Fair Lady	AQ115/100 AQ130/250 AQ130/250 AQ115/100	S S S S	13 x 15 14 x 17 14 x 14 14 x 13

AQUAMATIC 115/100

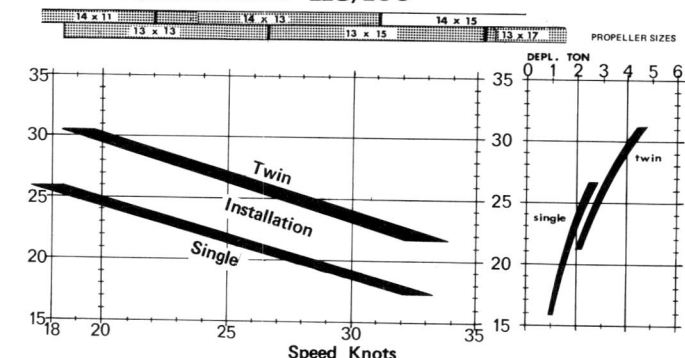

AQUAMATIC 130/250

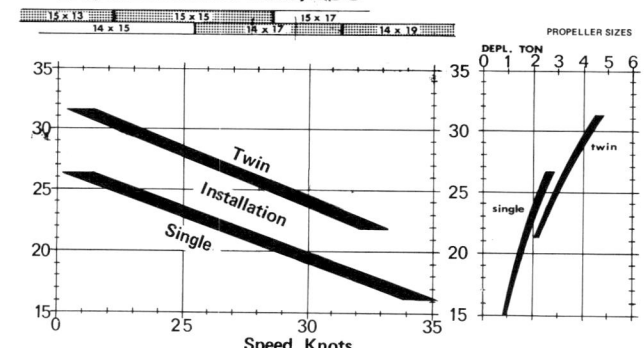

AQUAMATIC 170/250

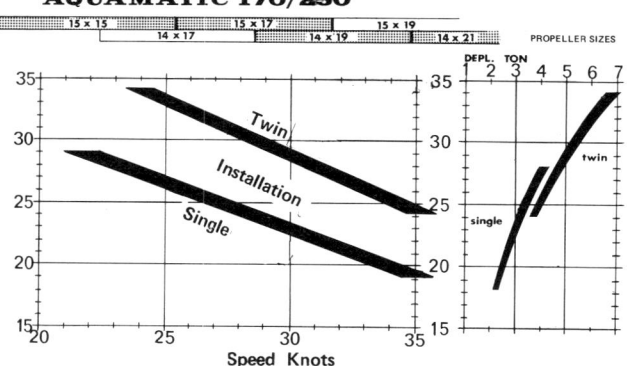

AQUAMATIC D21/250

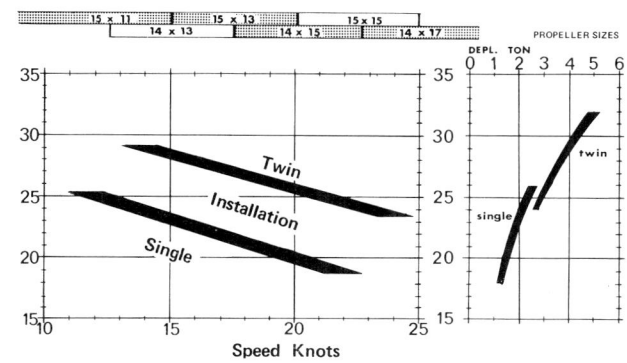

AQUAMATIC D32/250

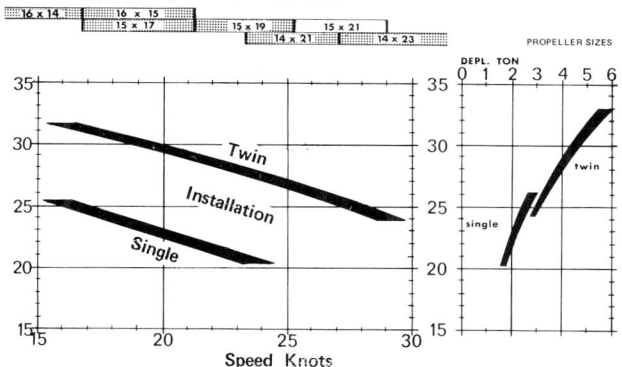

VOLVO PENTA AQ120B/270D

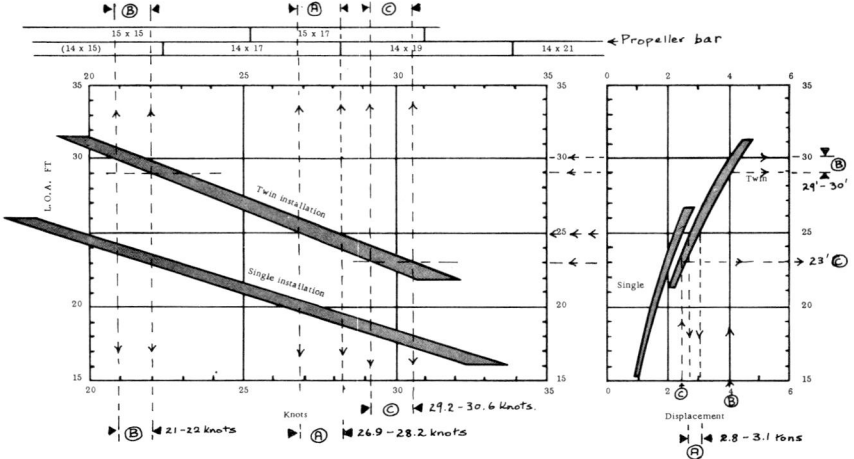

VOLVO PENTA AQ130D/280D

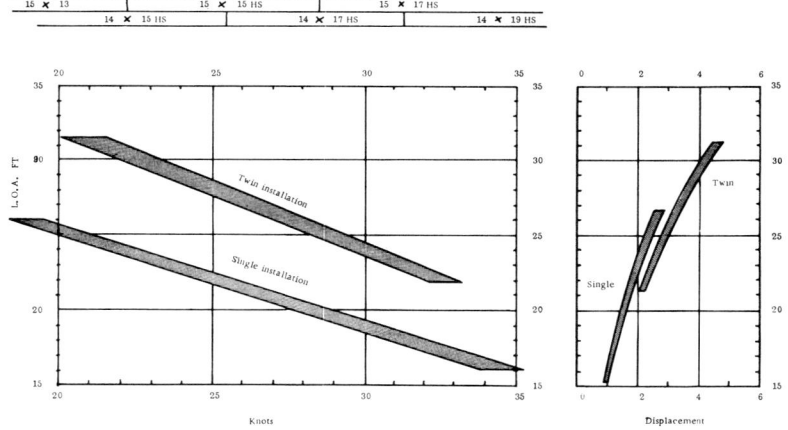

VOLVO PENTA AQ140A/280D

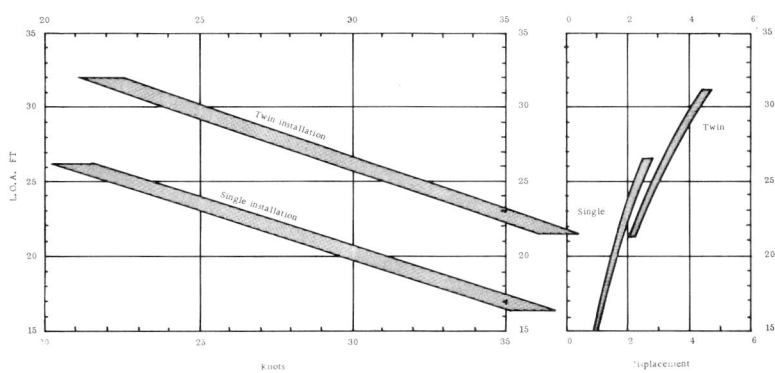

L.O.A. FT

Knots   Displacement

VOLVO PENTA AQ170C/280C

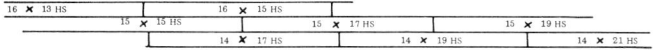

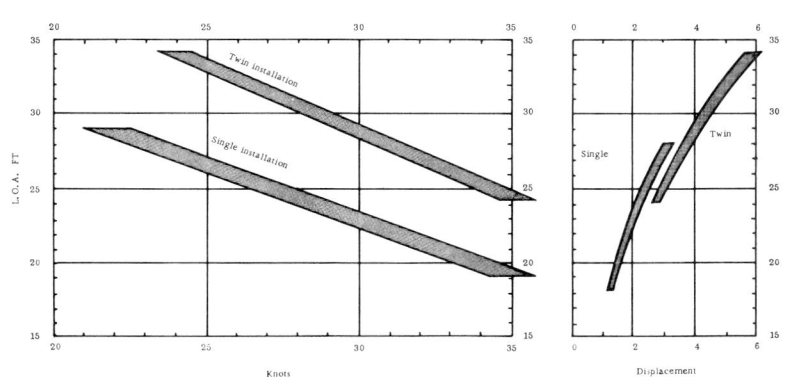

L.O.A. FT

Knots   Displacement

VOLVO PENTA AQ190A/280B

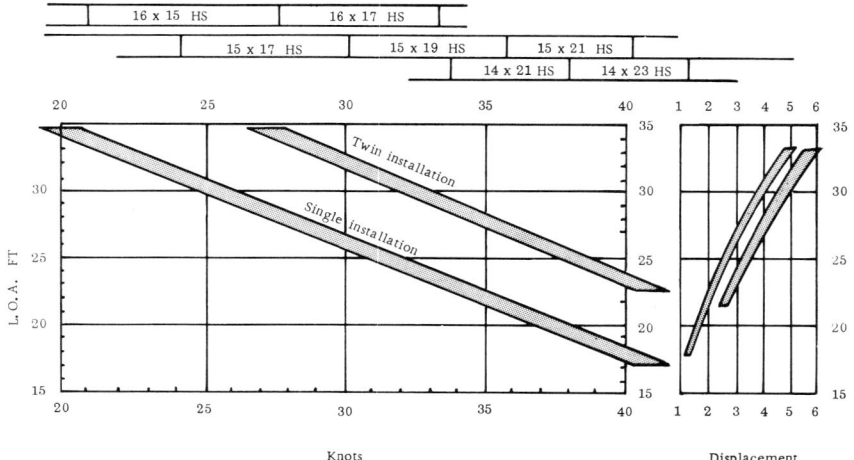

VOLVO PENTA AQ200D/280B

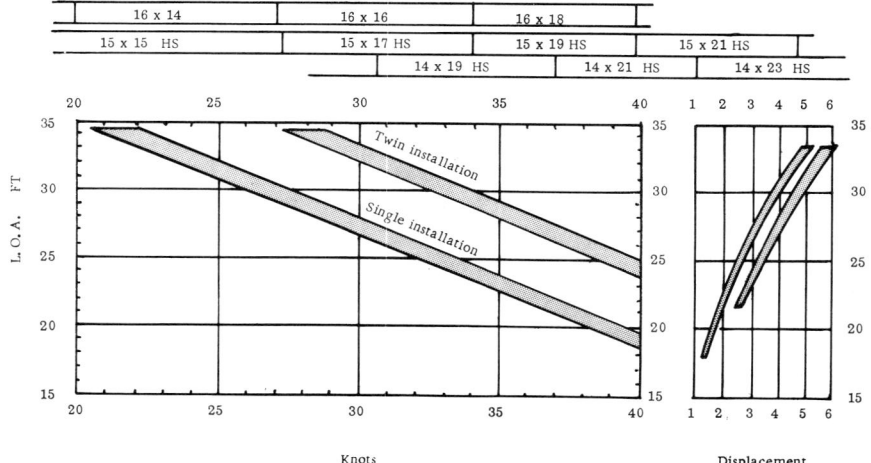

VOLVO PENTA AQ225D/280B

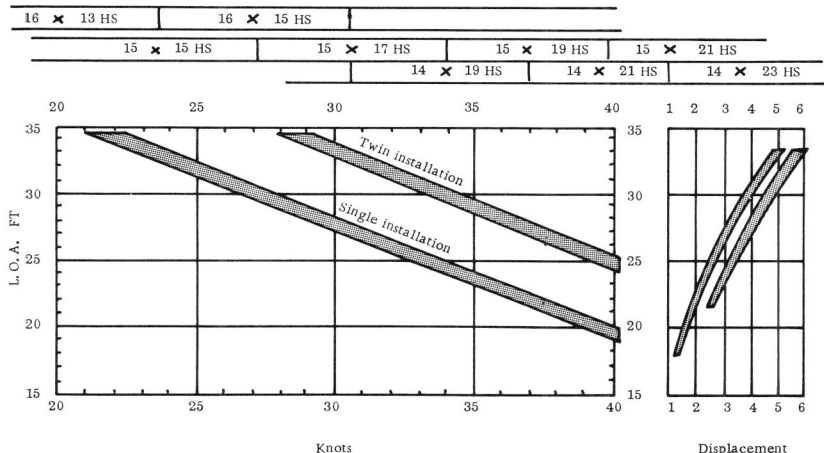

Knots   Displacement

VOLVO PENTA AQ260A/280B

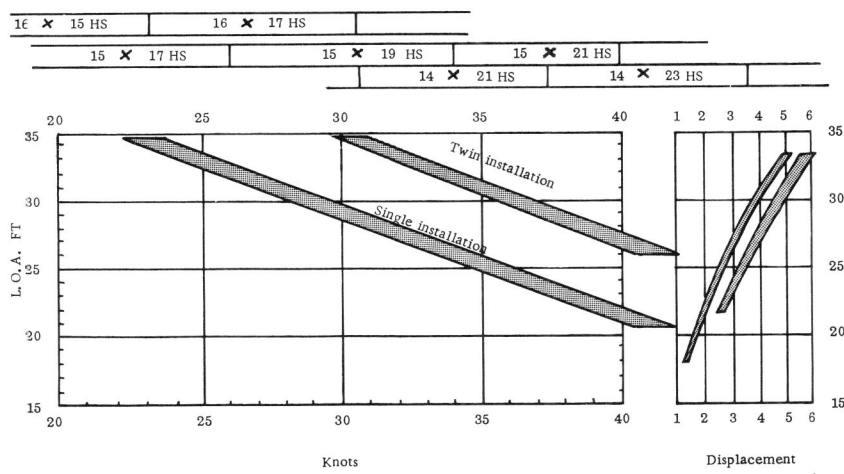

Knots   Displacement

VOLVO PENTA AQ290A/280B

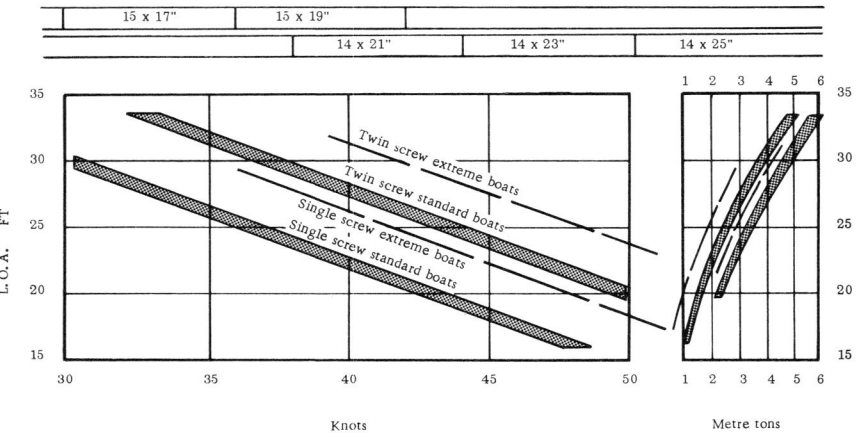

15 x 17"	15 x 19"			
	14 x 21"	14 x 23"	14 x 25"	

Twin screw extreme boats
Twin screw standard boats
Single screw extreme boats
Single screw standard boats

L.O.A. FT

Knots

Metre tons

VOLVO PENTA AQD21A/280D

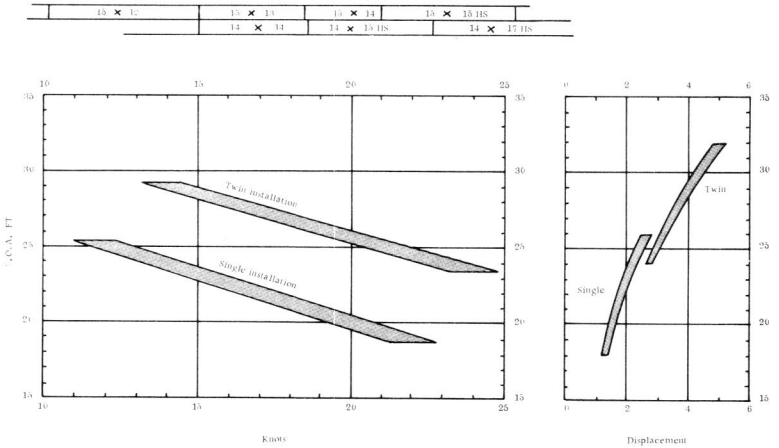

15 × 12	15 × 13	15 × 14	15 × 15 HS	
	14 × 14	14 × 15 HS	14 × 17 HS	

Twin installation
Single installation

L.O.A. FT

Twin

Single

Knots

Displacement

VOLVO PENTA AQD32A/280D

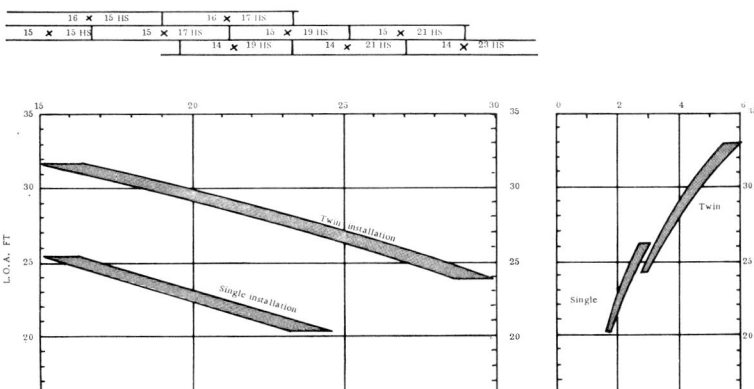

VOLVO PENTA AQD40A/280B

L = LEFT HAND ROTATION
R = RIGHT HAND ROTATION

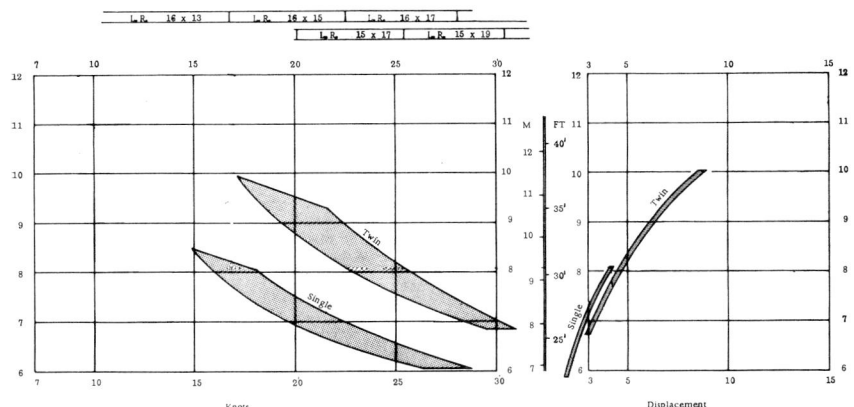

MOTOR/ENGINE AQD70C, CL, TAMD70C, THAMD70C

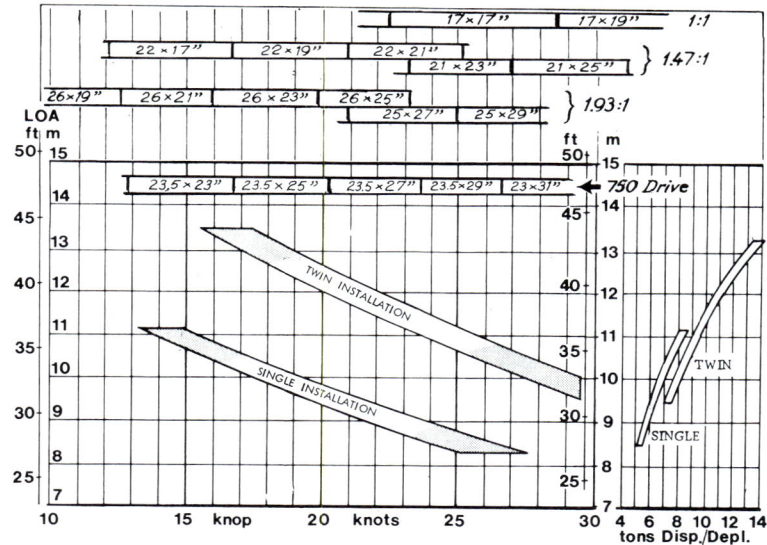

Speed and propeller diagram.

Planing pleasureboats. Displacement in metric tons.

7
The Diesels

From the early 1960s I/O manufacturers had seen the potential of linking diesel engines to outdrive units. Diesel engines are more economical, more robust and simpler (no spark ignition) than petrol engines. The fuel, considerably less volatile than gasoline, reduces fire risk on board and lowers insurance premiums. The drawbacks are the high initial cost; the low power-to-weight ratio, meaning low boat speed; and many owners fear of the technical mystique surrounding the diesel's compression-ignition system. The demand for diesel I/Os was primarily centred in Europe. American yachtsmen and powerboat owners enjoyed the lowest gasoline prices in the world and wanted high performance for their money.

Perkins Ltd, of Peterborough, England, adapted their 4.107 and 4.108 series engines in their Z-drive. These units, although never

72 Thirty-two-foot Coronet Oceanfarer powered by twin AQD40 engines

really successful for planing boats, are widely used for river craft, estuary craft and slower semi-planing offshore cruisers. The total I/O package was marketed at an extremely competitive price and achieved high sales, particularly in the UK, during the emergence of 'budget' boats in the late 1960s and during the boom of 1969–72.

Of the big-league I/O manufacturers only Volvo Penta and Mercruiser entered the diesel arena. Mercruiser marinised the UK-built Rover engine which had proved itself so well in the Land-Rover vehicles. As a marine engine it was not successful. Heavy, complicated and not powerful enough, it suffered the added embarrassment of being ineffective in astern. The high volume of exhaust gas being discharged at low velocity through the centre of the Mercruiser jet-prop caused chronic cavitation as the propeller in astern gear bit into gas instead of water. Mercruiser re-entered the diesel market in 1979 with a rather complicated four-cylinder engine advertised at 145hp followed by BMW with a lightweight engine of 136hp. This problem was to arise later for Volvo too with their AQD21/250 and 270 series, although to a lesser extent.

By 1962 Wiklund was becoming concerned by the ever increasing numbers of I/O competitors beginning to encroach on Volvo's three-year monopoly. The 100 drive with only minor modifications was virtually unchanged since the prototypes had appeared. Volvo were developing a new engine, the B.18, to replace the tough little B.16 and Wiklund decided that a new drive-unit should be developed. This was to evolve into the 200 series of 1965. Meanwhile to protect his flanks, particularly from the rumoured Perkins activity, Wiklund instructed his research team to investigate the possibility of mating diesels to the 100 drive, preferably of sufficient power and low weight to give planing speeds. Volvo were not without substantial diesel knowledge. The company had pioneered (at the same time as Mercedes-Benz) the concept of designing diesels for high turbocharging from the outset (as opposed to adding turbochargers later to obtain more power) and Volvo Penta were successfully marketing 4.7, 6.7 and 9.6 litre engines for yachts and commercial craft. At the lower end of the scale Penta had introduced a 'hand-built' pure marine direct injection single-cylinder engine in 1959 which as the MD1 was destined to become, along with the twin-cylinder MD2, the best known sailboat auxiliary in the world. Volvo Penta had also proved their ability to marinise

73 This Wynne-designed Formula 233 won the diesel class in the 1964
Around Nassau race. Engines were two early AQD27/100s giving a top
speed of around 37mph

other makes of engines, their MD4 being a conversion of a Mercedes
four-cylinder diesel. Unfortunately, none of these sources provided
the right combination of power and weight for the researchers to
adapt for the i/o unit. The MD4 was considered, and possibly
with supercharging could have been improved, but Mercedes-Benz
were contemplating marketing a marine version of this engine
themselves and eventually the MD4 was withdrawn from Penta's
range. The engine became the delightful Mercedes OM636.

Eventually, Volvo Penta found their diesel in France at Indenor/
Peugeot. The XDP series of four- and six-cylinder units, with their
Ricardo indirect injection and alloy cylinder heads, were the lightest
and most powerful production diesels available. The four-cylinder
engine was given a rating of 68hp SAE for pleasure boats at an
unbelievable, for a diesel, 4500rpm, and the six-cylinder engine
83hp at 4000rpm. These two units, designated AQD19/100 and
AQD27/100, were announced in 1965. They and their derivatives
dominated the i/o high-power diesel scene for the next eleven years,

74 Pair of snug fitting AQD29/200C units in a 35ft cruiser

75 This unusual application of AQD29/250s was a Prout Ranger catamaran, built in Essex, UK. The steering link between the drives was complicated!

the latest versions AQD21/280 and AQD32/280 producing 75hp and 106hp respectively.

The highly successful Indenor engines stayed predominantly in Europe, achieving a large following in Holland, France, Germany and the UK. A few were used commercially in pilot vessels, sea trucks, police and customs launches etc in Europe and the Third World. A large number were used in patrol boats during the Nigerian–Biafran crisis, but very few entered the USA.

The AQD40

Volvo Penta's researchers met with Wiklund in 1970 to give special consideration to the diesel Aquamatic programme. Rumblings about pending oil crises and consequent fuel shortages, allied to a growing awareness of environmental pollution, prompted the 'think tank' to look closely at the diesel i/o potential.

The co-operation with Indenor, although an overall success, did have quite substantial drawbacks. Firstly, Volvo had little influence

76 AQD40/280

on the technical development of the French engines and even less influence on availability and delivery from France. Volvo Penta could not expect priority allocation of basic engines during diesel booms in the French automotive industry. Secondly, the costing of the production was outside Volvo's own control and the price at which the i/os had to be sold was prohibitive. Finally, when operated under commercial heavy duty conditions the engines had proved too lightly constructed and extremely expensive to repair. The think tank knew that other manufacturers such as BMW, Perkins, Nissan and Mercedes were planning for high-speed light engines, but an approach to these would merely mean a new generation engine but with all the old generation inherent problems. Volvo Penta on the other hand could not go it alone and develop a purely marine diesel. The cost would be astronomical and the market potential too small.

Wiklund decided to discuss the problem with the young president of A. B. Volvo, Per Gyllenhammar, because Wiklund was convinced that, if the engine could be powerful enough to corner some of the US petrol i/o market and an automotive/industrial potential existed, it could be developed in-house. Wiklund was as convincing as he was far-sighted, for Gyllenhammar authorised the setting up of a development team at Volvo's Skövde engine factory with Volvo Penta to take on the lion's share of the costs. Wiklund set in motion what was to become the largest investment in a new product ever made by Volvo Penta. The creation of the AQD40 engine was also to prove a fitting climax to the career of Volvo Penta's remarkable and intuitive leader. Fifteen technicians were appointed to the D.40 development programme in 1971 with a brief to develop an engine of up to four litres' displacement incorporating high output, low weight, compact dimensions, long life, low maintenance costs, low fuel consumption, and environmental sympathy. Lastly, the engine should be dimensioned to allow for further development in the future.

During the following five years, the technicians were to build and test ninety-five prototypes which, on the test bed and in boats and trucks, was equivalent to running twenty times round the world.

Before establishing a production line the 40 series engine was compared with six engines manufactured by rival companies. The D.40 was obviously in a class of its own. Light and compact, it produced 36hp per litre (.6hp per cubic inch) of swept volume—more than twenty per cent higher than the average value of the six competitors. The weight per horsepower was more than twenty per cent lower. Although the engine developed 130shp at 3600rpm, Lloyds had approved the crankshaft for up to 230hp. The Ricardo Vb combustion system allied to the high speed turbocharger brought the D.40 emission control within the strictest regulations to be applied in California up to 1982! To set the seal on Wiklund's hopes for acceptability in America, Volvo's new diesel proved to have an identical marine performance to the AQ170/280 petrol engine with an added bonus of a 15–20 per cent fuel saving.

Vara

Production capacity at Volvo's Skövde engine factory was already fully committed when in 1975 it was decided to go ahead with manufacture of the 40 diesel. Volvo, always conscious of their social responsibilities, consulted the regional authorities who, because of the local availability of labour, recommended that the plant should be established in Vara, northeast of Gothenburg on the route to Skövde.

Here the factory designers could apply all the experience gained from the much publicised 'Volvo experiment' in which car production workers were formed into small, self-organising groups, placed

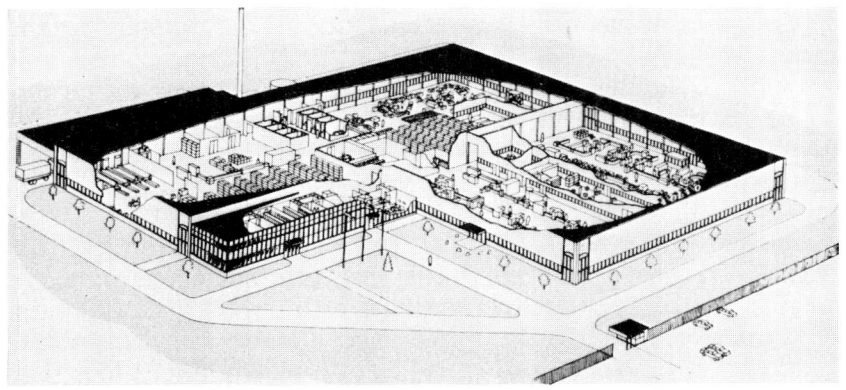

77 The Vara plant

131

78 Assembly line at Vara

in attractive surroundings and given responsibility for a complete vehicle or unit of production. This experiment had drastically reduced absenteeism in the car plant, had improved employee-management relations and provided more job satisfaction and prestige. These factors influenced the quality of the final product.

The Vara plant adopted an L-shaped layout with all central services, ie machine maintenance, component store, training departments, at the junction of the two main sprigs. The machining and assembly departments consist of small workshops within the greater whole, each department being heated and air-conditioned individually. A great deal of attention has been given to sound limitation both within the departments and between them. Machinery used in the factory has been built to very stringent noise control specifications. Assembly work throughout the plant is carried out with the engines stationary, all movements between functions being via air-cushion trolleys which at the flick of a switch and with little physical effort transport the units between stations. For the workers' comfort and to prevent feelings of claustrophobia the building has large windows to the outside. Colour schemes are lively, chosen

79 Coffee break in one of the Vara rest rooms

by the working teams in conjunction with management. Each department has its own coffee room, spacious and well decorated. Generally, flexitime prevails and each team is able to plan its own hours and break times within agreed guidelines.

Volvo are convinced that by removing heavy physical labour and drudgery from the factory environment a better attitude to work is created, thereby ensuring higher quality. The checking of that quality is as thorough at Vara as it is throughout the Volvo manufacturing plants. Laboratory-style test units are constantly monitoring the standards of construction and assembly. Every engine is test run and inspected for more than an hour under varying load conditions. The failure rate is minimal.

After Lindbergh

In the year of his retirement, 1977, Harald Wiklund had the satisfaction of seeing a large proportion of his AQD40/280 production heading for the United States. To his surprise one man brought his engine back to Europe from America—in an unexpected way.

Alan Cargile, a forty-six-year-old boatbuilder from Nashville, Tennessee, had always had a high regard for the transatlantic flight of Charles Lindbergh. Lindbergh, against great odds, succeeded in crossing the Atlantic in the single-engined aircraft *Spirit of St. Louis.* Fifty years later Alan Cargile determined to retrace this epic flight by crossing in his single-engined boat, *Spirit of Nashville.*

The press was highly sceptical about Cargile's chances of survival when they saw his boat: thirty feet long and only eight feet abeam, the boat had been designed as a trailable lakes cruiser. With its shallow draft and large windows it looked more like a houseboat than an ocean-going vessel. Cargile had chosen the new Aquamatic D40/280 as the power unit 'since it was important that the engine be really dependable'. In order to follow Lindbergh's route as accurately as possible, Cargile planned to leave New York for Paris via Le Havre and the River Seine. On 16 July 1977 he and two friends, Ed Gillespie and Billy Flanagan, left New York in fine weather carrying nearly four tons of fuel in an all-up eight-ton rig. Speed was kept down to about six knots to ensure that there would be enough fuel for the journey. An extract from the log reads:

After five days and about 1100 nautical miles from the start, we ran into a storm. Wind intensity of 26 metres/seconds results in very high waves. For a period of 12 hours we encountered waves 12–13 metres high. In order to avoid being swamped from astern, we laid out our drogue anchor in the bows and by combining this with running in reverse, we managed to stay on the right side of the wave peaks. We were very grateful to our Aquamatic which made it possible to keep the drive in the right direction the whole time. The three-blade propeller (16 x 15in) had an excellent braking effect when the waves tended to hurl us forward. Everything on board was soaked through and the radio also broke down. The storm gradually blew itself out, we got the radio working again and we decided to return

81 *Spirit of Nashville*

to Newfoundland to repair it. This was an unwelcome deviation from the Lindbergh route but we decided to accept this five-day extension of our trip.

The weather continued to be bad during the rest of the voyage with a choppy sea, rain and mist. In other words just about the sort of weather to be expected on the Atlantic at this time of the year. Lindbergh met the same conditions to a certain extent in 1927. The boat ran into yet another storm, not as long and troublesome as the first, but quite sufficient to cause the radio to break down once again. The rest of the voyage was carried out without any contact with land or other vessel.

The three men sighted Le Havre on Sunday 14 August and on Tuesday 16th moored near the Alexander III bridge in Paris. The voyage had taken a total of thirty-one days and the engine had run non-stop without any problems for 695 hours. The fuel consumption was 2.13 gallons per hour.

Cargile's voyage was practical proof of the reliability and economy of the new diesel. Although some heat exchanger problems were experienced during the first production year, Volvo quickly solved them and were left with one of the most technically excellent engines ever introduced. Already plans are in hand to develop further the 40 series for the 1980s.

8
The Future

Necessity is said to be the mother of invention. This old saw is fast achieving a pinnacle of poignancy, to judge by the frenetic activity of automotive engineers all over the world to anticipate and adapt to the diminishing supplies of oil and the attendant gloom-laden prophecies. The on-going oil crisis has prompted vast investments in exploring not only alternative fuels, but ways in which existing fuels can be used more efficiently. Governments are busily legislating for fuel preservation and actively discouraging the development of industrial or domestic apparatus with a high fuel demand. Alternative energy sources are being developed. Ergonomic and ecological studies are as commonplace as consumer researches and sociologists are finding a plethora of job opportunities in analysing and forecasting probable behavioural patterns in future oil-starved environments.

Parallel with their contemporaries Volvo too have delved deeply into research, both technical and sociological, in order to establish a forecast of probable trends for the 1980s. Researches and trend investigations have been pursued by the Volvo American Corporation of Rockley, New Jersey, in great detail. Already the world's largest consumer nation is proposing the most severe legislative action for 1982, directed in the main against the automobile. Environmental anti-pollution law in America is more stringent than in any other country and safety regulations for automobiles and automotive products require a high degree of compliance from manufacturers. With its highly developed leisure and marine market North America provides the ideal backdrop against which Volvo Penta can set their ideas and intentions for the next decade.

In 1978 the total worldwide market for i/o units was estimated at between 110,000 and 116,000. Of this total an incredible 95,000 are sold on the US market alone. Although Volvo claim to be

number two in America, Mercruiser commands a massive 70 per
cent market share on this their home ground, whilst the other home
team, OMC, have slightly less than Volvo's claimed 16–17 per cent.
All other I/os together, eg BMW and Chrysler, share one per cent
between them. Clearly, if the Aquamatic mouse is going to have
something to roar about in future he has to do most of it in the
USA, and future engine/drive designs will need to be very much
American-oriented.

A VAC market study concluded that the consumer group which
participates in boating is generally in a socio-economic bracket that
is less sensitive to increasing fuel costs. Trends also indicate that
in the period up to 1985 this group will expand and on 1979 values
will have an average disposable income of $25,000. Optimistically,
VAC researchers are confident that future legislation will be

primarily to control use of fuel for automobiles and that little attention will be given to the marine industry, as the total fuel take is proportionately small. (This observation is probably applicable to Europe too.) Nonetheless, any factors which potentially limit the use of the automobile can have a wide ranging influence on the marine leisure market and consequently on the future of the Aquamatic.

It is both price *and* availability of fuel that has to be considered. The next ten years may see permutations of a continued relatively low price coupled with low availability or a very high price with normal (or high) availability or, in the worst case, a high price level with low availability. Predictions for the future have been based largely on a prognosis somewhere between the last two possibilities. Despite VAC predictions of higher fuel costs being of little consequence to the yachtsman, he cannot help but be psychologically influenced by rising prices when receiving the bill for filling his boat tanks with anything between 100 and 500 gallons each time. He may simply reduce his frequency of boat use, or the speed of his boat, or change to a smaller craft to compensate for increased costs and lower fuel availability. As boat purchase is of a purely discretionary nature, potential customers may turn away and spend money on other activities. Such action on a wide scale could easily

VOLVO PENTA
AQ AD 40/280

have an adverse effect on the market for used boats, thereby reducing the investment incentive for new boat purchasers.

A reduction in use of the automobile would directly lead to a reduction in boat usage, particularly of trailable boats. A projection study of US car trends covering the period from 1976 to 1985 indicates a reduction in size and weight by up to 22 per cent, although by 1979 average kerb weight has only reduced by $2\frac{1}{2}$ per cent in spite of the compact, sub-compact, micro-compact etc. Assuming a hypothetical weight reduction of maximum 20 per cent of the towing vehicle a calculation can be made to determine the resultant effect on weights and sizes of boats that will be trailed in the mid-1980s. In 1979 a 15–20ft boat weighing 2100–3000lb, requiring 140–250shp would, by 1985, become 1700–2400lb and 115–200shp; the weight/power ratios for both ranges of boats being a constant. This means that small boats for trailer use would need to be constructed 400–600lb lighter over the six-year period—hardly a dramatic challenge for the boat builder or trailer manufacturers. Studies of boats of 20–25ft and over 25ft have produced similar results, the 1985 power requirement for these falling into the range of 150–280shp. Volvo Penta have drawn confidence from this study because, assuming boats are still being trailed in the years to come, the power requirement for 15–25ft craft fits the Aquamatic programme exactly: 115–280shp. Very few US-built pleasure boats over 25ft have I/O engine installations.

With considerable government pressure for smaller and lighter cars being applied, US auto manufacturers are looking at radical new designs to cut fuel consumption. A proposed legislative measure for 1982 specifies that the average fuel consumption for a manufacturer's fleet of cars should be a minimum 24mpg, rising to 27.5mpg by 1985. Even with vehicles of smaller sizes this regulation could not be adhered to with current engines and fuel systems. Engine design has to be re-thought and will most likely trend towards the transverse engine with integral gearbox and transmission, the concept beloved of Europeans. This type of engine, where good acceleration prevails at the cost of top end performance, is totally unsuitable for marinisation. The wider application of computerised ignition and fuel systems, too complex for the demanding marine environment, could further limit the choice of basic units for the future Aquamatic.

American engine manufacturers have also restricted the choice for the mariniser. From the entire output of the giant General Motors corporation, only the Chevrolet division continues to supply basic engines for marine conversion. But it is with General Motors and Ford in close contact that Volvo has been able to preconceive an Aquamatic programme for the next few years. Today the bulk of auto engine production is still centred around the V-8, which because of its sheer volume is cheaper to buy than a V-6. GM anticipates a strong trend towards the six-cylinder during the next two years, which will reduce unit cost. Ultimately, by the end of the next decade, GM expects the in-line four to be the most prominent engine type.

	V-8	V-6	in-line 4
1980	4.9mil	2.5mil	1.9mil
1985	2.5mil	4mil	3mil

The above shows the anticipated swing to smaller units in the first five years from 1980. The 1980 figure is less of a forecast than an actuality, as production plans are already laid. The increase in four-cylinder production is rising rapidly. Production of these engines in 1978 was only 800,000 compared to the planned 1.9 million of 1980. Volvo, therefore, can reasonably plan to continue the Aquamatic range through an interim V-8 and V-6 era, back into straight four-cylinder units which can still be produced in Sweden today at a lower cost than any American alternative. (With higher straight four-cylinder production in the US, this picture may change.) To give them added strength they already have a marked lead in the field of diesel i/os.

Given that their assessment of socio-economic trends, boat-usage and design trends and basic engine availability factors are reasonably accurate, Volvo predict a market growth of five per cent per annum, which is an improvement on the actual growth in 1979. With so much to be gained in terms of US market share they have reaffirmed their commitment to continue technical developments of the i/o and exploit to the full their unique ability to influence boat-builders with their innovative approach to marine propulsion. Already Volvo Penta of America are revising their distribution system and adapting their resources to the new market conditions. In Gothenburg the first phase of planning and technical development has already begun. Whilst the car division concentrates on increasing engine efficiency, Volvo Penta is directing its considerable R&D thinking towards more efficient transmissions and utilisation of available power. It is hard to conceive of any improvements to the 280 drive, particularly as the new power-trim system has a kick-up facility and safety tilt switch ensuring even more technical advance, but a new drive is on the drawing board, although several years and a lot of investment away from production reality. This, more than anything else reflects Volvo's commitment to their belief in the i/o future.

Meanwhile, Volvo Penta have succeeded in achieving a high level of performance from the new generation of aluminium and stainless steel propellers. The latter are equal to the best available and have given results parallel with the splendid Black Max propeller on test. Even now, a second generation is being evolved.

At the Chicago Boat Show in September 1979, Volvo Penta's new Aquamatic AQ145/280 was launched. Based on the new B.23 engine, it features redesigned combustion chambers, a new high lift camshaft and a new inlet manifold with downdraft carburettors. At 3000rpm it gains 12shp over the AQ140 and at the top end 13shp to give an overall 138shp. For the first time a Volvo Aquamatic in the same category can produce a higher speed than the Mercruiser 140, which in Volvo's test laboratory was unable to show more than 127shp. It is claimed that if the AQ140 is jacked up higher in the transom, as is the Mercruiser, the top speed would increase further. Volvo also intend to introduce a 'limited edition' AQ145 Turbo, a project that was first experimented with on a B.20 AQ130 engine in 1974.

Although Chevrolet V-6 engines are today more expensive than V-8s, this picture is expected to change by 1981 (see above). Volvo Penta intend to gamble on a falling V-6 price by introducing a 160–170hp unit based on a newly developed GM engine of just under four litres displacement. At the lower end of the scale, the AQ120 engine with the resurrected 270 drive has proved popular among first-time boat buyers by virtue of its reliability and low initial cost. Extending this success Volvo Penta have planned to reduce production costs even further and yet increase the power of the engine to 115shp DIN compared with the 107shp DIN of the present engine.

It is mooted that the engine will be termed AQ125/270.

The AQD40 diesel has given Volvo Penta a striking market lead in I/O propulsion of this type. However, several questionmarks hang over the future of the diesel I/O in the US. Once again, the possible trends of automotive engines will have a direct influence on the marine diesel versions. Government legislation restricting nitrous oxide content in the atmosphere could be so prohibitive that the diesel would be killed altogether. Assuming that good sense does not allow such stringency and that NOX content is limited to perhaps one part per million (.4ppm had been proposed), US diesel production could increase by 1985 to represent as much as twenty per cent of all automotive engines. In this event a whole new volume production of diesel and hybrid (adapted petrol engine blocks) diesel engines would be generated in America and Europe, thus bringing price levels down. A recent comparison showed that the automotive Volkswagen Rabbit diesel as opposed to the petrol option would cost an initial 200 dollars more but give a fuel saving of 16mpg. On an annual mileage of 15,000 it would take just over one and a half years to break even at current fuel prices. Similarly, the Peugeot diesel saloon would break even at just over five years. The same type of yardstick applied to the AQD40 portends a horrifying result. With a price differential of 6000 dollars over the equivalent petrol engine and an average use of 75 hours running per year, break-even on fuel saving would take over 98 years to achieve! In Europe where fuel is up to five times more costly the results are more moderate.

In the long term Volvo clearly need to extend their marketing of the 40 series engine into volume automotive markets in order to reduce unit cost and compete with the general production step-up predicted for diesels. Activities towards this end were initiated in 1978 and had achieved measurable success by the end of 1979. Meanwhile an indirect way of alleviating the problem in the shorter term is to provide more power from within the same basic engine unit. By the early autumn of 1980 Volvo expect to announce an aftercooled variant of the AQD40—not to replace it, but to supplement the range. This new engine will be designated AQAD40/280 and the power increase is to rise from the present 130shp DIN to 155shp DIN with an even lower smoke content than the already minimal 10–15 per cent of the D.40.

Summarising, the future for the Aquamatic depends on: (a) fuel availability and price; (b) legislation; (c) continued availability of basic petrol and diesel engines at acceptable cost, be they of American, European or Volvo origin; (d) Volvo Penta's continued innovative strength, particularly with regard to power transmission efficiency; (e) their ability to increase market share for their products in the USA. Both (a) and (b) are, of course, common influences on all marine engine and i/o manufacturers. Point (c) is particularly significant to the i/o builders, and Volvo Penta may just have an advantage with their in-house engines. The remaining two points are entirely down to Volvo Penta themselves and, as we can see, the investment has already begun.

Volvo Penta intend with great determination to keep the mighty mouse roaring like a lion, even more stridently—and never to see it reduced to an insignificant squeak!

Tables of Technical Data

B.16 Engines

General

	AQ80	AQ80 Sport
Aquamatic type	AQ80	AQ80 Sport
Specification Nos.	9419	9454
Engine type	4-stroke	O.H.V.
No. of cylinders	4 in-line	
Bore m.m. (ins.)	79.37 (3.125)	
Stroke m.m. (ins.)	80 (3.15)	
Capacity litres (cu.ins.)	1.58 (98)	
Compression ratio	8:2:1	
Max r.p.m./h.p.	4500/80	5000/88
Idling r.p.m.	600	
Total weight (incl.drive) kg. (lbs)	212(465)	213(467)

Cylinder Block

Material .... Special-alloy cast-iron
The cylinder bores are machined directly in the block
Bore, standard .... 3.125" (79.37 mm)
    0.020" oversize .... 3.145" (79.88 mm)
    0.030"   "   .... 3.155" (80.13 mm)
    0.040"   "   .... 3.165" (80.39 mm)
    0.050"   "   .... 3.175" (80.64 mm)

Pistons

Material .... Light-alloy
Weight .... 14.46 + 0.18 oz.
    (410 + 5 grams)
Permissible weight difference between pistons in
same engine .... 0.35 oz. (10 grams)
Total height .... 3.390" (86 mm)
Height from piston pin centre to piston top .... 1.81" (46 mm)
Piston clearance .... 0.0012"-0.0020"
    (0.03-0.05 mm)

Diameter, measured at right-angles to piston pin
at lower edge, standard .... 3.1230" (79.33 mm)
    0.020" oversize .... 3.1431" (79.84 mm)
    0.030"   "   .... 3.1535" (80.09 mm)
    0.040"   "   .... 3.1638" (80.35 mm)
    0.050"   "   .... 3.1736" (80.60 mm)

Piston Rings

Ring gap measured at gap opening .... 0.001"-0.002"
    (0.25-0.50 mm)
Piston ring oversizes .... 0.02"
    0.03"
    0.04"
    0.05"

Compression rings

Beveled on upper inner edge
Number on each piston 2
Height upper ring (chromed) .... 0.078" (1.97 mm)
    lower ring .... 0.078" (1.97 mm)
Ring clearance in groove .... 0.0027"-0.0031"
    (0.068-0.079 mm)

147

Oil rings

Number on each piston 1
Height .... 0.186" (4.73 mm)
Ring clearance in groove .... 0.0017"-0.0029"
                                                        (0.045-0.073 mm)

Piston Rings

Fully floating. Circlips at both ends in piston.
Fit in connecting rod .... Close running fit
Fit in piston .... Slide fit
Diameter, standard .... 0.748" (19 mm)
          0.05 mm oversize .... 0.750" (19.05 mm)
          0.10 mm   "   .... 0.752" (19.10 mm)
          0.20 mm   "   .... 0.754" (19.20 mm)

Cylinder Head

Height measured from cylinder head
contact surface to cylinder head nut flats .... 3.90" (99 mm)

Crankshaft

Replaceable bearing shells for main and big-end bearings.
Crankshaft end play .... 0.0004"-0.0040"
                                                        (0.01-0.10 mm)
Main bearings, radial play .... 0.0005"-0.0025"
                                                        (0.014-0.064 mm)
Connecting rod bearings, radial play .... 0.0020"-0.0036"
                                                        (0.051-0.091 mm)

Main Bearings

Main bearing journals

Journal diameter, standard .... 2.1240"-2.1244"
                                                        (53.950-53.960 mm)
                   0.010" undersize .... 2.1140"-2.1144"
                                                        (53.696-53.706 mm)
                   0.020"   "   .... 2.1040"-2.1044"
                                                        (53.442-53.452 mm)
                   0.030"   "   .... 2.0940"-2.0944"
                                                        (53.188-53.198 mm)
                   0.040"   "   .... 2.0840"-2.0844"
                                                        (52.934-52.944 mm)

Journal width, flange bearing, standard .... 1.5329"-1.5344"
                                                        (38.935-38.975 mm)
0.1 mm oversize (for 0.010" undersize shell) .... 1.5369"-1.5384"
                                                        (39.035-39.075 mm)
0.2 mm   "   (" 0.020"   "   ") .... 1.5407"-1.5423"
                                                        (39.135-39.175 mm)
0.3 mm   "   (" 0.030"   "   ") .... 1.5447"-1.5463"
                                                        (39.235-39.275 mm)
0.4 mm   "   (" 0.040"   "   ") .... 1.5486"-1.5502"
                                                        (39.335-39.375 mm)

Main bearing shells

Thickness, standard .... 0.0752"-0.0755"
                                                        (1.911-1.918 mm)
      0.010" undersize .... 0.0802"-0.0805"
                                                        (2.038-2.045 mm)
      0.020"   "   .... 0.0852"-0.0855"
                                                        (2.165-2.172 mm)
      0.030"   "   .... 0.0902"-0.0905"
                                                        (2.292-2.299 mm)
      0.040"   "   .... 0.0962"-0.0955"
                                                        (2.419-2.426 mm)

Connecting rod bearings

Connecting rod bearing journals.
Bearing seat width .... 1.2953"-1.2992"
                                                        (32.900-33.000 mm)
Journal diameter, standard .... 1.8736"-1.8740"
                                                        (47.589-47.600 mm)
         0.010" undersize .... 1.8635"-1.8640"
                                                        (47.335-47.347 mm)
         0.020"   "   .... 1.8536"-1.8540"
                                                        (47.081-47.092 mm)
         0.030"   "   .... 1.8436"-1.8440"
                                                        (46.827-46.838 mm)
         0.040"   "   .... 1.8336"-1.8520"
                                                        (46.573-46.584 mm)

Connecting rod bearing shells.
Thickness, standard .... 0.0614"-0.0617"
                                                        (1.560-1.568 mm)
      0.010" undersize .... 0.0664"-0.0667"
                                                        (1.687-1.695 mm)
      0.020"   "   .... 0.0714"-0.0717"
                                                        (1.814-1.822 mm)
      0.030"   "   .... 0.0764"-0.0767"
                                                        (1.941-1.949 mm)
      0.040"   "   .... 0.0814"-0.0817"
                                                        (2.068-2.076 mm)

Connecting rods

Marked 1-4 on side away from camshaft. Classified A-D
showing weight classification. Only connecting rods
with same weight classification may be used in the same
engine. Axial play at crankshaft .... 0.0060"-0.0140"
                                                        (0.15-0.35 mm)
Length, centre-centre ················· .... 5.905+0.004"
                                                        (150+0.1 mm)
Weight, Class A .... 20.39-21.44 oz.
                                                        (578-608 grams)
        B .... 21.44-22.50 oz.
                                                        (608-638 grams)
        C .... 22.50-23.56 oz.
                                                        (638-668 grams)
        D .... 23.56-24.62 oz.
                                                        (668-698 grams)

149

Camshaft

Drive	Fibre gear on camshaft
Number of bearings	3
Forward bearing journal, diameter ....,..............	1.8494"-1.8504"
	(46.975-47.000 mm)
Centre bearing journal, diameter	1.6919"-1.6929"
	(42.975-43.000 mm)
Rear bearing journal, diameter	1.4557"-1.4567"
	(36.975-37.000 mm)
Radial clearance	0.0010"-0.0029"
	(0.025-0.075 mm)
Valve clearance for check of camshaft setting	
(cold engine)	0.043" (1.1 mm)
Inlet valves should then open at	10° after T.D.C.

Camshaft bearings

Forward bearing, diameter	1.8514"-1.8524"
	(47.025-47.050 mm)
Centre bearing, diameter	1.6939"-1.6949"
	(43.025-43.050 mm)
Rear bearing, diameter	1.4577"-1.4587"
	(37.025-37.050 mm)

Timing gears

Crankshaft gear	20 teeth
Camshaft gear	40 teeth
Backlash	0.004"-0.0016"
	(0.01-0.04 mm)

Valve System

Valves

Inlet

Disc diameter	1.46" (37 mm)
Stem diameter	0.3094"-0.3100"
	(7.859-7.874 mm)
Valve seat angle	44.5°
Cylinder head seat angle	45°
Seat width in cylinder head	0.060" (1.5 mm)

Exhaust

Disc diameter	1.34" (34 mm)
Stem diameter	0.3082"-0.3089"
	(7.830-7.845 mm)
Valve seat angle	44.5°
Cylinder head seat angle	45°
Seat width in cylinder head	0.060" (1.5 mm)

Valve Clearances

Clearance - warm engine	
inlet mm. (ins.)	.50 (.020)
exhaust mm. (ins.)	.50 (.020)

Valve guides

Length	2.44" (62 mm)
Inner diameter	0.311"-0.312"
	(7.905-7.920 mm)
Length above cylinder head upper surface	0.83" (21 mm)
Clearance valve stem-valve guide, inlet valves	0.0012"-0.0024"
	(0.031-0.061 mm)
Clearance valve stem-valve guide, exhaust valves	0.0024"-0.0035"
	(0.060-0.090 mm)

Valve springs

Springs close-wound at one end. This end should be
turned downwards.
Length, unloaded .... 1.77" (45 mm)
        in./loading, lb. .... 1.54/56+4½
        mm/loading, kg. .... 39/25.5+2
        in./loading, lb. .... 1.20/145+8
        mm/loading, kg. .... 30.5/66+3.5

Lubricating System

Oil capacity of crankcase .... 4$\frac{7}{8}$ Imp. pints=5$\frac{3}{4}$ US pints
                                                 (2.75 litres)
Oil capacity, incl. oil cleaner .... 6$\frac{1}{4}$ Imp. pints=7$\frac{1}{2}$ US pints
                                                 (3.5 litres)
Oil pressure, warm engine .... 36-50 lb./sq.in.
                                                 (2.5-3.5 kg/cm^2)
Lubricant .... Engine oil (For Service MS
                                                        or PG)
      viscosity, below 32°F (0° C) .... SAE 10W
              from 32°F (0°C) to 90°F (30°C) ... SAE 20
              above 90°F (30°C) .... SAE 30

Oil pump

Type .... Gear pump
Number of teeth 10
Axial clearance .... 0.0008"-0.004"
                                                 (0.020-0.10 mm)
Radial clearance .... 0"-0.004"
                                                 (0.00-0.10 mm)
Backlash .... 0.006"-0.014"
                                                 (0.15-0.35 mm)

Relief valve spring

Length unloaded .... 1.575"+0.002" (40+0.5 mm)
    loaded with 5½+½lb. (2.5+0.2 kg) .... 1.340" (34 mm)
            8+½ lb. (3.5+0.2 kg) .... 1.230" (31.5 mm)

Fuel System

Carburettor .... Single Zenith 34 VN 2x Zenith C1799F
                                                              34V.N.
Main Jet 012471/120   012571/112
Fuel pump .... A.C. Diaphragm
Pressure max. kg/cm^2 (lbs ") .... .25 (3.5)
       min. kg/cm^2 (lbs ") .... .14 (2)
Fuel grade minimum .... 87 octane (research)

Cooling System

Thermostat opens .... 76°C (170°F) early production
                                            55°C (130°F) late production

Ignition System

Firing Order 1-3-4-2
Ignition Setting basic .... 4° B.T.D.C.
              Stroboscopic 3500-4000 r.p.m. 32° B.T.D.C.
Spark plugs .... Champion J6 or equivalent
Spark plug gap mm.(ins.) .... .71.8 (.027-.032)
Contact Breaker gap mm. (ins.)................ .4-.5 (.016-.020)

Electrical system

```
Voltage ................................................  12v.
generator output ......................................  75w.
starter output ........................................  .6 h.p.
battery capacity standard .............................  60 Ah.
specific gravity fully charged ........................  1.275-1.285
                         needs recharge ...............  1.230
drive belt ................................ HC 38 x 29      HC 38 x 30
```

Wear Tolerances

Cylinders
Rebore when worn (if consumption abnormal) .... 0.010" (0.25 mm)

Crankshaft

```
Maximum main bearing journal out-of-round .............  0.0020" (0.05 mm)
Maximum connecting rod journal out-of-round ...........  0.0028" (0.07 mm)
Maximum crankshaft end play ...........................  0.0060" (0.15 mm)
```

Valves

```
Maximum valve stem to valve guide clearance ...........  0.0060" (0.15 mm)
Maximum valve stem wear ...............................  0.0008" (0.02 mm)
```

Camshaft

```
Maximum out-of-round (with new bearings) ..............  0.0030" (0.075 mm)
Maximum bearing wear ..................................  0.0008" (0.02 mm)
```

Timing gears

Permissible backlash .... 0.0050" (0.12 mm)

Tightening Torques

	Lb. ft.	Kgm.
Cylinder head	50-60	7-8
Main bearings	60-70	8-10
Big-end bearings	30-35	4-5
Flywheel	17-20	2.3-2.7
Spark plugs, 14 mm	30	4
Camshaft nut	105	15
Tensioner ring and flywheel housing	25	3.5

152

GENERAL

Aquamatic, type	100/100	110/100	95/100	110/200	95A/100	120/200
Max. output, h.p.	100	110	95	110	95	120
Compression pressure (200 r.p.m.) kg/cm^2 (lb/sq.in.)	13-14 (185-200)	13-14 (185-200)	13-14 (185-200)	13-14 (185-200)	12-14 (170-200)	12-14 (170-200)
Compression ratio	9.5:1	10:1	10:1	10:1	9.7:1	9.7:1
Number of cylinders			4			
Bore,			84.14mm (3.313")			
Stroke			80mm (3.150")			
Displacement			1.78 litres (108.6 cu.in)			
Weight, incl. elec. equipment, carburetor			Approx. 180kg (396 lb)			
Idling speed, max.	600 r.p.m.		900 - 1000 r.p.m.			

CYLINDER BLOCK

Material	Special alloy cast iron
Bore, nominal, standard	84.14mm (3.313")
0.020" oversize	84.65mm (3.332")
0.030" "	84.90mm (3.342")
0.040" "	85.16mm (3.353")
0.050" "	85.41mm (3.362")

PISTONS

Material	Light-alloy
Permissible weight deviation between pistons in same engine	10g (0.35oz)
Height, overall, early production	83.5mm (3.29")
late production	71.0mm (2.79")
Height, piston pin centre - piston crown	46mm (1.81")
Piston clearance	0.02-0.04mm (0.0008-0.0016")

PISTON RINGS

Piston ring gap	0.25-0.50mm (0.010-0.020")
Piston ring oversizes	0.020"
	0.030"
	0.040"
	0.050"

* AQ90/100	Compression pressure at 200 r.p.m.	10-11kg/cm^2 (145-155)
	Compression ratio	7.6 : 1

COMPRESSION RINGS

Marked "TOP". Top ring chromed	
Number on each piston	2
Height	1.98mm (0.078")
Piston ring clearance in groove	0.054-0.081mm (0.0021-0.0032")

153

OIL SCRAPER RINGS

Number on each piston   1
Height ....   4.74mm (0.186")
Piston ring clearance in groove   0.044-0.072mm (0.0017-0.0028")

PISTON PINS

Floating fit. Circlips at both
ends in piston.
Fit:
  In connecting rod ....   Close running fit
  In piston ....   Push fit
Diameter, standard ....   22.00mm (0.866")
  0.05mm (0.002") oversize ....   22.05mm (0.868")
  0.10mm (0.004") "   ....   22.10mm (0.870")
  0.20mm (0.008") "   ....   22.20mm (0.874")

CYLINDER HEAD

Height, measured from cylinder
head contact face to face for
bolt heads 87mm   86.2mm   86.2mm   86.2mm   86.2mm   86.2mm
                                 (3.43")   (3.39")   (3.39")   (3.39")   (3.39")   (3.39")

CRANKSHAFT

Crankshaft, end float ....   0.017-0.108mm (0.0007-0.0042")
Main bearings,radial clearance.   0.038-0.089mm (0.0015-0.0035")
Big-end bearings, radial
clearance ....   0.039-0.081mm (0.0015-0.0032")

MAIN BEARINGS

Main bearing journals

Diameter, standard ....   63.441-63.454mm (2.4977-2.4982")
  0.010" undersize ....   63.187-63.200mm (2.4877-2.4882")
  0.020"   "   ....   62.933-62.946mm (2.4777-2.4782")
  0.030"   "   ....   62.679-62.692mm (2.4677-2.4682")
  0.040"   "   ....   62.425-62.438mm (2.4577-2.4582")
  0.050"   "   ....   62.171-62.184mm (2.4477-2.4482")
Width on crankshaft for pilot
bearing shell
Standard ....   38.930-38.970mm (1.5327-1.5342")
Oversize 1 (0.010" undersize
  shell) ....   39.031-39.072mm (1.5367-1.5383")
Oversize 2 (0.020") undersize
  shell ....   39.133-39.173mm (1.5407-1.5422")
Oversize 3 (0.030")   "   "   39.235-39.275mm (1.5447-1.5463")
Oversize 4 (0.040")   "   "   39.336-39.376mm (1.5487-1.5502")
Oversize 5 (0.050")   "   "   39.438-39.478mm (1.5527-1.5543")

Main bearing shells

Thickness, standard ....   1.985-1.991mm (0.0781-0.0784")
  0.010" undersize ....   2.112-2.118mm (0.0831-0.0834")
  0.020"   "   ....   2.239-2.245mm (0.0881-0.0884")
  0.030"   "   ....   2.366-2.372mm (0.0931-0.0934")
  0.040"   "   ....   2.493-2.499mm (0.0981-0.0984")
  0.050"   "   ....   2.620-2.626mm (0.1031-0.1034")

154

BIG-END BEARINGS

Big-end bearing journals

Width of bearing recess	31.950-32.050mm (1.2579-1.2618")
Diameter, standard	54.089-54.102mm (2.1295-2.1300")
0.010" undersize	53.835-53.848mm (2.1195-2.1200")
0.020" "	53.581-53.594mm (2.1095-2.1100")
0.030" "	53.327-53.340mm (2.0995-2.1000")
0.040" "	53.073-53.086mm (2.0895-2.0900")
0.050" "	52.819-52.832mm (2.0795-2.0800")

Big-end bearing snells

Thickness, standard	1.833-1.841mm (0.0722-0.0725")
0.010" undersize	1.960-1.968mm (0.0772-0.0755")
0.020" "	2.087-2.095mm (0.0822-0.0825")
0.030" "	2.214-2.222mm (0.0872-0.0875")
0.040" "	2.341-2.349mm (0.0922-0.0925")
0.050" "	2.468-2.476mm (0.0972-0.0975")

CONNECTING RODS

End float on crankshaft	0.15-0.35mm (0.006-0.014")
Length, centre - centre	14 ± 0.1mm (5.710 ± 0.004")
Max.permissible wt.deviation between connecting rods in same engine	6 g (0.21 oz.)

FLYWHEEL

Max.permissible axial throw....	0.05mm (0.002") at a diameter of 150mm (5 29/32")
Ring gear (chamfer facing forwards)	142 teeth

FLYWHEEL HOUSING

Max.axial throw for rear face..	0.05mm (0.002") at a diameter of 100mm (3 15/16")
Max.radial throw for rear guide	0.15mm (0.006")

CAMSHAFT

Marking	B	C	C	C	C	C
Number of bearings			3			
Front bearing journal, diameter.			46.975-47.000mm (1.8494-1.8504")			
Centre bearing journal, " ...			42.975-43.000mm (1.6919-1.6929")			
Rear bearing journal, " ...			36.975-37.000mm (1.4557-1.4567")			
Radial clearance			0.020-0.075mm (0.0008-0.0030")			
End float			0.020-0.060mm (0.0008-0.0024")			
Valve clearance for check of camshaft setting(cold engine)..	1.1mm (0.043")		1.45mm (0.057")			
Intake valve should then open at	T.D.C.		T.D.C.			

CAMSHAFT BEARINGS

Front bearing,diameter	47.020-47.050mm (1.8512-1.8524")
Centre bearing,diameter	43.025-43.050mm (1.6939-1.6949")
Rear bearing, diameter	37.020-37.045mm (1.4575-1.4585")

TIMING GEARS

Crankshaft drive,number of teeth	21
Camshaft gear,number of teeth..	42
Backlash	0.04-0.08mm (0.0016-0.0032")
End float, camshaft	0.02-0.06mm (0.0008-0.0024")

VALVES

INTAKE

Valve head diameter	40mm (1.58")	40mm (1.58")	40mm (1.58")	40mm (1.58")	42mm (1.65")	42mm (1.65")
Stem diameter	8.685-8.700mm (0.3419-0.3425")				7.859-7.874mm (0.3094-0.3099")	
Valve seat angle	44.5°				44.5°	
Seat angle in cylinder head ...	45°				45°	
Seat width in cylinder head ...	1.5mm (0.059")				1.5mm (0.059")	
Clearance,both warm and cold engine	0.50-0.55mm (0.020-0.022")				0.50-0.55mm (0.020-0.022")	

EXHAUST

Valve head diameter	35mm (1.38")	35mm (1.38")
Stem diameter	8.645-8.660mm (0.3403-0.3409")	8.645-8.660mm (0.3403-0.3409")
Valve seat angle	44.5°	44.5°
Seat angle in cylinder head ...	45°	45°
Seat width in cylinder head ...	1.5mm (0.059")	1.5mm (0.059")
Clearance,both warm and cold engine	0.50-0.55mm (0.020-0.022")	0.50-0.55mm (0.20-0.022")

VALVE GUIDES

Length, exhaust	62.7-63.0mm (2.4684-2.4803")	62.7-63.0mm (2.4684-2.4803")
intake	62.7-63.0mm (2.4684-2.4803")	61.7-62.0m (2.4291-2.4410")
Inner diameter, exhaust	8.725-8.740mm (0.3435-0.3441")	8.725-8.740mm (0.3435-0.3441")
intake	8.725-8.740mm (0.3435-0.3441")	7.905-7.927mm (0.3112-0.3121")
Height above upper face of cylinder head	21mm (0.83")	21mm (0.83")
Clearance,valve stem-guide, intake	0.025-0.055mm (0.0010-0.0022")	0.031-0.068mm (0.0012-0.0027")
Clearance,valve stem-guide, exhaust	0.065-0.095mm (0.0026-0.0037")	0.065-0.095mm (0.0026-0.0037")

VALVE SPRINGS

Length, unloaded,approx.	46mm (1.81")
With load of 29.5±2.3kg(65±5 lb.)	40mm (1.57")
With load of 82.5±4.3kg (181.5±9.5 lb.)	30mm (1.18")

LUBRICATING SYSTEM

Oil capacity,including oil filter....	3.75 litres (6½ Imp.pints=8 US pints)
excluding " " ...	3.25 litres (5¾ Imp.pints= 7 US pints)
Oil pressure at 2000 r.p.m. (with warm engine and new oil filter)	2.5-6.0 kp/cm^2(36-85 lb/sq.in)
Oil grade	Multigrade oil Service MS
Oil viscosity	SAE 10W/30

OIL FILTER

Type	Full-flow filter
Make	Wix or Mann

OIL PUMP

Type	Gear
Number of teeth on each gear...	10
End float	0.02-0.10mm (0.0008-0.0040")
Radial clearance	0.08-0.14mm (0.0032-0.0055")
Backlash	0.15-0.35mm (0.0060-0.0140")

Relief valve spring
(in oil pump)

Early type (100/100)	
Length, unloaded	31mm (1.22")
loaded with 4.0±0.2kp (8.8±0.44 lb.)	27.5mm (1.08")
9.5±0.3kp(20.9±0.66 lb.)	22.5mm (0.89")
Late type	
Length, unloaded	32.5mm (1.28")
loaded with 8.0±0.8kp (17.6±1.76 lb.)	22.5mm (0.89")

FUEL SYSTEM

FUEL PUMP

Type	Diaphragm pump
Make	AC-7950757 UE
Fuel pressure,measured at same level as pump	0.11-0.25 kp/cm^2(1.5-3.5 lb/sq.in)
Suction height	Max. 1.80m (5.9ft.)
Fuel grade, minimum .... 92(ROT)	97 (ROT)

ROT = Research Method

157

CARBURETTORS

	100/100	110/100	95/100	110/200	95A/100	120/200
No. of carburettors...........	2	2	1	2	1	2

100/100 110/100

Type .... Down-draught carburettors
Make and designation .... Zenith 36 VNP
Venturi 32
Main jet 135
Compensating jet 120
Idling jet 50
Air jet for idling 50
Air jet for partial
acceleration 140
Acceleration jet 60
Float valve 1.75
Gasket for float valve,
thickness .... 1mm (0.04")

95/100 95A/100 110/100 110/200

Type .... Horizontal carburettors
Make and designation .... Zenith Stromberg 150 CD
Metering needle 95/100,95A/100,
marked 6A
Metering needle 110/100,110/200
marked 6B
Float level("A"Fig.60) .... 18.5-19.5mm (0.73-0.77")

120/200

Type .... Horizontal carburettors
Make and designation .... Zenith Stromberg 175 CD
Metering needle,marked 3B
Float level("A"Fig.60) .... 15.5-16.5mm (0.61-0.65")

BATTERY

Earthed .... Negative terminal
Voltage .... 12 V
Battery capacity,standard ..... 60 Ah
Specific gravity of electrolyte:
  Fully charged battery 1.275-1.285
  When charging is necessary... 1.230
Recommended charging current... 4.5A

DYNAMO/ALTERNATOR

Type 95/100,95A/100,110/100 ...	Bosch LJ/GEH 90/12	1800 FR 20
100/100	Bosch LJ/REE 75/12	1800 CR 2
100/100	Bosch LJ/REE 75/12	1800 CR 2S
110/100, 110/200, 120/200 ...	S.E.V. MOTOROLA	

Voltage .... 12 V
Rated output:Bosch LJ/GEH90/12
  1800 FR 20 90 W
  Bosch LJ/REE75/12 1800 CR 2.. 75 W
  Bosch LJ/REE75/12 1800 CR2S.. 75 W
  S.E.V.MOTOROLA .... 450 W
Max.current:Bosch LJ/GEH90/12
  1800 FR 20 .... 7.5A
  Bosch LJ/REE75/12 1800 CR 2.. 6.25A
  Bosch LJ/REE75/12 1800 CR2S.. 6.25A
  S.E.V. MOTOROLA .... 38 A
Earthed .... Negative terminal
Direction of rotation .... Clockwise

158

STARTER MOTOR

Type 95/100,100/100,110/100,
  110/200 ....   Bosch EGD 1/12   AR 37
  95/100,95A/100,110/100,
  110/200 ....   Bosch GF (R)   12 V 1 PS
  120/200 ....   Bosch GF (R)   12 V 1 PS
Voltage ....   12 V
Earthed ....   Negative terminal
Direction of rotation ....   Clockwise
Output ....   Approx. 1 h.p.

IGNITION SYSTEM

Order of firing ....   1 - 3 - 4 - 2
Spark plug type ....   Bosch W 225T1, or corresponding
Spark plug thread ....   14 mm
Spark plug gap ....   0.7 mm (0.028")

IGNITION SETTING

Engine	Carburettor	Distributor	Basic setting	Stroboscope setting
120/200	Stromberg 175 CD	0231153003 or 0231153007	10°B.T.D.C.	18-20°B.T.D.C./1500 r.p.m.
95A/100	Stromberg 150 CD	0231153003 or 0231153007	8° B.T.D.C.	15-17°B.T.D.C./1500 r.p.m.
110/100 110/100 95/100	Stromberg 150 CD	0231110038 (VJ4BL32TMK)	2°A.T.D.C.	31-33°B.T.D.C./3500 r.p.m.
110/100 110/200 95/100	Stromberg 150 CD	0231153003 or 0231153007	4°B.T.D.C.	31-33°B.T.D.C./4500 r.p.m.
110/100 110/200	Zenith 36 VNP	0231110038 (VJ4BL32TMK)	2°A.T.D.C.	28-30°B.T.D.C./3500 r.p.m.
110/100 110/200	Zenith 36 VNP	0231153007	0° T.D.C.	28-30°B.T.D.C./4500 r.p.m.
100/100	Zenith 36 VNP	0231110038 (VJ4BL32TMK)	2°A.T.D.C.	28-30°B.T.D.C./3500 r.p.m.
100/100	Zenith 36 VNP	0231153007	0° T.D.C.	28-30°B.T.D.C./4500 r.p.m.
AQ90[1]	Zenith 36 VNP	VJ4BL32TMK 0231153007	5°B.T.D.C. 7°B.T.D.C.	35-37°B.T.D.C./3500 r.p.m. 35-37°B.T.D.C./4500 r.p.m.
AQ90[2]	Zenith 36 VNP	VJ4BL32TMK 0231153007	0° 2°B.T.D.C.	30-32°B.T.D.C./3500 r.p.m. 30-32°B.T.D.C./4500 r.p.m.

The settings apply to fuel 97 octane ROT (Research Method) and higher.

   1) apply to fuel 87 octane ROT and higher.
   2) apply to fuel less than 87 octane ROT.

159

DISTRIBUTOR

Type 95/100,100/100,110/100, 110/200	Bosch 0231 110 038 (VJ 4 BL 32 TMK)
Dwell angle	60°
Breaker points, gap	0.40-0.50mm (0.016-0.020")
Direction of rotation	Anti-clockwise
Type 95/100,95A/100,110/100, 110/200,120/200	Bosch 0231 153 003
Dwell angle	60°
Breaker points, gap	0.40-0.50mm (0.016-0.020")
Direction of rotation	Anti-clockwise
Type 100/100, 110/100, 95/100, 110/200, 95A/100, 120/200....	Bosch 0321 153 007
Dwell angle	60°
Breaker points, gap	0.40-0.50mm (0.016-0.020")
Direction of rotation	Anti-clockwise

COOLING SYSTEM

THERMOSTAT

Type	Bellows thermostat
Marked	54
Begins opening at	51-56°C(124-131°F)
Fully open at	67°C (153°F)

WEAR TOLERANCES

CYLINDERS

To be rebored when wear amounts to (if engine has abnormal oil consumption)	0.25mm (0.010")

CRANKSHAFT

Max.permissible out-of-round on main bearing journals	0.05mm (0.0020")
Max.permissible out-of-round on big-end bearing journals	0.05mm (0.0020")
Max.crankshaft end float	0.15mm (0.0060")

VALVES

Max.permissible clearance between valve stem and valve guide	0.15mm (0.0060")
Max.permissible wear,valve stem	0.02mm (0.0008")

CAMSHAFT

Permissible out-of-round (with new bearings),max	0.07mm (0.0028")
Bearings, permissible wear,max.	0.02mm (0.0008")

TIMING GEARS

Permissible backlash,max. .....   0.12mm (0.0048")

TIGHTENING TORQUES

Cylinder head	9 kpm(65 lb.ft.)
Main bearings	12.5kpm(90 lb.ft.)
Big-end bearings	5.5kpm(40 lb.ft.)
Flywheel	5 kpm(35·lb.ft.)
Spark plugs	4 kpm(30 lb.ft.)
Camshaft nut	13-15 kpm(95 - 108 lb.ft.)
Bolt for crankshaft belt	
pulley	7- 8 kpm(51 - 58 lb. ft.)
Nipple for oil filter	4.5-5.5kpm(33 - 40 lb. ft.)
Oil sump bolts	0.8-1.1kpm(6 - 8 lb. ft.)
Tensioning ring - flywheel	
casing	3.5 kpm(25 lb. ft.)

161

B.20 and B.30 Engines

GENERAL

	AQ105A	AQ115A	AQ130A	AQ130B	AQ130C	AQ165A	AQ170A
Aquamatic, engine version	AQ105A	AQ115A	AQ130A	AQ130B	AQ130C	AQ165A	AQ170A
Max.output,h.p.(SAE)	105	115	130	115	130	165	170
Max.engine speed r.p.m.	5100¹⁾	5100¹⁾	5100¹⁾	5100¹⁾	5100¹⁾	5000	5000
Compression ratio	9.5:1	9.5:1	9.5:1	8.4:1	9.5:1	9.2:1	9.5:1
Compression pressure (at starter motor speed 200 r.p.m.)kg/cm²(lb/sq.in)	11-13(155-185)	12-14(170-200)	12-14(170-200)	10-12(145-170)	12-14(170-200)	10-12(145-170)	12-14(170-200)
Number of cylinders	4	4	4	4	4	6	6
Bore, mm (in)	88.90(3.50)	88.90(3.50)	88.90(3.50)	88.90(3.50)	88.90(3.50)	88.90(3.50)	88.90(3.50)
Stroke, mm (in)	80.0(3.15)	80.0(3.15)	80.0(3.15)	80.0(3.15)	80.0(3.15)	80.0(3.15)	80.0(3.15)
Capacity,litres (cu.in)	1.986(121)	1.986(121)	1.986(121)	1.986(121)	1.986(121)	2.979(182)	2.979(182)
Weight,incl.elec. equipment,carburettor,approx. kg (lb)	180(396)	180(396)	180(396)	180(396)	180(396)	220(485)	220(485)
Idling speed,r.p.m.	900 - 1000	900 - 1000	900 - 1000	900 - 1000	900 - 1000	800 - 900	900 - 1000

CYLINDER BLOCK

Material: Special alloy cast iron

Bore,nominal,standard mm(in.): 88.90(3.50)   88.92 (3.508) 2)   89.68 (3.530) 2)

Bore,0.030" oversize mm (in.): 89.66(3.529)

PISTONS

Material: Light-alloy

Permissible weight deviation between pistons in the same engine,g(oz.): 10 (0.35)

height,overall,mm (in.): 71.0(2.79)

Weight standard,g(oz): 495-505(19.48-19.88), 502-512(19.74-20.14) 4)

Height,piston pin centre-piston crown,mm(in.): 46 (1.81)

Piston clearance: 0.02-0.04 (0.0008-0.0016)   0.04-0.06 (0.0016-0.0024) 2)

PISTON RINGS

Piston ring gap,mm(in): 0.40-0.55 (0.0158-0.0217)

Piston ring oversizes: 0.030"

COMPRESSION RINGS

Marked "TOP". Top ring chromed.	
Number on each piston	2
Height, mm(in.)	1.98 (0.078)
Piston ring clearance in groove, mm (in.)	0.045-0.072 (0.0018-0.0028)

OIL SCRAPER RINGS

Number on each piston	1
Height, mm (in.)	4.74 (0.186)
Piston ring clearance in groove, mm (in.)	0.045-0.072 (0.0018 - 0.0028)

PISTON PINS

Floating fit. Circlips at both ends in piston.

Fit:	
In connecting rod	Close running fit
In piston	Push fit
Diameter, standard, mm(in.)	22.00 (0.866)
0.05mm (0.002")oversize, mm (in.)	22.05 (0.868)

CYLINDER HEAD

Height, measured from cylinder head contact face to face for bolt heads, mm (in.)	86.7(3.413)
Cylinder-head gasket, thin mm (in.)	0.8 (0.0315)[3]
Cylinder-head gasket, thick[5], mm (in.)	2.5 (0.098)[5]

1) In light boats with a speed exceeding 30 knots (35 m.p.h) the maximum speed of the 4-cyl. engine may reach 5500 r.p.m.

2) AQ170A from No. 520

3) Not AQ130B

4) AQl05A - 130A from No. 5929
   AQ165A   "   "   1379
   AQ170A   "   "   all

5) Engines equipped with thick cylinder-head gasket is only marketed in countries where there is no premium petrol (gasoline) with an octane rating of at least 97 (Research Method).

CRANKSHAFT	AQ105A	AQ115A	AQ130A	AQ130B	AQ130C	AQ165A	AQ170A
Crankshaft, end float, mm (in)			0.047 – 0.138 (0.0019 – 0.0054)				
Main bearings, radial clearance, mm (in.)			0.028 – 0.079 (0.0011 – 0.0031)				
Big-end bearings, radial clearance, mm (in.)			0.029 – 0.071 (0.0011 – 0.0028)				
MAIN BEARINGS							
Main Bearing Journals							
Diameter. standard, mm (in.)			63.451–63.464 (2.4981 – 2.4986)				
0.010" undersize, mm (in.)			63.197–63.210 (2.4881 – 2.4886)				
0.020" " mm (in.)			62.943–62.956 (2.4781 – 2.4786)				
Width on crankshaft for pilot bearing shell Standard, mm (in.)			38.930 – 38.970 (1.5327 – 1.5343)				
Oversize 1 (0.010" undersize shell), mm (in.)			39.031 – 39.072 (1.5367 – 1.5736)				
Oversize 2 (0.020" undersize shell), mm (in.)			39.133 – 39.173 (1.5407 – 1.5422)				
Main Bearing Shells							
Thickness, standard, mm (in)			1.985 – 1.991 (0.0781 – 0.0784)				
0.010" undersize, mm (in)			2.112 – 2.118 (0.0831 – 0.0834)				
0.020" " mm (in)			2.239 – 2.245 (0.0881 – 0.0884)				
BIG-END BEARINGS							
Big-End Bearing Journals							
Width of bearing recess, mm (in.)			31.950 – 32.050 (1.2579 – 1.2618)				
Diameter standard, mm (in)			54.099 – 54.112 (2.1650 – 2.1304)				
0.010" undersize, mm (in)			53.845 – 53.858 (2.1199 – 2.1204)				
0.020" " mm (in)			53.591 – 53.604 (2.1099 – 2.1104)				
Big-End Bearing Shells							
Thickness, standard, mm (in.)			1.833 – 1.841 (0.0722 – 0.0725)				
0.010" undersize, mm (in)			1.960 – 1.968 (0.0772 – 0.0725)				
0.020" " mm (in)			2.087 – 2.095 (0.0822 – 0.0825)				

CONNECTING RODS

End float on crankshaft. mm (in.)	0.15 - 0.35 (0.006 - 0.014)	
Length, centre - centre, mm (in.)	144.9 - 145.1(5.706-5.714)	
Max. permissible wt.deviation between connecting rods in the same engine g (oz.)	6 (0.21)	

FLYWHEEL

Max.permissible axial throw. mm (in.)	0.05(0.002) at a diameter of 150(5.906)	
Ring gear (chamfer facing forwards), teeth	142	153

FLYWHEEL HOUSING

Max.axial throw for rear face,mm(in.)	0.05(0.002) of a diameter of 100(3.937)
Max.radial throw for rear guide, mm (in.)	0.15 (0.006)

CAMSHAFT

Marking	C	
Number of bearings	3	4
Front bearing journal, mm (in.)	46.975-47.000 (1.8494 - 1.8504)	46.975-47.000)1.8494-1.8504)
Centre bearing journal, mm (in.)	42.975-43.000 (1.6919 - 1.6929)	46.975-47.000(1.8494-1.8504)
Rear bearing journal, mm (in.)	36.975-37.000(1.4557 - 1.4567)	46.975-47.000(1.8494-1.8504)
Radial clearance,mm(in)	0.020 - 0.075 (0.0008-0.0030)	
End float, mm(In.)	0.020-0.060 (0.008-0.0024)	
Valve clearance for check of camshaft setting(cold engine), mm (in.)	1.45 (0.057)	
Intake valve should then open at T.D.C.	0	

	AQ105A	AQ115A	AQ130A	AQ130B	AQ130C	AQ165A	AQ170A
CAMSHAFT BEARINGS							
Front bearing, mm(in.)		47.020 - 47.050 (1.8512 - 1.8524)				47.020-47.050 (1.8512-1.8524)	
Centre bearing, mm(in.)		43.025 - 43.050 (1.6939 - 1.6949)				47.020-47.050 (1.8512-1.8524)	
Rear bearing, mm(in.)		37.020 - 37.045 (1.4575 - 1.4585)				47.020-47.050 (1.8512-1.8524)	
TIMING GEARS							
Crankshaft drive, teeth			21				
Camshaft gear, teeth			42				
Backlash, mm (in.)			0.04 - 0.08 (0.0016 - 0.0032)				
End float, camshaft, mm(in)			0.02 - 0.06 (0.008 - 0.0024)				
VALVES							
Intake							
Valve head diameter, mm(in.)				42 (1.65)			
Stem diameter, mm (in.)			7.955 - 7.970 (0.3132 - 0.3138)				
Valve seat angle, °				44.5			
Seat angle in cylinder head°				45			
Seat width in cylinder head, mm (in.)				2 (0.079)			
Clearance both warm and cold engine, mm (in.)			0.50 - 0.55 (0.020 - 0.022)				
Exhaust							
Valve head diameter, mm(in)				35 (1.38)			
Stem diameter, mm (in.)				7.925-7.940			
Valve seat angle°				44.5			
Seat angle in cylinder head°				45			
Seat width in cylinder head, mm (in.)				2 (0.079)			
Clearance,both warm and cold engine, mm (in.)			0.50 - 0.55 (0.020 - 0.022)				

VALVE GUIDES

Length, exhaust, mm(in.)	59 (3.32)	
intake, mm(in.)	52 (2.05)	
Inner diameter, mm(in.)	8.000 - 8.022 (0.3150 - 0.3158)	
Height above upper face of cylinder head, mm(in.)	17.5 (0.6890)	
Clearance,valve stem-guide, intake, mm (in.)	0.030 - 0.067 (0.0012 - 0.0022)	
Clearance,valve stem-guide, exhaust, mm (in.)	0.060 - 0.097 (0.0024 - 0.0038)	

VALVE SPRINGS

Length,unloaded,approx. mm(in.)	46 (1.81)	45 (1.77)
With load of 23.5-27.5 kp(51.4-61.020 lb.) mm (in.)	40 (1.57)	39 (1.54)
With load of 62.5-69.5kp (137.8-193.2 lb.),mm(in.)	30 (1.18)	30.5 (1.20)

LUBRICATING SYSTEM

Oil capacity,including oil filter, l	3.75(6½ Imp pints = 8 US pints)	6.0 (10½;13)
excluding oil filter, l	3.25(5¾ " " = 7 " ")	5.2 (9½;11)
Oil pressure at 2000 r.p.m. (with warm engine and new oil filter), kp/cm²(lb/sq.in)	2.5 -6.0 (35.56-85.34)	
Oil grade	Multigrade oil Service MS	
Oil viscosity	SAE 10W-30 alt. 20W-40	

Oil filter

Type	Full-flow filter
Make	Wix or Mann

Oil pump

Type	Gear
Number of teeth on each gear	9
End float, mm (in.)	0.02 - 0.10 (0.0008- 0.0040)
Radial clearance, mm (in.)	0.08 - 0.14 (0.0032 - 0.0055)
Backlash, mm (in.)	0.15 - 0.35 (0.0060 - 0.0140)

	AQ105A	AQ115A	AQ130A	AQ130B	AQ165A	AQ170A
Relief valve spring (in oil pump)						
Length, unloaded, mm (in)				39.0 (1.54)		
Length, loaded with 4.6–5.4 kp(10.1–11.9 lb.),mm(in)				26.3 (1.04)		
Length, loaded with 6.2–7.8 kp(13.6–17.2 lb), mm (in)				21.0 (0.83)		
FUEL SYSTEM						
Fuel pump						
Type						
Make				Diaphragm pump Pierburg: PE15572		
Fuel pressure, measured at same level as pump kp/cm^2 (p.s.i.)				0.22 (3.2)		
Carburettors						
No. of carburettors	1	1	2	2	2	3

AQ115A, AQ130C, AQ170A

	AQ115A	AQ130C	AQ170A
Type	Down-draught carburettors		
Make and designation	Solex 44 PAI		
Main jet	145		
Idling jet	55		
Emulsion jet	145 E5	190 E5	210 E5
Pump jet	70	70	70
Needle seating	2		

AQ105A, AQ130A, AQ165A

	AQ105A	AQ130A	AQ165A
Type	Horizontal carburettors		
Make and designation Zenith-Stromberg	150CD	175CDSE	175CDSE
Metering needle marked	8B	3D	2AA
Float level ("A" Fig.F5), mm (in.)	17–18 (0.67–0.71)	15–17 (0.59–0.67)	15–17 (0.59–0.67)

Float level ("R" Fig.F5), mm (in.)	14.5 (0.5716) 11.0 (0.4331)
Float needle valve, mm (in.)	2 (0.08) 1.5 (0.06)
Washer thickness under float needle valve, mm (in.)	1.0 (0.04) 1.6 (0.06).
Air valve spring colour marking	Red Blue Uncoloured
Air valve spring coil thickness, mm (in.)	1.0 (0.040) 0.9 (0.036) 0.8 (0.032)
Oil for damper	Same as in engine

BATTERY

Earthed	Negative terminal
Voltage, V	12
Battery capacity, standard, Ah	60
Specific gravity of electrolyte:	
Fully charged battery, g/cm^3	1.275-1.285
When charging is necessary, g/cm^3	1.230
Recommended charging current, A	4.5

DYNAMO/ALTERNATOR

Type	Bosch LJ/6EH90/12 1800 FR20 S.E.V. Motorola
Voltage, V	12
Rated output, W	90
Max.current,A	7.5
Earthed	Negative terminal
Direction of rotation	Clockwise

STARTER MOTOR

Type	Bosch 0 001 311 032
Voltage, V	12
Earthed	Negative terminal
Direction of rotation	Clockwise
Output, hp	Approx. 1

IGNITION SYSTEM

	AQ105A	AQ115A	AQ130A	AQ130B	AQ130C	AQ165A	AQ170A
Order of firing			1-3-4-2			1-5-3-6-2-4	
Spark plug type			Bosch W 225T35 or corresponding				
Spark plug gap (in.)			0.7 (0.028)				

DISTRIBUTOR

	AQ105A	AQ115A	AQ130A	AQ130B	AQ130C	AQ165A	AQ170A
Type Bosch			0 231 153 012			0 231 152 060	
Dwell angle, °			59-65			37-43	
Breaker points, gap, mm(in)			0.40-0.50(0.016-0.020)			0.25-0.35(0.010-0.014)	
Basic setting °, BTDC	9		12			15 4)	
Stroboscope setting (2000 r.p.m.)8, BTDC	22-24	24-26	27-29	26-28	27-29	22-24 3)	28-30 3) 4)

COOLING SYSTEM

	AQ105A	AQ115A	AQ130A	AQ130B	AQ130C	AQ165A	AQ170A
Thermostat Type			Bellows thermostat				
Marked			54			55	
Begins opening at, °C(°F)			51-56(124-133)			53-56(127-133)	
Fully open at, °C(°F)			67 (153)			66-70(151-158)	

WEAR TOLERANCES

Cylinders

	AQ105A	AQ115A	AQ130A	AQ130B	AQ130C	AQ165A	AQ170A
To be rebored when wear amounts to (if engine has abnormal oil consumption,) mm (in.)				0.25 (0.010)			

Crankshaft

	AQ105A	AQ115A	AQ130A	AQ130B	AQ130C	AQ165A	AQ170A
Max.permissible out-of-round on main bearing journals, mm (in.)				0.05 (0.0020)			
Max.permissible out-of-round on big-end bearing journals, mm (in.)				0.07 (0.0028)			
Max.crankshaft end float, mm (in.)				0.15 (0.0060)			

Valves

	kpm	(ft.lb.)
Max.permissible clearance between valve stem and valve guide, mm (in.)		0.15 (0.0060)
Max.permissible wear, valve stem, mm (in.)		0.02 (0.0008)

Camshaft

Permissible out-of-round (with new bearings),max., mm (in.)		0.07 (0.0028)
Bearings, permissible wear, max., mm (in.)		0.02 (0.0008)

Timing Gears

Permissible backlash,max., mm (in.)		0.12 (0.0048)

TIGHTENING TORQUES

	kpm	(ft.lb.)
Cylinder head	9	(65)
Main bearings	12.5	(90)
Big-end bearings	5.5	(40)
Flywheel	5	(35)
Spark plugs	4	(30)
Camshaft nut	13–15	(95–108)
Bolt for crankshaft belt pulley	7–8	(51–58)
Nipple for oil filter	4.5–5.5	(38–40)
Oil sump bolts	1.0–1.2	(7.3–8.7)
Tensioning ring-flywheel casing	3.5	(25)
Nut, oil cooler	3.0–3.5	(21.7–25.3)
Centre bolt,oil cooler	1.2–1.4	(8.7–10[1])
V-belt A.C. generator approx.	1.5[1],1.7[2])	(10.85[1] , 12.30[2])
V-belt D.C. generator approx.	0.9	(6.51)

1) AQ130A-C   2) AQ165A-170A

3) AQ165A, with vacuum governor uncoupled.

4) AQ165-170A, engines equiped with thick cylinder-head gasket.

Late B.20 and B.30 Engines

	AQ130D/280D	AQ170C/280C
General		
Engine designation	AQ130D/280D	AQ170C/280C
Operation	4-stroke carburettor engine with overhead valves	
Outboard drive, model	280D	280C
Reduction ratio	2.15:1	1.89:1
Number of cylinders	4	6
Max.output[1]kW at 91.7 rev/s(5500 rev/min)	81	
Max.output[1]kW at 83.3 rev/s(5000 rev/min)		118
Max.operating speed rev/s(rev/min)	91.7(5500)	82.2(5000)
Max.cruising speed rev/s(rev/min)	5-8(300-500 below max.speed reached)	
Cylinder bore, mm (in)	88.90(3.50)	
Stroke, mm (in)	80 (3.15)	
Capacity, dm³ (in³)	1.986(122)	2.979(181)
Compression pressure kgf/cm²(lbf/in²) (starter motor speed)	12-14(170-200)	10-12(140-170)
Idling speed rev/s (rev/min)approx.	15(900)	
Direction of rotation seen from the crankshaft pulley	clockwise	
Engine weight including drive,approx.kg(lb)	245(540)	320(705)

Valves
Valve clearance,warm or cold engine

Inlet valve, mm (in)	0.50-0.55 (0.020-0.022)	
Exhaust valves, mm (in)	0.50-0.55 (0.020-0.022)	

Lubricating system
Engine
Oil capacity,dm³=litres (Imp.qts=USqts.).excl.

filter	3.25(2¾-3¼)	5.2(4¾-5½)
incl. filter	3.75(3¼-4)	6.0(5¼-6½)
Oil quality	Multigrade Oil Service SE	
Viscosity	SAE 10W/40[2])	

Outboard drive

Oil quality/viscosity	Same as for the engine	
Oil capacity,dm³(Imp.quarts/US quarts)..........	2.6(2.3-2.7)	
Oil capacity between max. and min. marks on dipstick,dm³(Imp.pint)approx.	0.15(0.25)	

Cooling system

Thermostat, begins to open at °C(°F)	54(129)	

Fuel system

Fuel quality	Min.90 octane (Research Method) (the engine can be run on petrol (gasoline)without lead additives)	
Carburettor,Solex	44PAI	44PAI
Number	2	3

[1] Flywheel output according to DIN 6270 Leistung B.

[2] Volvo Penta Multigrade oil.

172

Ignition system	AQ130D/280D	AQ170C/280C
Firing order	1-3-4-2	1-5-3-6-2-4
Ignition distributor, Bosch type	0231 178 011	0231 311 002
Basic setting, B.T.D.C.	8°	12°
Stroboscope setting 50 rev/s (3000 rev/min)	$25-27^o$	$32-34^o$
Cam angle	$62+3^o$	$40+3^o$
Spark plug, Bosch type	W225T35 (or corresponding type)	
Electrode gap, spark plug, mm (in)	0.7-0.8 (0.028-0.032)	

Electrical system		
Voltage, V	12	
Battery capacity, standard, Ah	60	
Battery electrolyte specific gravity		
Fully charged battery	1.275-1.285	
Recharge at	1.230	
Alternator		
Type	Alternating current	
Output max.	450 W(35 A)	
Starter motor output, hp	1	

Tightening torques	Nm	kpm	lb.ft
Cylinder head bolts	90	9	65
Spark plugs	40	4	30
Clamp ring, flywheel housing	35	3.5	25

173

B.21 and B23 Engines

General

Engine designation	AQ 120B
Operation	4-stroke fresh-water cooled carburettor engine with over-head camshaft and valves
Drive, model	270D
Reduction ratio	2.15:1
Number of cylinders	4
Max. output[1] kW at 83.3 r/s(5000 r/m)	79.4
Recommended full throttle rpm (rps)	4400-4800 (73.3-80.0)
Max.cruising speed rev/sec (rev/min)	5-8(300-500) below max. speed obtained
Bore, mm (in.)	92(3.622)
Stroke, mm (in.)...........,..................	80(3.150)
Displacement, dm^3 (in^2)	2.13(130)
Compr.pressure, kp/cm^2(lbf/in^2)(starter motor speed)	10-12(142-170)
Idling speed rev/sec (rev/min),approx.	15(900)
Direction of rotation looking at crankshaft pulley	Clockwise
Engine weight, incl.drive approx.kg(lb.)	240(528)

Valves

Valve clearance adjustment,hot engine	
Inlet, mm (in.)	0.40-0.45(0.016-0.018)
Exhaust, mm (in.)	0.40-0.45(0.016-0.018)
Valve clearance adjustment,cold engine	
Inlet, mm (in.)	0.35-0.40(0.014-0.016)
Exhaust, mm (in.)	0.35-0.40(0.014-0.016)
Valve clearance check,hot engine	
Inlet, mm (in.)	0.30-0.50(0.012-0.020)
Exhaust, mm (in.)	0.30-0.50(0.012-0.020)
Valve clearance check, cold engine	
Inlet, mm (in.)	0.25-0.45(0.010-0.018)
Exhaust, mm (in.)	0.25-0.45(0.010-0.018)

Lubricating system

Engine

Oil capacity,engine dm^3=litres(Imp.qts/US qts)	
excl. filter	3.5(3.0/3.7)
incl. filter	4.0(3.6/4.3)
Oil quality	Multigrade oil Service SE
Viscosity	SAE 10W/40[2]
Oil pressure hot engine, at full speed,kp/cm^2 (lbf/in^2)	2.5-6(35-85)

Outboard drive

Oil quality/viscosity	Same as in engine
Oil capacity, dm^3=litres(Imp.qts./US qts.)......	2.2(1.9/2.3)
Oil capacity between Max. and Min.marks on dipstick,dm^3=litres(Imp.qts./US qts.)approx. ...	0.15(0.13/0.16)

[1]
  Flywheel output according to DIN 6270 Leistung B
[2]
  Volvo Penta Multigrade oil

Cooling system

Thermostat, start opening at $^{o}C(^{o}F)$ .... 82(180)
            fully open at $^{o}C(^{o}F)$ .... 92(197)
Fresh-water quantity in dm^3=litres(Imp.qts/US
  qts.) approx. .... 6.75(6.0/7.0)

Fuel system

Fuel quality .... Min 90 octane (RON) engine can
                            be run on unleaded fuel
Carburettor, Solex .... PHN
Number 1
Float height from housing face,mm (in.) .... 4(0.16)
Idle-trimming screw,screwed out no.of times .... $1\frac{1}{4}$
Mixing screw,screwed out no.of turns .... $4\frac{1}{2}$

Ignition system

Firing sequence 1-3-4-2
Ignition distributor:Bosch type JF4 .... 0 231 178 017
Basic setting 0-12.5 r/s(0-750r/m) .... 10° B.T.D.C.
Stroboscope setting 61.6-80.0 r/s(3700-4800rm).. 36-38° B.T.D.C.
Ignition distributor,contact gap,mm (in.) ...... 0.40-0.50(0.016-0.018)
Dwell angle .... 62 ± 3°
Spark plug, Bosch type .... W 200 T30(or equivalent)
Electrode gap,spark plug, mm(in.) .... 0.7-0.8(0.028-0.032)

Electrical system

Voltage 12
Battery capacity,standard, Ah 60
Battery electrolyte specific gravity:
    Fully charged battery 1.275-1.285
    When battery is to be re-charged........... 1.230
Alternator
    Output,max. .... 450 W(38 A)
Starter motor output,h.p. 1

Tightening torques

Cylinder head bolts
    1st tightening .... 60 Nm (6kpm=43 lb.ft.)
    2nd tightening .... 110 Nm(11kpm=79 lb.ft.)
Spark plug .... 25 Nm(2.5kpm=18 lb.ft.)
Tension ring, flywheel casing .... 40 Nm(4kpm=30 lb.ft.)
Steering helmet Allen-bolt .... 50-60 Nm,5-6kpm/36-43 ftlbs

General

Engine designation .... AQ 140A
Operation .... 4-stroke fresh-water cooled
                            carburettor engine with over-
                            head camshaft and valves
Outboard drive, model 280D
Reduction ratio 2.15:1

```
Number of cylinders ...........................   4
Max.output 1)kW at 91.7 rev/sec(5500 rev/min) ..   92
Max.operating speed, rev/sec(rev/min) ..........   91.7(5500)
Max.cruising speed rev/sec(rev/min) ............   5-8 (300-500)below max. speed
                                                   reached
Bore, mm (in.) .................................   92(3.622)
Stroke, mm (in.) ...............................   80(3.150)
Displacement, dm$^3$(in$^3$) .......................   2.13(130)
Compr.pressure,kp/cm$^2$ (lbf/in$^2$)(starter motor
  speed) ........................................   10-12(142-170)
Idling speed rev/sec(rev/min),approx. ..........   15(900)
Direction of rotation looking at crankshaft
  pulley .......................................   Clockwise
Engine weight, incl.drive approx.kg(lb.) .......   245(540)
```

Valves

```
Valve clearance adjustment,hot engine
  Inlet,mm (in.) ...............................   0.40-0.45(0.016-0.018)
  Exhaust,mm (in.) .............................   0.40-0.45(0.016-0.018)
Valve clearance adjustment,cold engine
  Inlet,mm (in.) ...............................   0.35-0.40(0.014-0.016)
  Exhaust, mm(in.) .............................   0.35-0.40(0.014-0.016)
Valve clearance check,hot engine
  Inlet, mm (in.) ..............................   0.30-0.50(0.012-0.020)
  Exhaust,mm(in.) ..............................   0.30-0.50(0.012-0.020)
Valve clearance check,cold engine
  Inlet,mm (in.) ...............................   0.25-0.45(0.010-0.018)
  Exhaust,mm(in.) ..............................   0.25-0.45(0.010-0.018)
```

Lubricating system

Engine
```
  Oil capacity, engine, dm$^3$=litres(Imp.qts=US
  qts.), excl. filter ..........................   5.0(4.4=5.3)
          incl. filter ..........................   5.7(5.0=6.0)
  Oil quality ..................................   Multigrade oil Service SE
  Viscosity ....................................   SAE 10W/40$^{2)}$
  Oil pressure not engine, at full speed, kp/cm$^2$
  (lbf/in$^2$) ...................................   2.5-6(35-85)
```

Outboard drive

```
Oil quality/viscosity ..........................   Same as in engine
Oil capacity, dm$^3$=litres(Imp.qts=US qts.) ......   2.6(2.3=2.7)
Oil capacity between max. and min. marks on
  dipstick,dm$^3$=litres(Imp.qts=US qts.),approx...   0.15(0.13-0.16)
```

1)
  Flywheel output according to DIN 6270 Leistung B
2)
  Volvo-Penta Multigrade oil

Cooling system

Thermostats, start opening at $^{O}C(^{O}F)$ .... 82(180)
                 fully open at $^{O}C(^{O}F)$ .... 92(197)
Fresh-water quantity in dm^3=litres(Imp.qts.=US
  qts.) approx. .... 6.75(6.0=7.0)

Fuel system

Fuel quality .... Min 90 octane (RON) engine can
                                               be run on lead-free fuel
Carburettors, Solex .... PHN
Number 2
Float height from housing face,mm (in.) .... 4(0.16)
Idle-trimming screw,screwed out no,of times..... $1\frac{1}{4}$
Mixing screw, screwed out no.of turns .... $4\frac{1}{2}$

Ignition system

Firing sequence 1-3-4-2
Ignition distributor:
  Early prod.yellow marked
  Bosch type JF4 .... 0231 178 010
  Basic setting 0-12.5 r/s(0-750 r/m) .... 6° B.T.D.C.
  Late prod.
  Bosch type JF4 .... 0231 178 010
  Basic setting 0-12.5 r/s (0-750 r/m) .... 10° B.T.D.C.
Stroboscope setting 46.6-83.3 r/s(2800-5000rm).. 36-38° B.T.D.C.
Ignition distributor, contact gap,mm(in.) ...... 0.40-0.50(0.016-0.018)
Dwell angle .... $62^{+}_{-}3^{O}$
Spark plug, Bosch type .... W 200 T30(or corresponding type of
                                               another make)
Electrode gap,spark plug,mm (in.) .... 0.7-0.8(0.028-0.032)

Electrical system

Voltage 12
Battery capacity, standard, Ah 60
Battery electrolyte specific gravity:
    Fully charged battery 1.275-1.285
    When battery is to be re-charged 1.230
Alternator
    Output, max. .... 450 W(38A)
Starter motor output, h.p. 1

Tightening torques

Cylinder head bolts
  1st tightening .... 60 Nm(6kpm=43 lbf)
  2nd tightening .... 110 Nm(11kpm=79 lb.ft.)
Spark plug .... 25 Nm(2.5kpm=18 lbf)
Tension ring, flywheel casing .... 40 Nm (4kpm=30 lbf)

177

General

Engine designation	AQ 145A
Operation	4-stroke fresh-water cooled carburettor engine with overhead camshaft and valves
Outboard drive, model	280 D
Reduction ratio	2.15:1
Number of cylinders	4
Max.output [1] kW at 91.7 r/s(5500rpm)	101 (138) [4]
Max.operating speed,r/s (rpm)	85 (5100) [4]
Max.cruising speed r/s (rpm)	5-8(300-500)below max.speed obtained
Bore, mm (in.)	96 (3.779)
Stroke, mm (in.)	80 (3.150)
Displacement, $dm^3(in^3)$	2.31 (141)
Compr. pressure $kp/cm^2(lbf/in^2)$(starter motor speed)	10-12 (142-170)
Idling speed r/s (rpm), approx	15 (900)
Direction of rotation looking at crankshaft pulley	Clockwise
Engine weight,incl.drive approx.kg(lb)	245 (540) [3]

Valves

Valve clearance adjustment,hot engine	
Inlet, mm(in.)	0.40-0.45 (0.016-0.018)
Exhaust, mm (in.)	0.40-0.45 (0.016-0.018)
Valve clearance adjustment,cold engine	
Inlet, mm (in.)	0.35-0.40 (0.014-0.016)
Exhaust,mm(in.)	0.35-0.40 (0.014-0.016)
Valve clearance check,hot engine	
Inlet, mm (in.)	0.30-0.50 (0.012-0.020)
Exhaust,mm(in.)	0.30-0.50 (0.012-0.020)
Valve clearance check, cold engine	
Inlet, mm (in.)	0.25-0.45 (0.010-0.018)
Exhaust,mm(in.)	0.25-0.45 (0.010-0.018)

Lubricating system

Engine

Oil capacity,engine, dm^3=litres(Imp.qts. =US qts.) excl.filter	4.5 (3.96-4.77)
incl.filter	5.0 (4.4-5.3)
Oil quality	Multigrade oil Service SE
Viscosity	SAE 10W/40 [2]
Oil pressure hot engine,at full speed,kp/cm^2 (lbf/in^2)	2.5-6(35-85)

[1]
Flywheel output according to SAE J-607
[2]
Volvo-Penta Multigrade oil
[3]
With Power Trim, 275 (606)

Outboard drive

```
Oil quality/viscosity .........................  Same as in engine
Oil capacity, dm³=litres(Imp.qts=US qts.) ......  2.6(2.3=2.7)
Oil capacity between max.and min. marks on
  dipstick,dm³=litres(Imp.qts.=US qts.)approx...  0.15(0.13-0.16)
Oil capacity, hydraulic system drive 280 with
  Power Trim,dm³/litres(Imp.qts=US qts.) .......  1.5(1.32-1.56)
Oil quality ..................................  Same as in engine
```

Electrical system

```
Voltage ......................................  12
Battery capacity, standard, Ah ................  60
Battery electrolyte specific gravity:
    Fully charged battery ....................  1.275-1.285
    When battery is to be re-charged ..........  1.230
Alternator
    Output, max. .............................  450 W (38A)
    Starter motor output, h.p. ................  1.5
```

Cooling system

```
Thermostats, start opening at °C(°F) ..........  82(180)
              fully open at °C(°F) .............  92(197)
Fresh-water quantity in dm³=litres(Imp.qts.=US
  qts.) approx. ..............................  6.75(6.0=7.0)
```

Fuel system

```
Fuel quality .................................  See Ignition timing
Carburettors, Solex ...........................  PAI
Number .......................................  2
Float height from housing face,mm(in.) ........  4(0.16)
Idle-trimming screw,screwed out no.of turns ....  3/4
Mixing screw, screwed out no.of turns ..........  1
```

Ignition System

```
Firing order .................................  1-3-4-2
Ignition timing from factory for regular type of
  gasoline min.90 Octane (ROT):
    Basic timing 0-12.5r/s(0-750rpm) ..........  4° B.T.D.C.
    Stroboscopic setting 66.6r/s(4000rpm) ......  30° B.T.D.C.
Ignition timing for premium type of gasoline
min. 94 Octane (ROT):
    Basic timing 0-12.5r/s(0-750rpm) ..........  10° B.T.D.C.
    Stroboscopic setting 66.6r/s(4000 rpm) .....  36° B.T.D.C.
Distributor,breaker point gap,mm(in.) ..........  0.40(.0157)
Spark plugs ..................................  P/N 1276513
    Electrode gap, mm (in.) ...................  0.7-0.8(.0275-.0315)
```

Tightening torques

```
Cylinder head bolts
    1st tightening ...........................  60 Nm (6kpm=43 lbf)
    2nd tightening ...........................  110 Nm (11kpm=79 lb.ft.)
Spark plug ...................................  40 Nm (4kpm=30 lb.ft.)
Tension ring, flywheel casing .................  35 Nm (3.5kpm=26 lb.ft.)
Steering helmet screw .........................  60 Nm (6kpm=43 lb.ft.)
```

179

V-6 Engines

General

```
Type designation ..............................  AQ150, 150A, 150B
Output, h.p. at r.p.m. (SAE) ..................  150/4200
Compression pressure (warm engine and starter
motor speed)  ...............................  11-12 kg/cm² (160 lb./sq.in.)
Compression ratio .............................  9:1
Number of cylinders (two banks 90° V-shape) ....  6
Cylinder numbering (from front to rear)
                    Left cylinder bank ..........  1-3-5
                    Right cylinder bank .........  2-4-6
Bore ..........................................  95.25 mm (3.750 in.)
Stroke ........................................  86.36 mm (3.400 in.)
Piston displacement ...........................  3.7 litres (225 cu.in.)
Operating speed, max.  ........................  4200 r.p.m.
Idle speed (warm engine) ......................  600-700 r.p.m.
Weight, engine unit approx.  ..................  280 kg (506 lb.)
150 Weight, engine and drive ..................  275 kg (605 lb.)
150A    "        "      "    "   ..................  322 kg (710 lb.)
150A & B "      "      "    "   with rizers .......  340 kg (750 lb.)
```

Cylinder Block

```
Material ......................................  Cast iron
Cylinder bore, nominal standard ...............  95.250 mm (3.750 in.)
               0.010" oversize ................  95.504 mm (3.760 in.)
               0.020"    "     ................  95.758 mm (3.770 in.)
               0.030"    "     ................  96.012 mm (3.780 in.)
```

Cylinder Heads

```
Material ......................................  Cast iron
Number ........................................  2
```

Pistons

```
Material ......................................  Cast alloy iron
Piston clearance ..............................  0.025-0.038 mm (0.0010-0.0015 in.)
Piston diameter, nominal standard .............  95.225 mm (3.749 in.)
                 0.010" oversize ..............  95.479 mm (3.759 in.)
                 0.020"    "     ..............  95.733 mm (3.769 in.)
                 0.030"    "     ..............  95.987 mm (3.779 in.)
```

Piston Rings

```
Ring gap measured in ring opening:
                compression ring .............  0.254-0.508 mm (0.010-0.020 in.)
                oil ring .....................  0.381-0.889 mm (0.015-0.035 in.)
Oversizes on piston rings .....................  0.508 mm (0.020 in.)
                                                 0.762 mm (0.003 in.)
```

No. 1 Compression ring

```
Marked with letter or "TOP". Chromium-plated.
Number on each piston .........................  1
Width .........................................  1.994-2.007 mm (0.0785-0.0790 in.)
Piston ring clearance in groove ...............  0.076-0.127 mm (0.003-0.005 in.)
```

No. 2 Compression ring

Marked with letter or "TOP".
Number on each piston 1
Width .... 1.956-1.981 mm (0.0770-0.0780 in.)
Piston ring clearance in groove .... 0.076-0.127 mm (0.003-0.005 in.)

Oil ring

Number on each piston 1
Type .... Expanding
Width .... 4.597-4.750 mm (0.180-0.187 in.)
Piston ring clearance in groove................ 0.089-0.241 mm (0.0035-0.0095 in.)

Gudgeon Pin

Floating journalled in piston. Circlips are
not fitted.
Fit:
In connecting rod .... Press fit
In piston .... Slide fit
Diameter .... 23.861-23.868 mm (0.9394-0.9397 in.)

Crankshaft

Crankshaft end play .... 0.102-0.203 mm (0.004-0.008 in.)
Main bearing to journal clearance .... 0.013-0.053 mm (0.005-0.0021 in.)
Connecting rod bearing clearance .... 0.051-0.058 mm (0.0020-0.0023 in.)

Main bearings

Main bearing journals

Diameter, standard .... 63.487 mm (2.4995 in.)
          undersize 0.001" .... 63.462 mm (2.4672 in.)
          "   0.002" .... 63.437 mm (2.4985 in.)
          "   0.010" .... 63.233 mm (2.4895 in.)

Main bearing shells

                                    Standard sizes
                                    Undersize 0.001"
                                        "   0.002"
                                        "   0.010"

Crankshaft bearings

Crankshaft bearing journals

Diameter, standard .... 50.800 mm (2.0000 in.)
          undersize 0.001" .... 50.775 mm (1.9932 in.)
          "   0.002" .... 50.750 mm (1.9980 in.)
          "   0.010" .... 50.546 mm (1.9899 in.)

Crankshaft bearing shells

                                    Standard sizes
                                    Undersize 0.001"
                                        "   0.002"
                                        "   0.010"

181

Connecting Rods

End play at crankshaft (total for both rods).... 0.152-0.356 mm (0.006-0.014 in.)

Camshaft

Number of bearings 4
Diameter: Bearing journal 1 .... 44.577-44.602 mm (1.755-1.756 in.)
      "   "   2 .... 43.815-43.840 mm (1.725-1.726 in.)
      "   "   3 .... 43.053-43.078 mm (1.695-1.696 in.)
      "   "   4 .... 42.291-42.316 mm (1.665-1.666 in.)
Journal clearance in bearings .... 0.038-0.102 mm (0.0015-0.0040 in.)

Timing Gears

Crankshaft drive, number of teeth on gear 20
Camshaft gear (nylon), number of teeth 40

Valve System

Rocker arm clearance on shaft .... 0.043-0.081 mm (0.0017-0.0032 in.)
Valve lifter diameter .... 21.392-21.405 mm (0.8422-0.8427 in.)
Valve lifter clearance in crankcase .... 0.038-0.076 mm (0.0015-0.0036 in.)
Height from valve stem end to valve spring
surface on the cylinder head .... 48.895 mm (1.9250 in.)

Valves

Intake

Head diameter .... 41.225 mm (1.625 in.)
Stem diameter .... 8.666 mm (0.3412 in.)
Valve seat angle .... 45°
Cylinder head seat angle .... 45°
Seat width in cylinder heads .... 1.6 mm (0.0630 in.)

Exhaust

Head diameter .... 34.925 mm (1.3750 in.)
Stem diameter .... 8.654 mm (0.3407 in.)
Valve seat angle .... 45°
Cylinder head seat angle .... 45°
Seat width in cylinder heads .... 1.6 mm (0.0630 in.)

Valve Guides

Not replaceable.
Drift with 0.10 mm (1/64") oversize available.
Clearance valve stem - guide, intake valves..... 0.025-0.089 mm (0.0010-0.0035 in.)
                        exhaust valves ... 0.038-0.102 mm (0.0015-0.0040 in.)

Valve Springs

Length - with load .... 41.6 mm-29$\pm$2.5 kg (1.727 in.-.64$\pm$5.5lb.)
    "   "   " .... 32.0 mm-76$\pm$3.0 kg (1.340 in.-1.64$\pm$6.6lb.)

182

Lubricating System

```
Oil capacity, incl. oil filter ................  4.7 litres (8¼ Imp. pints = 4 US quarts)
              excl. oil filter ................  3.8 litres (6½ Imp. pints = 5 US quarts)
Oil pressure at 2400 r.p.m. (warm engine) ......  2.3 kg/cm² (33 lb/sq.in.)
Lubricant ....................................  Multigrade oil, Service MS SAE 10W-30
```

Oil filter

```
Type .........................................  Full flow oil filter
```

Oil pump

```
Oil pump, type ...............................  Gear-driven
         number of teeth on each gear .........  8
```

Fuel System

Fuel pump

```
Fuel pump, diaphragm type .....................  AC
Min.fuel pressure at carburettor level
(idling speed) ...............................  0.27 kp/cm² (4 lb/sq.in.)
```

Carburettor

```
Type .........................................  Two barrel down draught carburettor
Make and designation .........................  Rochester 2GC
Diameter at throttle flap ....................  36.5 mm (1 7/16in.)
Venturi, large ...............................  31.8 mm (1¼ in.)
         small ...............................  3.2 mm (⅛ in.)
Main jet (2) No. .............................  61
Idling speed .................................  600-700 r.p.m.
```

Electrical System

```
Voltage ......................................  12 V
Alternator, output S.E.V. Motorola ...........  450 W
Alternator, output Motorola USA ..............  520 W
Regulator, type ..............................  Fully-transistorized
Control voltage (charging current near zero) ...  14.4-14.8 V
```

Ignition System

```
Firing order .................................  1-6-5-4-3-2
Ignition timing, 92 octane Research Method at
550 r.p.m. (vacuum regulator disconnected) .....  5° before T.D.C.
Spark plugs ..................................  Champion J 10 Y
Spark plug electrode gap .....................  0.9 mm (1/32 in.)
```

Distributor

```
Make .........................................  Delco Remy
Breaker contact points, gap ..................  0.4 mm (0.016 in.)
                contact pressure .......  0.5-0.65 kg (1.10-1.40 lb.)
Dwell angle ..................................  30° ± 1°
Direction of rotation ........................  Clockwise
Condenser, make and capacity .................  Delco Remy, 18-23 micro-farad
```

183

Cooling System

Type .... Pressurized
Capacity, AQ150 (fresh-water cooled) approx. ... 10 litres (17½ Imp. pints=11.2 US quarts)

Thermostat

Begins opening at AQ 150 .... $60^{\circ} - 63^{\circ}C (140^{\circ} - 147^{\circ}F)$
              AQ 150A .... $54^{\circ} - 55^{\circ}C (129^{\circ} - 131^{\circ}F)$
              AQ 150B .... $76^{\circ} - 78^{\circ}C (169^{\circ} - 171^{\circ}F)$

Wear Tolerances

Cylinder

To be rebored when wear amounts to (if engine
has abnormal oil consumption) .... 0.127 mm (0.0050 in.)
To be rebored when out-of-round amounts to
(if engine has abnormal oil consumption) .... 0.076 mm (0.0030 in.)

Crankshaft

Permissible out-of-round on main bearing
journals, max. .... 0.038 mm (0.0015 in.)
Permissible out-of-round on big-end bearing
journals, max. .... 0.038 mm (0.0015 in.)
Max. end play for main bearings .... 0.076 mm (0.0030 in.)
   " " "   " big-end bearings .... 0.076 mm (0.0030 in.)

Tightening Torques

	kpm	lb.ft.
Cylinder heads	9-11	65-80
Main bearings	13-16	95-120
Big-end bearings	4-5.5	30-40
Flywheel	7-9	50-65
Vibration damper, min.	19	140
Crankshaft pulley	2.5-3.5	17-25
Sump	1.2-1.8	9.13
Sump drain plug	3.5-5	25-35
Oil pump cover	1.1-1.6	8-12
Relief valve	3.5-4	25-30
Oil screen in sump	0.8-1.2	6-9
Baffle in sump	1.2-1.8	9-13
Plugs for oil galleries	3-4	20-30
Timing gear cover	2.5-3	17-23
Circulation pump	0.8-1.1	6-8
Circulation pump pulley	2.5-3	17-23
Intake manifold	6-7.5	45-55
Exhaust manifold	4-5	30-35
Carburetor	1.5-2	10-15
Fuel pump	2.5-3	17-23
Camshaft centre bolt	5.5-7.5	40-55
Rocker arm covers	0.4-0.7	3-5
Rocker arm shaft bearing brackets	3.5-5	25-35
Starter motor to cylinder block	4-5.5	30-40
Starter motor brace to cylinder block	1.2-1.8	9-13
Distributor holddown clamp	1.4-2	10-15
Spark plugs	3.5-5	25-35
Coupling flywheel-crankshaft	5.5-7	40-50

V-8 Engines

General

```
Specification number ...............................  9714
Output at maximum speed ............................  180 h.p. (SAE)
Maximum speed ......................................  5000 r.p.m.
Number of cylinders (2 banks, V-form) .............  8
Bore ...............................................  84.14 mm (3.313")
Stroke .............................................  80 mm (3.15")
Capacity ...........................................  3.6 litres (219 cu.in.)
Compression ratio ..................................  9.5:1
Idling speed .......................................  600 r.p.m.
Compression pressure at starter speed .............  11.5-12.5 kg/cm$^2$
                                                      (160-175 lb./sq.in.)
Approx. weight of engine including outboard drive..  330 kg (730 lb.)
```

Valve clearances

```
Valve clearances (warm engine), inlet and exhaust..  0.45 mm (0.018")
```

Lubricating system

Engine

```
Oil grade ..........................................  "Service MS"
Oil capacity, including oil filter, approx ........  5.5 litres (9½ quarts)
 "         "     excluding oil filter, approx ........  5.0 litres (9 quarts)
Viscosity, over 30°C (90°F) .......................  SAE 30
 "         0-30°C (32-90°F) .......................  SAE 20
 "         below 0°C (32°F) .......................  SAE 10W
Oil pressure .......................................  3-4 kg/cm$^2$ (42-56)
                                                      lb./sq.in.)
Oil filter, full-flow designation .................  AC-A700
 "      "      insert ..............................  AC 70
```

Fuel system

```
Carburetters (2) ...................................  Carter WGD
Fuel pump ..........................................  AC diaphragm pump
Fuel pressure ......................................  0.15-0.25 kg/cm$^2$
                                                      (2.1-3.5 lb./sq.in.)
```

Cooling system

```
Thermostat: starts to open at .....................  54°C (130°F)
 "          fully open at .........................  68°C (155°F)
```

Electrical system

```
Battery voltage ....................................  12 V

Battery electrolyte specific gravity:
  Fully charged battery ...........................  1.275-1.285
  When battery needs re-charging ..................  1.230

Order of firing          ..........................  1-8-4-3-6-5-7-2
Spark plugs, type, normal running ................  Bosch W 225 T3
 "     "      "   , heavy duty running ............  Bosch W 240 T3
Spark plug electrode gap...........................  0.7-0.8 mm (0.028"-0.032")
```

185

```
Basic ignition timing setting, stationary .........  12-14° before T.D.C.
Timing setting at 1500 r.p.m.  ....................  24-26° before T.D.C.
Distributor, type ................................  Bosch ZV/LAU 8 AL 2
     "       rotation ...........................  Anti-clockwise
     "       contact breaker gap ................  0.35-0.40 (0.013"-0.016")
     "       cam dwell angle ....................  32°
Ignition coil, type .............................  Bosch TK12A4
Dynamo (generator), type ........................  Bosch LJ/GG 130/12 2000
                                                   AR 24
Charging relay, type ............................  Bosch RS/UAA 130/12/23
Dynamo (generator) output .......................  130 W
Starter motor, type .............................  Bosch EGD 1/12 AL 33
                                                   or EGF 1/12 AL 33
```

Wear tolerances

Cylinders
    The cylinders should be re-bored and the pistons
    with piston rings replaced when wear reaches
    0.25-0.30 mm (0.010"-0.012") or when out-of-round
    reaches 0.08 mm (0.003") (if oil consumption
    is abnormally high)

Crankshaft

Permissible out-of-round on main bearing journals, max.	0.05 mm (0.002")
Permissible out-of-round on big-end (connecting rod) journals, max.	0.07 mm (0.003")
Permissible taper on main and big-end (connecting rod) bearing journals, max.	0.05 mm (0.002")
Maximum crankshaft end play	0.30 mm (0.012")

Valves

Valve stems, permissible wear	0.05 mm (0.002")
Permissible clearance between valve stems and valve guides:	
Inlet valves	0.13 mm (0.005")
Exhaust valves	0.17 mm (0.006")
Valve disc edges must be at least	1 mm (0.040")

Camshaft

Permissible out-of-round (with new bushings)	0.07 mm (0.003")
Bushings, permissible wear	0.05 mm (0.002")

Tightening torques

	kgm	lb.ft.
Cylinder heads	10	72
Main bearings	12.5	90
Big-end (connecting rod) bearings	6.5	47
Flywheel	8	58
Spark plugs	3.5	25
Oil filter bolt	2	15

General

```
Type designation ...............................  AQ210A/270B
Max. output, h.p. ..............................  210
Type of engine .................................  4-stroke
Number of cylinders (2 banks, 90° V-form) .......  8
Bore, mm .......................................  98.43
                                                  (3.88")
Stroke, mm .....................................  82.55
                                                  (3.25")
Capacity, litres ...............................  5.0
                                                  (307 cu.in.)
Compression ratio ..............................  8:1
Max. operating speed r.p.m. ....................  4000[1]
Max. idling speed r.p.m.  ......................  500
Direction of rotation, viewed from ahead .......  Clockwise
Reduction ratio, outboard drive unit type B,
  overall ("forward" and "reverse") ............  1.61:1
Total weight, engine with risers and outboard
  drive kg .....................................  470 (1036 lb.)
```

[1]
At cruising speed the number of revolutions should be 400 r.p.m. below the max. speed obtained.

Valves
```
Valve  system ..................................  Overhead
Valve clearances ...............................  Hydraulic tappets (no valve clearance
                                                  adjustment necessary)
```

Lubricating system

Engine
```
  Oil grade ....................................  Multigrade oil Service MS
  Oil viscosity ................................  SAE 10W-30
  Oil capacity including oil filter,litres.......  5.7-6.6 (4.5-5.7 Imp. qts.=6-7 US qts)
```
Outboard drive unit
```
  Oil quality/viscosity ........................  Same as in engine
  Oil capacity, approx. litres (Imp.quarts/
  US quarts) ...................................  2.2 (2 2¼)
  Oil capacity between max. and min. marks,
  approx. litres ...............................  0.15 (¼ pint)
```

Cooling system

```
Thermostat by-pass type, °C ....................  60-74 (140-165°F)
```

Fuel system

```
Carburettor, type...............................  Carter
```

Fuel grade

Gasoline of at least 92 octane rating = (Research Method)

Ignition system

Order of firing 1-8-7-2-4-3-6-5
Contact point dwell angle .... 28°

Electrical system

Voltage, V 12
Battery, capacity, standard, Ah 60
Spark plugs .... Champion UJ-6
Spark plug, electrode gap mm .... 0.7 (0.028")
Contact breaker point gap mm .... 0.5 (0.020")
Generator type .... alternator
Output, max. 450W (38A)
Battery electrolyte specific gravity:
    Fully charged battery 1.275-1.285
    When re-charging is necessary 1.230

Tightening torques

	kgm	lb.ft.
Cylinder head	9	65
Main bearings	9	65
Connecting rod bearings	7	50
Flywheel	8.2	60
Spark plugs	3.2	23
Tensioner - flywheel housing	3.5	25
Intake manifold	4.1	30
Exhaust manifold	2.8	20

General

Type designation .... AQ200B/280[1]   AQ225B/280
Type of engine 4-stroke
Number of cylinders (2 banks,90°V-form) 8
Bore, mm (in.) .... 98.43(3.875)
Stroke, mm (in.) .... 82.55(3.25)
Capacity, dm^3(cu.in.) .... 5.05(307)
Compression ratio 8.01:1   8.25:1
Compression pressure(starter motor),MPa(kp/cm^2). 100-110(10.0-11.0=142-156 p.s.i.)
Max. speed, rev/sec .... 73(4400 rev/min)[2]
Max. operating speed, long running periods
(cruising speed), rev/sec. .... 5-8(300-500 rev/min) lower than
                                       max. speed obtained
Idling speed, rev/sec. .... 10.0-10.8(600-650 rev/min)
Direction of rotation, viewed from front .... Clockwise
Outboard drive with electro-mech.lift .... Aquamatic 280
Tilt-up angle, drive 280 .... 0°-60°
Reduction ratio("Forward" and "Reverse") 1.61:1
Max. propeller diameter .... 16"
Total weight, engine, risers and outboard drive,
approx. kg .... 420(925 lb.)

Valves

Valve system .... Overhead
Valve clearances .... Hydraulic valve lifters
                                       (no valve clearance
                                       adjustment necessary)

[1]
  Marketed in North America.

188

Cooling system

Thermostat limit values, $^{\circ}C(^{\circ}F)$ ....   71-86(161-187)

Fuel system

Carburetor, Carter 2-port, type .... BBD 64785
            Carter 4-port, type Quadra Jet   7044288
Fuel pump Carter, type M-3961-S

Fuel grade

Petrol (gasoline) lower than 92 octane rating (=Research
Number) should not be used.

Lubricating system	AQ200B/280	AQ225B/280

Engine
  Oil grade ....   Service SE[3]

  Oil viscosity ....   Multigrade oil
                                                         SAE 10W-30 or
                                                         10W/40[4]
                                                         20W-40

  Oil capacity, including oil filter, litres
  (Imp. qts./US qts.) ....   6.1(5.4/6.4)
  Oil capacity, excluding cleaner litres (Imp.qts
  /US qts.) ....   5.7(5.0/6.0)
  Oil capacity between max. and min. marks,
  approx. litre (Imp.qts./US qts.) ....·..........   1.0(1.0 qt.)
Outboard drive
  Oil grade/viscosity ....   Same as in engine
  Oil capacity, approx.litres(Imp.qts./US qts.)..   2.6(2.3/2.8)
  Oil capacity between max. and min.marks,
  approx. litre ....   0.15($\frac{1}{4}$ pint)

Ignition system

Firing order 1-8-4-3-6-5-7-2
Ignition distributor, type Mallory YL-585-AV
Basic setting (idling speed) .... 4°B.T.D.C.
Ignition distributor,contact gap,mm .... 0.45(0.018")
Dwell angle .... 30°
Spark plugs, type Champion RBL-9Y
            type AC R44T
Spark plugs, electrode gap, mm .... 0.7(0.028")

[3]
  Earlier designation, Service MS
[4]
  Volvo Penta oil has viscosity SAE 10W/40

Electrical system

Voltage, V .... 12 V Negative Ground
Battery, capacity, standard, Ah 60
Battery electrolyte specific gravity:
    Fully charged battery 1.275-1.285
    When re-charging is necessary 1.230
Generator, type .... Alternator
    Output, max. .... 420 W(35A)
Starter motor, type Prestolite .... MHA 7013
    Output, kW .... 0.96(1.3 hp)

Tightening torques

	Nm	kgm	lb.ft
Cylinder head bolts(7/16"-14)	90	9	65
Main bearings(7/16"-14)	102	10.2	75
Connecting rod bearings($\frac{3}{8}$"-24)	62	6.2	45
Flywheel(7/16"-20)	82	8.2	60
Spark plugs, 14mm ($\frac{5}{8}$")	21	2.1	15
Tensioner - flywheel housing	35	3.5	25
Intake manifold($\frac{5}{16}$"-16)	41	4.1	30
Exhaust manifold ($\frac{5}{16}$-16)	28	2.8	20

General

Type designation	AQ200D	AQ225D	AQ260A	AQ290A
Type of engine	4-stroke	4-stroke	4-stroke	4-stroke
Number of cylinders(2 banks, 90°V-form).	8	8	8	8
Max output at 73r/s(4400r/m)	200hp	225hp	260hp	-
	(147kW)	(166kW)	(190kW)	
Max output at 87r/s(5200r/m)	-	-	-	290hp
				(215kW)
Bore, mm (in.)	95(3.74)	95(3.74)	101.6(4)	101.6(4)
Stroke, mm (in.)	88.4(3.48)	88.4(3.48)	88.4(3.48)	88.4(3.48)
Capacity, dm³(cu.in.)	5(305)	5(305)	5.74(350)	5.74(350)
Compression ratio	8.5:1	8.5:1	8.5:1	9:1

Compression pressure(starter motor).
Mpa (kp/cm²) .... 100-110(10.0-11.0=142-156 p.s.i.)
Max.speed, rev/sec. .... 73(4400 rev/min)   87(5200 rev/min)
Max.operating speed, long running
periods(cruising speed),rev/sec .... 5-8(300-500 rev/min)lower than max.speed obtained
Idling speed, rev/sec .... 10.0-10.8(600-650 rev/min)
Direction of rotation, viewed from front   Clockwise
Outboard drive .... Aquamatic 280B
Tilt-up angle drive 280 .... 0°-60°
Reduction ratio("Forward" and "Reverse")   1.61:1
Max.propeller diameter .... 16"
Total weight, engine risers and
outboard drive, approx.kg. .... 405kg(893 lb.)   410(900 lb.)
Total weight engine risers and
outboard drive,with Power trim kg(lbs).. 435kg(957 lb.)   440(978 lb.)

Valves

Valve system .... Overhead
Valve clearances .... Hydraulic valve lifters (no valve clearance
adjustment necessary).

Cooling system

Thermostat limit values, °C(°F)........ 62-72(143-160)

Lubricating system

Engine

Oil grade	Service SE			
Oil viscosity	SAE 10W-30 or 10W/40[2]			
Oil capacity including oil filter, litres(Imp.qts./US qts.)	5(4.4/5.3)	5.2(4.6/5.5)	5.2(4.6/5.5)	-
Oil capacity including oil filter and oil cooler litres(Imp.qts/US qts).....	-	-	-	5.5(4.8/5.7)
Oil capacity excluding cleaner litres (Imp.qts/US qts/	4.6(4.0/4.9)	4.8(4.2/5.1)	4.8(4.2/5.1)	4.8(4.2/5.1)
Oil capacity between max. and min. marks,approx litre(Imp.qts/US qts)....	1.0(1.0qt)	1.0(1.0qt)	1.0(1.0qt)	1.0(1.0qt)

Outboard drive

Oil grade/viscosity ....   Same as in engine
Oil capacity, approx.litres
(Imp.qts./USqts.) ....   2.6(2.3/2.7)
Oil capacity, hydraulic system drive
280 with Power trim,litres (Imp.qts/
US qts.) ....   1.5(1.5 qt)
Oil grade ....   ATF, Type F
                                          A   or Dexron [1]

Ignition system

Firing order   1-8-4-3-6-5-7-2
Ignition distributor,type Prestolite ... IBM 70 11-A
Basic setting (idling speed) .... 8° B.T.D.C.
Ignition distributor, contact gap,mm ... 0.36-0.48(0.14-0.19")
Dwell angle ....   31° ± 3°
Spark plugs ....   AC43MT or similar
Spark plugs, electrode gap, mm .... 0.7(0.028")

Electrical system

Voltage, V ....   12 V Negative Ground
Battery, capacity, standard, Ah 60
Battery electrolyte specific gravity:
    Fully charged battery 1.275-1.285
    When re-charging is necessary 1.230
Generator, type ....   Alternator
    Output, max. ....   490 W (38 A)
Starter motor, type Prestolite MDY-7054
    Output kW 0.96 (1.3hp)

Tightening torques

	Nm	kgm	lb.ft.
Cylinder head bolts	90	9	65
Main bearings	102	10.2	75
Main bearings inner (AQ290)	95	9.5	70
Main bearings outer (AQ290)	88	8.8	65
Connecting rod bearings	62	6.2	45
Flywheel	82	8.2	60
Spark plugs	21	2.1	15
Tensioner - flywheel housing	35	3.5	25
Intake manifold	41	4.1	30
Exhaust manifold	28	2.8	20
Cranksnaft bolts	90	9	65
Steering helmet Allen-bolt	60	6	43

1) Only if type F is not available

2) Volvo Penta oil has viscosity SAE 10W/40

AQD40 Diesel

General

Engine designation	AQD40A
Operation	4-stroke turbo-charged diesel engine with swirl chambers
Number of cylinders	6
Valve system .... [1]	Overhead valves
Flywheel output [1] HP(kW) at 60 r/s (3600 r/m)	130(96) –
Max. operating speed r/s (r/m)	60(3600)
Idling speed, r/s (r/m)	11(650)
Bore/stroke mm (inch)	92(3.62)/90(3.54)
Displacement dm^3 (in^3)	3.59 (220)
Compression ratio	21:1
Firing order, No. 6 cylinder closest to flywheel ...	1-5-3-6-2-4
Engine weight incl. outdrive kg(lbs)	465(1025) – –

Valves

Valve clearance, cold engine	
inlet, mm (inch)	0.40(0157)
outlet, mm (inch)	0.40(0157)

Lubricating system

Engine	
Oil capacity, dm^3 (UK pints-US pints)	
excl. filter	10.0(17.6-20.7)
incl. filter	11.0(19.4-22.8)
Oil quality (Acc. to API)	Diesel lubricating oil CD
Viscosity, above + 10^oC (+ 50^oF)	SAE 20W/30 [2]
below + 10^oC (+ 50^oF)	SAE 10W [3]
Oil pressure, warm engine,	
idling speed, kp/cm^2 (lbs/in^2)	2.2-2.5(31.3-35.6)
at full speed, kp/cm^2 (lbs/in^2)	3.5-4.5(49.8-64.0)
Outboard drive	
Oil capacity, dm^3 (UK pints-US pints)	2.6(4.6-5.4)
Oil quality and viscosity	Same as engine
Oil volume between max. and min. marks on dipstick dm^3 (UK pints-US pints)	0.15(0.25-0.31)

Cooling System

Thermostat 1 begins opening at, ^oC (^oF)	70(158)
2 begins opening at, ^oC (^oF)	76(169)
Freshwater system capacity incl. heat-exchanger, dm^3 (UK pints-US pints)	21(37-43.5)

Fuel system

Fuel injection pump, Bosch	EP VE 6 11F
Injectors, Bosch	KBE 36 S 2/13
Fuel filter, Bosch	FJ DBR 1 W6 225

[1] According to "DIN 6270 Leistung B"
[2] Volvo Penta CD Oil Double Grade
[3] Volvo Penta CD Oil Single Grade

Electrical system

```
Voltage ..........................................    12
Battery capacity, Ah .............................    114
Battery, spec. gravity of electrolyte:
    Fully charged battery ........................    1.275-1.285
    To be recharged at, ..........................    1.230
Glow plugs, Bosch ................................    RSK
```

Alternator

```
    Type .........................................    S.E.V.
    Max. output ..................................    490W (35A)
    Starter motor output, kW (HP) ................    2.5 (3.4)
```

Outdrive

```
Outdrive model ...................................    280 B
Ratio ............................................    1.61:1
```

Tightening torques

```
Steering helmet Allen-bolt (AQD40A) kpm(Nm)/ft lbs..    5-6(50-60)/36-43
Cylinder-head bolts:
    1st tightening, kpm (Nm)/ftlbs ................    3(30)/22
    2nd tightening, kpm (Nm)/ftlbs ................    9(90)/65
    3rd tightening, kpm (Nm)/ftlbs ................    13(130)/94
```

Engine designation	AQ 60 F
Output, max. SAE, h.p.	60
Max. running speed, r.p.m.*)	5000
Idling speed, r.p.m.	800
Compression ratio	6.0:1
Compression pressure at 200 r.p.m.	7-8 kg/cm^2
	(100-114 lb./sq.in.)

Fuel system

Fuel, paraffin (kerosene) engine fuel, octane rating (Research Method)	at least 55

Main carburetter

Down-draught carburetter (1), type	Zenith 30 VNN
Main jet	100
Compensation jet	100
Idling air jet	50
Idling jet	65
Acceleration jet	65
Venturi	26

Starting carburetter

Fuel jet	50
Air jet	50

Electrical system

Distributor, type designation, Bosch	VJ4BL 37 Tmk
Spark plugs, Bosch	W 145 T 1 **)
Spark plug electrode gap	0.9 mm (0.035)
Ignition timing at 4000 r.p.m.	46-48° before T.D.C.
" " with engine stationary	12° before T.D.C.

Cooling system

Thermostat marking	170
Thermostat starts to open at	73-78°C
	(163-172°F)

*) With the correct propeller dimension, the engine speed of the AQ 60F should attain 4500 r.p.m. but not exceed 5000 r.p.m. at full throttle.

**) or corresponding types.

195

Lubricating system

AQ 60 F

Oil capacity, including filter, litres
   (Imp. quarts/US quarts) 6.0
                                                 (5¼/6¼)

Oil capacity, excluding filter, litres
   (Imp. quarts/US quarts) 5.5
                                                 (4¾/5¾)

Oil grade ....   MS
Oil viscosity ....   SAE 20W-40
                                                (Multigrade)

Interval between oil changes ....   Every 50 hours of
                                                operation

The above details are peculiar to AQ60F/100 only. For other information see AQ95/100.

AQD2/100B

GENERAL

Engine designation	AQD2/100B
Number of cylinders	2
Output h.p. at 2500 r.p.m.	25
Max. operating speed r.p.m.	2500
Bore mm (in.)	88.9 (3.5)
Stroke mm (in.)	90.0 (3.54)
Displacement, litres (cu.in.)	1.12 (68.4)
Compression pressure kp/cm^2 (p.s.i.)	20–24
Starter motor r.p.m.	285–340
Idling speed r.p.m.	550–650
Direction of rotation	Clockwise
Engine weight approx. kg (1b)	236 (520)

VALVES

Valve clearance, warm engine	
inlet mm (in.)	0.30 (0.012)
exhaust mm (in.)	0.35 (0.014)
Decompression device, max. depression of exhaust	
valve, mm (in.)	0.5 (0.020)

LUBRICATING SYSTEM

Oil capacity, engine, litres (Imp.qts. – US qts.)	3.0 (2.6–3.2)
Filter (Imp. qts. – US qts.)	0.25 (0.3–0.2)
Oil quality	Diesel lub. oil Service CD or DS
Viscosity	SAE 10W/20
Oil pressure, warm engine	
Idling speed kp/cm^2 (p.s.i.)	0.8 – 1.5 (14–21)
full speed kp/cm^2 (p.s.i.)	2–3 (28–43)

COOLING SYSTEM

Thermostat opens at $^\circ C$ ($^\circ F$)	60 (140)
is fully open at $^\circ C$ ($^\circ F$)	75 (167)

FUEL SYSTEM

Fuel injection pump, Bosch AQD 2B	PFR 2K 75A/381/11
Feed pressure kp/cm^2 (p.s.i.)	0.75 (11)
Injectors, Bosch, Holder	KBL 87S78/4
spray nozzles	DLLA 150S720
opening pressures, kp/cm^2 (p.s.i.)	170–178 (2417–2531)
Pre injection angle, crankshaft degrees	$23^\circ – 26^\circ$

ELECTRICAL SYSTEM

Battery voltage	12
Battery capacity, max. Ah AQD 2B	60
Alternator output max. W	450
Starter generator AQD 2B	
Generator output max. W	135
continuous W	90
Starter motor output HP	1
Battery electrolyte, specific gravity	
Battery to be recharged at g/cm^3	1.230
Fully charged battery g/cm^3	1.275–1.285

TIGHTENING TORQUES

Cylinder head bolts (width across flats, 19mm=3/4 in).
  kpm (lb ft)
  width across flats 15mm = 19/32 in.) kpm(lb.ft.)........ 4.5 (33)
Connecting rod bolts kpm (lb.ft.) 6.5 (47)
Crankshaft main bearings (intermediate bearing) kpm(lb.ft) 8.0 (58)
Injector nuts kpm (lb.ft.) 2.0 (14)

Indenor Diesels

General

	AQD 19 Indenor XDP4/88	AQD 27 Indenor XDP6/85	AQD 29 Indenor XDP6/88 4-stroke Diesel engine with swirl chambers	AQD 21A Indenor XDP 4/90	AQD 32A Indenor XDP 6/90
Type designation					
Engine designation					
Type					
Number of cylinders	4	6	6	4	6
Valve system	Overhead	Overhead	Overhead valves	Overhead valves	Overhead valves
Max.output, pleasure boats, SAE	68h.p. at 4500	83h.p. at 4000	92h.p. at 4000	75h.p. at 4500rpm	106h.p. at 400rpm
Max.output, other installations in planing boats, SAE			83h.p. at 4000rpm	–	94h.p. at 4000rpm
Max.output, work boats, SMMT			67h.p. at 3000rpm	51h.p. at 3000rpm	75h.p. at 3000rpm
Max.intermittent torque	12kgm(87 lb.ft) at 2000 r.p.m.	17.2kgm(124 lb.ft)at 2200r.p.m.	18.2kgm(132 lb.ft) at 2000 r.p.m.	13.2kgm(95 lb.ft) at 2000 r.p.m.	20.6kgm (156 lb.ft) at 2000 r.p.m.
Bore	88mm (3.465")	85mm (3.346")	88mm (3.465")	90mm (3.543")	90mm (3.543")
Stroke	80mm (3.150")	80mm (3.150")	80mm (3.150")	83mm (3.268")	83mm (3.268")
Displacement	1.95 litres (119 cu.in)	2.72 litres (166 cu.in.)	2.92 litres (178 cu.in.)	2.11 litres (129 cu.in.)	3.17 litres (193 cu.in)
Compression ratio			21 : 1		
Compression pressure cold engine (at starter motor speed)			24-25kg/cm^2 (340-356 lb/sq.in.)	24-27^2) kg/cm^2 341-384 lb/sq.in)	24-27^2)kg/cm^2 (341-384 lb/sq.in.)
Order of injection, cylinder no. 1 nearest the flywheel	1-3-4-2	1-5-3-6-2-4	1-5-3-6-2-4	1-3-4-2	1-5-3-6-2-4
Direction of rotation, viewed from forward end of engine	Clockwise	Clockwise	Clockwise	Clockwise	Clockwise
Cylinder liners	Wet-type, replaceable	Wet-type, replaceable	Wet-type, replaceable	Wet-type, replaceable	Wet-type,replaceable
Total weight, approx.kg (lb)	approx.275kg (605 lb.)	approx. 330kg (726 lb.)	about 350kg (770 lb.)	.300 (660)	355 (785)

Engine speed

	AQD 19	AQD 27	AQD 29	AQD 21	AQD 32
Pleasure boats and other installations in planing boats					
Max.permissible operating speed during a short period of time	4500 r.p.m.	4000 r.p.m.	4000 r.p.m.	4500 r.p.m.	4000 rp.m.
Max.speed without load on engine	4750 r.p.m.	4250 r.p.m.	4350 r.p.m.	4850 r.p.m.	4350r.p.m.
Idling speed	650 r.p.m.	650 r.p.m.	650 r.p.m.	650 r.p.m.	650 r.p.m.
Work boats					
Max.operating speed			3000 r.p.m.	3000 r.p.m.	3000 r.p.m.
Max.speed, without load on engine			3400 r.p.m.	3400 r.p.m.	3400 r.p.m.
Idling speed			650 r.p.m.	650 r.p.m.	650 r.p.m.

Valves

	AQD 19	AQD 27	AQD 29	AQD 21	AQD 32
Valve clearance, cold engine					
Inlet valves	0.15mm (0.006")	0.15mm (0.006")	0.15mm (0.006")	0.15mm (0.006")	0.15mm (0.006")
Exhaust valves	0.25mm (0.010")	0.25mm (0.010")	0.25mm (0.010")	0.25mm (0.010")	0.25mm (0.010")

Lubricating system

	AQD 19	AQD 27	AQD 29	AQD 21	AQD 32
Engine					
Oil grade			Service DS		
Oil viscosity			SAE 30		
below 0°C (32°F)			SAE 20/20W		
Oil capacity including oil filter	6 litres (5¼ Imp. qts=6¼ US qts)	6.5 litres (5¾ Imp.qts=6¾ US qts)	5.0-6.5 litres approx.5.3 US qts= (4.4 Imp.qts= -5.7 Imp.qts= approx.6.9 US qts)[1]	approx.5.5 litres (4.8 Imp.qts=5.8 US qts.)	approx. 8 litres (7.0 Imp.qts= approx.8.4 US qts)

Fuel system

	AQD 19	AQD 27	AQD 29	AQD 21	AQD 32
Injection pump,make and designation	Silto distributing pump with hydraulic governor	Silto distributing pump with hydraulic governor	CAV ROTO-DIESEL DPA	CAV ROTO-DIESEL DPA	CAV ROTO-DIESEL DPA

			CAV/DES 583-6100	CAV/DES 583-6100	CAV/DES 583-6100
Fine filter, make and designation			CAV/DES 583-6100	CAV/DES 583-6100	CAV/DES 583-6100
Timing, injection begins	13.5° B.T.D.C.	13.5° B.T.D.C.	16° B.T.D.C.	19° B.T.D.C.	16° B.T.D.C.
Injectors			RKB 35 S 5246	RKB 35 S 5246	RKB 35 S 5246
Injector nozzles	DNOSD 210	ODGD 230	RDN OSD 21	RDN 12SD 65½7	RDN OSD 21
Injector opening pressure	115^{-5} kg/cm² (1635^{+70} lb./sq.in)	$115^{+}5$ kg/cm² (1635^{+70} lb./sq.in)	$120^{+}5$ kg/cm² (1705^{+70} lb./sq.in.)	$130^{+}5$ kg/cm² (1850^{+70} lb./sq.in.)	$120^{+}5$ kg/cm² (1700^{+70} lb./sq.in)
Marking on injection pump data plates					
Pleasure boats			R-34-62-031-6/88 -4350	R-34-42-490-4/90 -4850	R-34-62-091-6/90- 4350
Other installations in planing boats			R-34-62-031-6/88 -D4350	–	R-34-62-091-6/90- D4350
Other installations			R-34-62-031-6/88 -3400	R-34-42-4/90- 3400	R-34-62-091-6/90- 3400
Cooling system					
Capacity, fresh-water system	approx.11 litres (2¼ Imp.galls= 3 US galls.)	approx.12 litres (2⅝ Imp.galls= 3⅛ US galls.)	about 12 litres (2.65 Imp.galls = approx.3.15 US galls.)	about 9.5 litres (8.5 Imp.qts = 10 US qts.)	about 11.5 litres (10 Imp.qts = 12.5 US qts.)
Thermostat begins to open at	68-72°C (154-162°F)	68-72°C (154-162°F)	68-72°C (154-162°F)	68-72°C(154-162°F)	68-72°C(154-162°F)
Electrical system					
Voltage	12 V	12 V	12V	12 V	12 V
Alternator output					
Generator, effect	240 W	240 W	450 W	240 W	450 W
Starter motor, output	1.8 h.p.	2.7 h.p.	3 h.p.	1.8 h.p.	3 h.p.
Battery capacity, standard	114 Ah	114 Ah	114 Ah	114 Ah	114 Ah
Electrolyte specific gravity:					
Fully charged battery	1.275-1.285	1.275-1.285	1.275-1.285	1.275-1.285	1.275-1.285
Battery to be re-charged at	1.230	1.230	1.230	1.230	1.230
Glow plugs, Bosch	KE/GSA 10/1	KE/GSA 10/1	KE/GSA 10/1	KE/GSA 10/1	KE/GSA 10/1

Tightening torques

Cylinder head bolts	6.5-7.5kgm (47-54 lb.ft.)	6.5-7.5kgm (47-54 lb.ft.)	6.5-7.5kgm (47-54 lb.ft.)	6.5-7.5kgm (47-54 lb.ft.)
Main bearing bolts	9.5-10.5kgm (69-76 lb.ft.)	9.5-10.5kgm (69-76 lb.ft.)	9.5-10.5kgm (69-76 lb.ft.)	9.5-10.5kgm (69-76 lb.ft.)
Connecting rod bolts	5.5-6.5kgm (40-47 lb.ft.)	5.5-6.5kgm (40-47 lb.ft.)	5.5-6.5kgm (40-47 lb.ft.)	5.5-6.5kgm (40-47 lb.ft.)
Flywheel	5.5-6kgm (40-43 lb.ft.)	5.5-6kgm (40-43 lb.ft.)	6-7 kgm (43-50 lb.ft.)	6-7kgm (43-50 lb.ft.)
Flywheel damper	16-18kgm (116-130 lb.ft.)	16-18 kgm (116-130 lb.ft.)	16-18 kgm (116-130 lb.ft.)	16-18kgm (116-130 lb ft.)
Injector retaining nuts	1.5-2.5kgm (11-18 lb.ft.)	1.5-2.5kgm (11-18 lb.ft.)	1.5-2.5kgm (11-18 lb.ft.)	15.-2.5kgm (11-18 lb. ft.)
Glow plugs	4-5 kgm (29-36 lb.ft.)	4-5 kgm (29-36 lb.ft.)	4-5 kgm (29-36 lb.ft.)	4-5 kgm (29-36 lb.ft.)

*Later models

	AQD 19	AQD 27
Fuel injection pump	Roto-Diesel D.P.A.	
Pre-injection angle	21° B.T.D.C.	16° B.T.D.C.
Injector nozzle	RDN 125D 6236	RDN OSD 21
Injector opening pressure	140±5kp/cm²	120±5kp/cm²
	(1990±70 lb ")	(1710-70 lbs ")
Idling speed	650 r.p.m.	650 r.p.m.
Max.offload speed	4850 r.p.m.	4350 r.p.m.

Type designation	AQD70C TAMD70C (vertical)	AQD70CL THAMD70C (horizontal)
Number of cylinders	6	
Bore .... mm (inch)	104.77(4.13)	
Stroke .... mm (inch)	130.(5.12)	
Displacement.................... dm^3/litres(cu.in.)	6.73 (410)	
Output, measured on shaft (at the reverse gear flange) at 41.7 r/s(2500 rpm)[1] Only pleasure boats .... kW (hp) (reduce rpm for cruising speed with 200 rpm from that, under actual conditions of load, max. obtained rpm.)	198 (270)	
Output, measured on shaft (at the reverse gear f lange) at 36.7 r/s (2200 rpm)[2]. Other installations, light duty .... kW (hp)	152 (206)	
Inboard engines, inclination underway, max. .... degrees	18	
Idling speed .... r/s (rpm)	9.2 (550)	
Compression pressure at starter motor speed (180 rpm) .... MPa(kp/cm^2=1bf/in^2)	2.35 (24=341)	
Firing order (No.6 cylinder nearest flywheel)	1-5-3-6-2-4	
Direction of rotation viewed from engine front end..	Clockwise	
Cylinder liners	Wet, replaceable	
Valve system	Overhead	
Valve clearance(cold or at operating temp.):		
Inlet .... mm (inch)	0.40 (0.016)	
Outlet .... mm (inch)	0.55 (0.022)	
Weights of engine without reverse gear		
AQ-version .... kg (lbs)	840(1850)	900(1985)
Inboard version .... kg (lbs)	810(1785)	870(1920)

Lubrication system, engine

Oil grade, according to API-Standards	CD(For Service DS)	
Viscosity,above+20°C (68°F)	SAE 30)	
between +20°C and -10°C (68°F and 14°F) ..	SAE 20/20W) or 20W/30	
below -10°C (14°F)	SAE 10W	

Oil capacity (AQ version and inboard version without inclination) .. dm^3/litres (Imp.gals./US. gals.)	27(5.9/7.1)	24(5.3/6.3)
Inboard version (inclination 18°) .. dm^3/litres (Imp.gals./US gals.)	16(3.5/4.2)	23(5.1/6.1)

Oil pressure, warm engine at operation rpm ....MPa(kp/cm^2=1bf/in^2)	0.3-0.5(3-5=42-71)	

[1] DIN 6270 Leistung B [2] DIN 6270 Leistung B für Dauerbetrieb

Reverse gear

Make	Twin Disc MG506
Ratios ,...	1:1, 1.5:1, 2:1, 3:1
Oil grade and viscosity	Same as in engine
Oil quantity(incl. cooler) ....dm^3/litres(Imp (Imp.gals./US.gals.)	6.5 (1.4/1.7)
Operational oil pressure at oil temperature 82°C/ 180°F(engaged, 1800rpm) .... MPa(kp/cm^2=lbf/in^2)	2.1-2.2(21-22.5=300-320)
at cruising speed, min. .. MPa(kp/cm^2=lbf/in^2)	1.9(19.0=270)
Weight .... kg(lbs)	100(220)

Hydraulic system

(AQ-version)	AQD70C TAMD70C	AQD70CL THAMD70C
Oil grade and viscosity	Same as in engine	
Oil quantity ....dm^3/litres (Imp.gals./US gals.)	7(1.5/1.8)	

Fuel system

Type	Diesel/Direct injection
Fuel injection pump Bosch	PE6P 110A320RS260Z
Setting BTDC .... 20-21°	18-19°
Injectors, holders, Bosch	KBAL 112S28/4
nozzles, Bosch	DLLA 150 S 634
hole diameter(4 holes)......... mm (inch)	0.40(0.016)
opening pressure......MPa(kp/cm^2=lbf/in^2)	19.2(195=2774)
Centrifugal governor,Bosch ....,.....,.	EP/RSV 250-1250 PO/374/2R
Feed pump, operational pressure..kPa(kp/cm^2=lbf/in^2)	100-150(1.0-1.5=14.2-21.3)

Turbo-compressor

Make	Holset 3LD-530A
Lubrication	Pressure lubricating from engine
Cooling	Fresh-water cooled
Axial clearance .... mm (inch)	0.10-0.20(0.004-0.008)
Radial clearance, max. .... mm (inch)	0.61(0.024)

Cooling system

Capacity, incl.heat exchanger.......... dm^3/litres.. (Imp.gals./US gals.)	28(6.2/7.4)
Thermostats start opening at .... C°(F°)	74-78(165-172)
fully open at .... C°(F°)	84-88(183-190)

Electrical system

Voltage of electrical system	V	24 (12 alt.)
Alternator output (S.E.V.Marchal stand.)	W	600
(CAV optional)....................	W	1450
Starter motor output ....kW(hp)		3 (4)
Battery (2 units 12 V) capacity .... Ah		152
Battery electroylte density:		
fully charged at		1.275-1.285
needs recharging at		1.230
Stop solenoid, clearance at contacts, rod pulled fully backwards .... mm (inch)		2(0.08)

Tightening torques

	Nm	kpm	lbftf
Cylinder head bolts*, long	190	19	138
short	140	14	101
Main bearing bolts	140	14	101
Connecting rod bolts	160	16	116
Flywheel	170	17	123
Fuel injection pump:			
Discharge valve retainers	85	8.5	61
Injectors, attaching nuts	20	2.0	15

*

The bolt thread should be moistened in rustproofing agent
before fitting. Never use a cylinder head gasket twice.
Always fit a new gasket.

List of Drives, Ratios and rpm Limits

Reduction ratio	Engine/Drive Models	Optimum Prop. RPM	
1.18:1	AQ155/270E stage I and II	5100	B20 Competition
	AQ200/270E stage I and II	4900	B30 Competition
1.26:1	AQ155/170R stage I and II	4260	B20 Competition
1.35:1	250 drive 'A' ratio	-	Limited production for USA
1.41:1	AQ155/170R stage I and II	4250	B20 Competition
1.45:1	AQ155/270E stage I and II	4130	B20 Competition
	AQ200/270E stage I and II	4000	B30 Competition
1.59:1	AQ150/200 'B' ratio	2640	Production drive
1.61:1	250, 270, 280 drive 'B' ratio	2735	Production drive, V-8 engines, AQD40
1.66:1	100 drive standard ratio	1500/3310	All 100 drive production
1.67:1	AQ135/100CTH,AQ155/100CTH	3600	B18, B20 Comp. with 'slimline drive'
1.85:1	200 drive 'C' ratio	2700	Production drive on B18 engines
1.89:1	250, 270, 280 drive 'C' ratio	2700	Production drive on B30 engines
2.15:1	250, 270, 280 drive 'D' ratio	2700	Production drive on B18, B20, AQD21/32, B21, B23

206

Outboard Drives

Model 100:   Part no. 804400 L.H. rotation; Part no. 809870 R.H.
                                         rotation.

Shift mechanism ....   Dog-clutch
Tilt-up angle ....   45°
Upper gears ....   Bevel (spiral)
Lower gears ....   Spur
Reduction ratio 1.66:1
Propeller shaft ....   Splined, 13/16" dia.
Max. prop. dia. ....   14"
Lubrication system ....   Upper - pressure
                                      Lower - oil bath
Oil capacity ....   Upper - approx 1 litre (1 US quart)
                                      Lower - approx 1 litre (1 US quart)
Oil grade ....   S.A.E. 90 Hypoid.

Model 100:   Part no. 809881 L.H. rotation; Part no. 809891
                                         R.H. rotation.

Shift mechanism ....   Dog-clutch
Tilt-up angle ....   60°
Lift unit ....   Electro-hydraulic
Upper gears ....   Bevel (spiral)
Lower gears ....   Bevel (spiral)
Reduction ratio 1.66:1
Propeller shaft ....   Splined 13/16" dia.
Max. prop. dia. ....   14"
Lubrication system ....   Single chamber - pressure
Oil capacity ....   approx. 2.5 litres (2.5 US quarts)

Model 100:   Part no. 810000 L.H. rotation; Part no. 814000
                                         R.H. rotation.

Shift mechanism ....   'Silent-shift' cone clutch
Tilt-up angle ....   60°
Lift unit ....   Electro - hydraulic
Upper gears ....   Bevel (spiral)
Lower gears ....   Bevel (spiral)
Reduction ratio 1.66:1
Propeller shaft ....   Cylindrical with drive pin
Max. prop. dia. ....   14"
Lubrication system ....   Single chamber - pressure
Oil capacity ....   approx. 2 litres (2 US quarts)
Oil grade ....   S.A.E. 90 Hypoid

Model 100B: L.H. only

Shift mechanism ....   'Silent-shift' cone clutch
Tilt-up angle ....   60°
Lift unit ....   Electro-hydraulic
Upper gears ....   Bevel (spiral)
Lower gears ....   Bevel (spiral)
Reduction ratio 1.66:1
Propeller shaft ....   Cylindrical with drive pin
Max. prop. dia. ....   14"
Lubrication system ....   Single chamber - pressure
Oil capacity ....   approx. 3.1 litres (3.2 US quarts)
Oil grade ....   Multigrade S.A.E. 10W/30 or 20W/40

The 100B drive is easily distinguishable as the only 100 series drive to adopt
blue/grey paint finish as per 270/280 units.

207

Model 100 C.T.H.Competition

Part no. 814117 L.H. rotation; Part no. 814118 R.H. rotation.

Shift mechanism	'Silent-shift' cone clutch
Tilt-up angle	60°
Lift unit	Electro – hydraulic
Upper gears	Bevel (spiral)
Lower gears	Bevel (spiral)
Reduction ratio	1.66:1
Propeller shaft	Splined 13/16"
Max. prop. dia.	14"
Lubrication system	Single chamber – pressure
Oil capacity	approx. 2 litres (2 US quarts)
Oil grade	S.A.E. 90 Hypoid

Model 200:

Part no. 814050 B ratio; Part no. 814200 C ratio.

Snift mechanism	'Silent-shift' cone clutch
Tilt-up angle	60°
Lift Unit	Electro-mechanical
Upper gears	Bevel (spiral)
Lower gears	Bevel (straight cut)
Reduction ratios	200B 1.59:1
	200C 1.85:1
Propeller shaft	Splined 1⅛" dia.
Max. prop. dia.	15"
Lubrication system	Single chamber – pressure
Oil capacity	2.2 litres (2.3 US quarts)
Oil grade	S.A.E. 90 Hypoid (or as engine)

Model 250:

Part no. 832501 250A; Part no. 832502 250B; Part no. 832503 250C; Part no. 832504 250D.

Snift mechanism	'Silent-shift' cone clutch
Tilt-up angle	60°
Lift unit	Electro-mechanical
Upper gears	Bevel (spiral)
Lower gears	Bevel (straight cut)
Reduction ratios	250A 1.35:1, 250B 1.61:1, 250C 1.89:1, 250D 2.15:1.
Propeller shaft	Splined 1⅛" dia.
Max. prop. dia.	16"
Lubrication system	Single chamber – pressure
Oil capacity	2.2 litres (2.3 US quarts)
Oil grade	As engine

Model 250E/270E

Shift mechanism	'Silent-shift' cone clutch
Tilt-up angle	60°
Lift unit	Electrical-mechanical
Upper gears	Bevel (spiral)
Lower gears	Twin shaft system, straight cut bevel.
Reduction ratio	1.41:1
Propeller shaft	Splined 1⅛" dia.
Max. prop. dia.	14"
Lubrication system	Single chamber – pressure
Oil capacity	2.2 litres (2.3 US quarts)
Oil grade	S.A.E. 90 Hypoid

Model 270:   Refers 270 and 270T with powertrim.

Shift mechanism ....   'Silent-shift' cone clutch with servo-disengagement
Tilt-up angle ....   60°
Lift unit ....   Electro-mechanical
Upper gears ....   Bevel (spiral)
Lower gears ....   Bevel (moderate spiral)
Reduction ratios 270B 1.61:1, 270C 1.89:1, 270D 2.15:1
Propeller shaft ....   Splined 1⅛" dia.
Max. prop. dia. ....   16"
Lubrication system ....   Single chamber - pressure
Oil capacity ....   2.2 litres (2.3 US quarts)
    with 1" extension ....   2.2 litres (2.3 US quarts)
    with 4" extension ....   2.4 litres (2.5 US quarts)
Oil grade ....   As engine

Model 280:   Refers 280 and 280T with early type power trim.

Shift mechanism ....   'Silent-shift' cone clutch with servo disengagement
Tilt-up angle ....   60°
Tilt-up angle 280T
    a) 'Trim' position ....   From -4° to +5°
    b) 'Beach' position ....   From +5° to 30°
    c) 'Tilt' position ....   From 30° to 60°
Lift unit 280 ....   Electro-mechanical
          280T ....   Hydraulic
Reduction ratios 280B 1.61:1, 280C 1.89:1, 280D 2.15:1
Propeller shaft ....   Splined 1⅛" dia.
Max. prop. dia. ....   16"
Lubrication system ....   Single chamber - pressure
Oil capacity ....   2.6 litres (2.5 US quarts)
Oil grade ....   As engine
Oil capacity hydraulic system
    280T ....   1.5 litres (1.5 US quarts)
Oil grade hydraulic system 280T ..   Automatic Transmission Fluid Type F

Model 750:   Gearbox for fwd, neutral, reverse is not incorporated.

Reduction ratio 1.89:1
Tilt-up angle ....   80°
Lift unit ....   Hydraulic
Steering system ....   Hydraulic 30° each way
Max. prop. dia. ....   23.5"
Lubrication system ....   Pressure via circulating pump
Oil capacity - drive ....   17 litres (18 US quarts)
             - hydraulic system ..   7 litres (7 US quarts)
Oil grade ....   Diesel lub. oil Service D.S.
Weight - drive only ....   150kg (330 lbs.)
       - drive, shield &
         propeller ....   300kg (660 lbs.)

209

AQ155A based on B.20 block 1969-73

output hp DIN rpm	155/5700
torque kgm/rpm (lb ft)	19.5/4.500/(140)
max running speed rpm	5800
compression ratio	11.2:1
compression pressure kg/cm^2 (lb/in^2)	14-16 (199-228)
weight engine, shield and instruments kg (lb)	170 (375)
flywheel kg (lb)	45 (99)
camshaft marking	G
camshaft timing check (cold) at .4mm (.016")	
valve clearance inlet valve on cyl 1	
should open	55° BTDC
valve clearances (warm) inlet and	
exhaust mm (in)	.4-.45 (.016-.018)
fuel pump pressure at 100rpm $kg/cm^2(lb/in^2)$	.15-.25 (2-3.5)
carburettors, 2 off type	Solex 45 DDH-M
outer venturi	38
main jet	190
air jet	155
idling jet	62.5
idling air jet	120
emulsion pipe	C24186
starting jet	100
needle valve	1.8
packing for valve housing mm (in)	1 (.039)
packing for valve mm (in)	1.5 (.059)
float weight g (ozs)	13.6 (.48)
pump jet	45 (horizontal)
inner venturi	C23352 no 1
float level from plane of packing	20.5mm (.807in)
idling speed	900-1000rpm
spark plugs	Bosch W290 T16
spark plug gap	.35mm (.014in)
distributor	
basic setting at low idle	11° BTDC
max advance at 5800rpm	38° BTDC

AQ155A based on B.20 block 1974-7

	stage 1	stage 2
output hp DIN/rpm	145/5800	160/5800
torque kgm/rpm/lb/ft	19.5/4500/140	19.3/5000/139
max running speed rpm	6000	
compression ratio	11.2:1	11:1
compression pressure $kg/cm^2(lb/in^2)$	12-13.5 (170-190)	
weight engine, shield and instruments		
kg (lb)	170 (375)	
flywheel kg (lb)	45 (99)	
camshaft marking	G	
camshaft timing check (cold) at .4mm		
(.016in) valve clearance inlet valve on		
cyl 1 should open at	55° BTDC	
valve clearance (warm) inlet and exhaust		
mm/in	.4-.45 (.016-.018)	
fuel pump pressure at 100rpm kg/cm^2		
(lb/in^2)	.15-.25 (2-3.5)	
carburettors, 2 off type	Solex 45 DDHM	
outer venturi	38	40
main jet	190	150
air jet	155	120

idling jet	62.5
idling air jet	120
emulsion pipe	C24186
starting jet	100
needle valve	1.8
packing for valve housing	1mm (.039in)
packing for valve	1.5mm (.059in)
float, weight	13.6g (.48oz)
pump jet	45 (horizontal)
inner venturi	C23352 no 1
float level from plane of packing	20.5mm (.807in)
idling speed rpm	900-1000
spark plugs	Bosch W290 R16
spark plug gap	.35mm (.014in)
distributor	
basic setting at low idle	11° BTDC
max advance at 5800rpm	38° BTDC

AQ200A based on B.30 block 1969-73

output hp DIN/rpm	200/5700
torque kgm/rpm/lb/ft	28/4500/200
max running speed rpm	5800
compression ratio	11.2:1
compression pressure kg/cm^2 (lb/in^2)	14-16 (199-228)
weight engine, shield and instruments kg	
kg(lb)	233 (514)
flywheel kg/(lb)	55 (121)
camshaft marking	G
camshaft timing check (as for 155A)	55° BTDC
valve clearances (as for 155A)	.4-.45 (.016in-.018in)
carburettors, 3 off type	Solex 45-DDH-M
outer venturi	38
main jet	190
idling jet	55
idling air jet	120
emulsion pipe	C24186
starting jet	100
needle valve	1.8
packing for valve housing	1mm (.039in)
float, weight	13.6g (.48oz)
pump jet	45 (horizontal)
inner venturi	C23352 no 1
float level from plane of packing	20.5mm (.807in)
idling speed rpm	900-1000
spark plugs	Bosch W290 T16
spark plug gap	.35mm (.014in)
distributor	
basic setting at low idle	18° BTDC
max advance at 2500rpm	38° BTDC

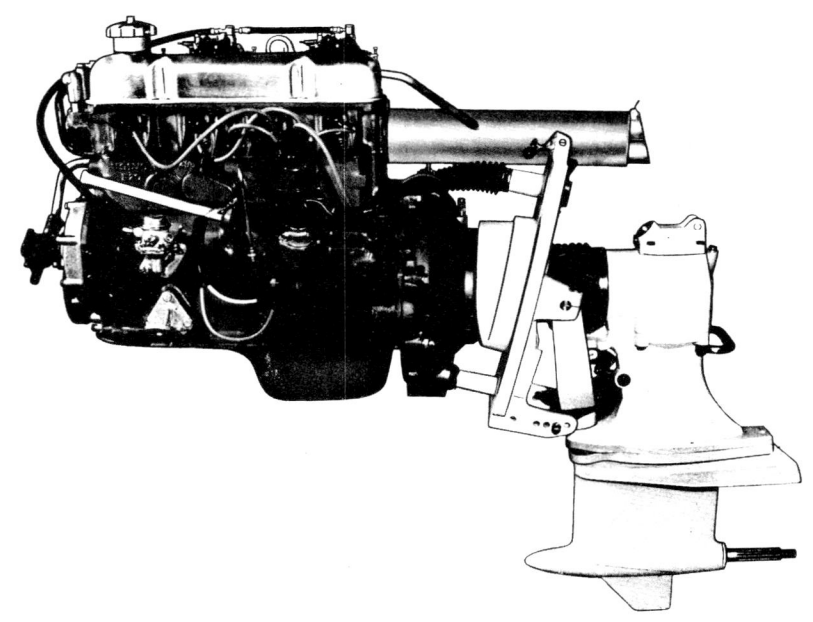

83 AQ155A/170R stage 1 and stage 2

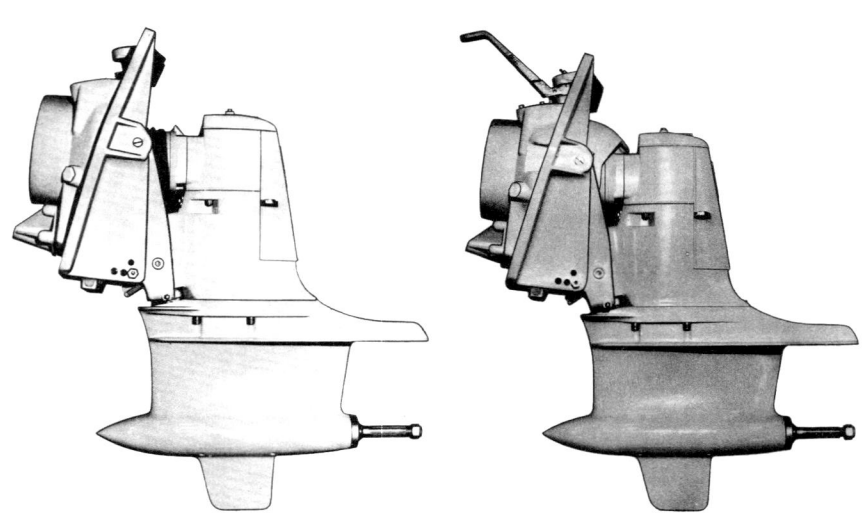

84 Drive 270E with external steering; 84a Drive 270E with internal steering

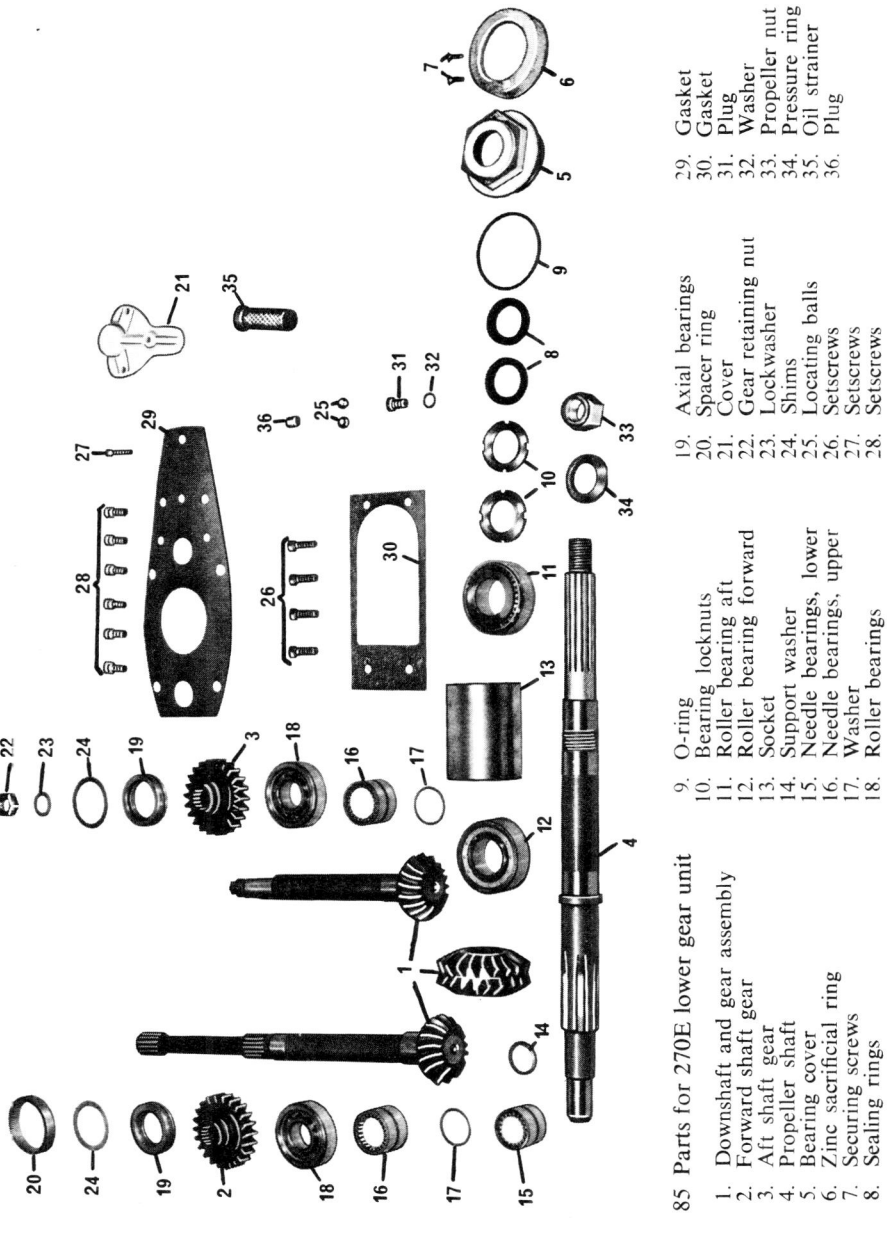

85 Parts for 270E lower gear unit

1. Downshaft and gear assembly
2. Forward shaft gear
3. Aft shaft gear
4. Propeller shaft
5. Bearing cover
6. Zinc sacrificial ring
7. Securing screws
8. Sealing rings
9. O-ring
10. Bearing locknuts
11. Roller bearing aft
12. Roller bearing forward
13. Socket
14. Support washer
15. Needle bearings, lower
16. Needle bearings, upper
17. Washer
18. Roller bearings
19. Axial bearings
20. Spacer ring
21. Cover
22. Gear retaining nut
23. Lockwasher
24. Shims
25. Locating balls
26. Setscrews
27. Setscrews
28. Setscrews
29. Gasket
30. Gasket
31. Plug
32. Washer
33. Propeller nut
34. Pressure ring
35. Oil strainer
36. Plug

	stage 1	stage 2
output hp DIN/rpm	200/5800	230/5800
torque kgm/rpm/lb/ft	26.5/4500/195	28/5500/205
max running speed rpm	5800	
compression ratio	11.2:1	11:1
compression pressure kg/cm^2(lb/in^2)	12-13.5 (170-190)	
weight engine, shield and		
instruments kg (lb)	233 (514)	
flywheel kg (lb)	55 (121)	
camshaft marking	G	
camshaft timing check (as for AQ155)	55°BTDC	
valve clearances mm (in) (as for AQ155)	.4-.45 (.016-.018)	
carburettors, 3 off type	Solex 45-DDH-M	
outer venturi	38	40
main jet	190	150
air jet	155	120
idling jet	62.5	
idling air jet	120	
emulsion pipe	C24186	
starting jet	100	
needle valve	1.8	
packing for valve housing	1mm (.039in)	
float weight	13.6g (.48oz)	
pump jet	45 (horizontal)	
inner venturi	C23352 no 1	
float level from plane of packing	20.5mm (.807in)	
idling speed rpm	900-1000	
spark plugs	Bosch W290 R16	
spark plug gap	.35mm (.014in)	
distributor		
basic setting at low idle	18° BTDC	
max advance at 2500rpm	38° BTDC	

From 1969 onwards, Volvo Competition Service made available a range of special propellers suitable for the E,R and CTH drives. The propellers were manufactured from bronze to eliminate flexing and featured especially slender bosses when designed for use with the slim torpedo of E and R drives. It was necessary to remove the propellers after each use if the boat were to remain afloat, as the electrolytic interaction between the bronze and the aluminium would swiftly cause damage.

214

Two-bladed bronze racing propellers for CTH drive

	Volvo part no	
dia x pitch	LH	RH
13⅛ x 16in	813350	813351
13⅛ x 17in	813352	813353
13¼ x 18in	813354	813355
13⅛ x 19in	813356	813357
13¼ x 20in	813358	813359
13¼ x 21in	813360	813361
13⅛ x 22in	813362	813363

Three-bladed bronze R-type propellers for E and R drives

	Volvo part no	
dia x pitch	LH	RH
12 x 22in	832176	832177
12 x 23in	832178	832179
12 x 24in	832180	832181
13 x 20in	832182	832183
13 x 21in	832184	832185
13 x 22in	832186	832187

Three-bladed bronze supercavitating surface propellers for E and R drives

	Volvo part no	
dia x pitch	LH	RH
13 x 20in	832790	832791
13 x 21in	832792	832793
12 x 23in	832794	832795
12 x 24in	832796	832797
12 x 25in	832798	832799

215

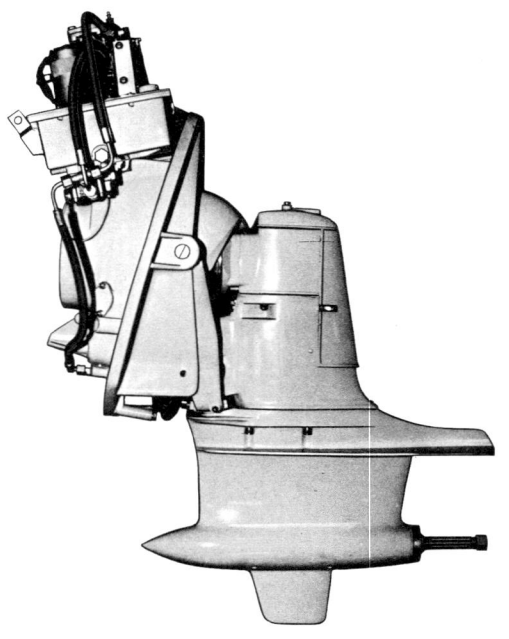

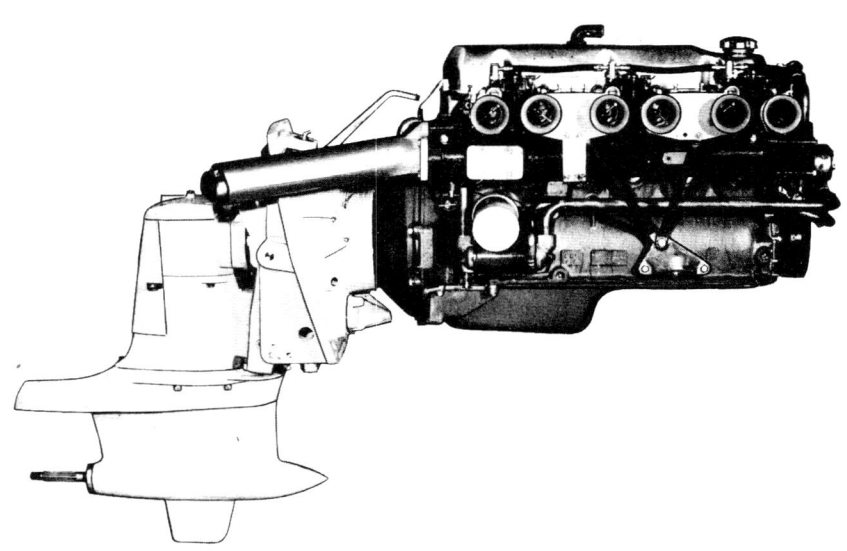

87 AQ200/280E, stage 1 and stage 2

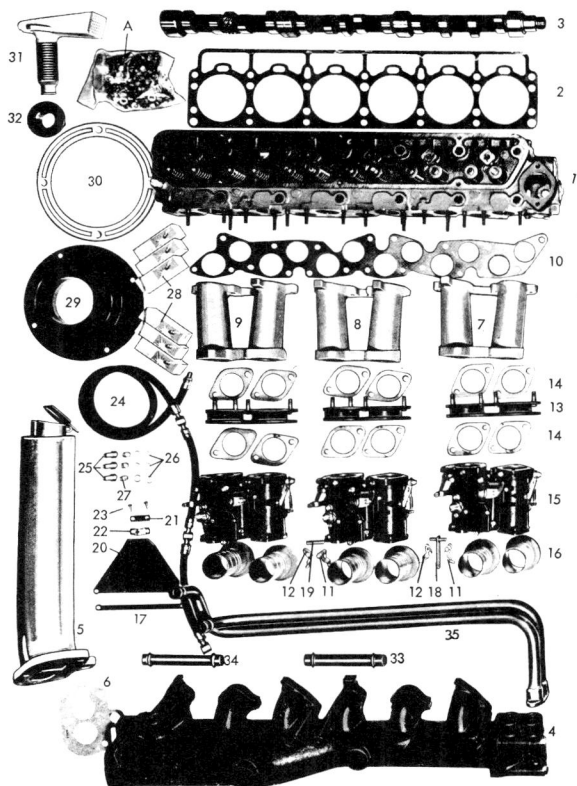

88 Tuning parts AQ200

1. Cylinder head
2. Cylinder head gasket
3. Camshaft 'G' profile
4. Exhaust manifold
5. Exhaust bend and overboard discharge
6. Gasket
7. Inlet manifold, front
8. Inlet manifold, centre
9. Inlet manifold, rear
10. Inlet/exhaust manifold gasket
11. Throttle levers, forward
12. Throttle levers, aft
13. Rubber flanges for carburettors
14. Carburettor gaskets
15. Carburettors
16. Air intake trumpets
17. Carburettor interlink bracket

18. Control rod front to centre carb
19. Control rod centre to rear carb
20. Bracket for throttle cable
21. Backing plate
22. Throttle cable clamp
23. Clamp bolts
24. Fuel feed hose
25. Banjo bolts
26. Copper washers for banjo bolts
27. Fuel line filters
28. Spark plugs
29. Rubber bellows for exhaust pipe
30. Attachment ring for bellows
31. Cooling water intake
32. Nut for intake
33. Cooling water pipes, oil cooler to exhaust manifold
34. Cooling water pipe, thermostat to pump
35. Cooling water pipe, pump to cooler
A. Nuts, bolts, screws and washers

217

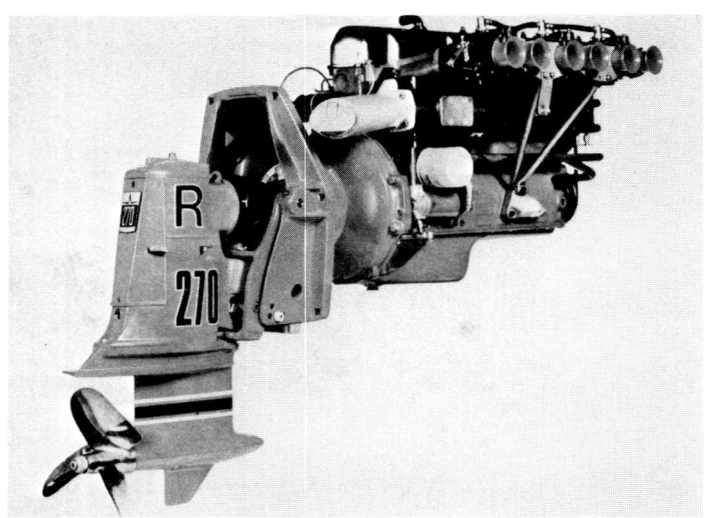

89 Prototype 270R drive in proposed new livery of gloss red with black and white bands on lower unit. Both drive and colour scheme have been dropped

90 AQ200/280E in similar style. Note the lugs each side of rear cover for external steering

Index

Numbers in *italic* indicate illustrations